Governance, Accountability and Sustainable Development

Governance, Accountability and Sustainable Development

Edited by

David Crowther, Mourad Oubrich,
Redouane Barzi and Sara Abdaless

Cambridge
Scholars
Publishing

Governance, Accountability and Sustainable Development

Edited by David Crowther, Mourad Oubrich, Redouane Barzi
and Sara Abdaless

This book first published 2015

Cambridge Scholars Publishing

Lady Stephenson Library, Newcastle upon Tyne, NE6 2PA, UK

British Library Cataloguing in Publication Data
A catalogue record for this book is available from the British Library

ISBN (10): 1-4438-6884-1
ISBN (13): 978-1-4438-6884-6

TABLE OF CONTENTS

Part III: Regional Understandings

LIST OF TABLES AND FIGURES

ABOUT THE EDITORS

David Crowther is Professor of Corporate Social Responsibility and Head of the Centre for Research into Organisational Governance, De Montfort University, UK. His current research is concerned with factors affecting corporate sustainability.

Sara Abdaless is a doctoral researcher at Henley Business School, University of Reading, UK.

Redouane Barzi is currently a research professor of Marketing/ Management at the National School of Business and Management (ENCG - Ibn Tofail University) and a research associate at Val de Loire Research on Management (VALLOREM - University of Orleans). He is also Vice-president of Studies and Research at the Competitive Intelligence and Strategic Management Center (CIEMS).

Mourad Oubrich is President of CIEMS and professor at INPT, Rabat, Morocco.

ABOUT THE AUTHORS

Ismail Adelopo is Associate Professor, University of the West of England, UK.

Ruby Melody Agbola lectures in the Department of Management Studies, Central Business School, Central University College, Tema, Ghana.

Samir Aguenaou is in the School of Business Administration, Al Akhawayn University, Ifrane, Morocco.

Myriam Boudiche is in the Department of Finance, Faculty of Economic Sciences and Management of Tunis, El Manar University, Tunis Cedex, Tunisia.

Brahim Boulafdour is a doctoral student at the Faculty of Juridical, Economic and Social Sciences, Fez, Morocco.

Eme Joel Efiong is Assistant Professor in the Department of Accounting, University of Caalabar, Nigeria.

Hicham Elachgar is a doctoral student at the National School of Computer Science and Systems Analysis, Rabat, Morocco.

Omar Farooq is in the Department of Business and Management, Aalborg University, Aalborg, Denmark.

Michael von Gagern is NCB Chair for Corporate Social Responsibility, King Saud University, Riyadh, Saudi Arabia.

Georgiana Grigore is Senior Lecturer in the Media School, Bournemouth University, UK.

Suan Gulliver is an independent researcher based in the UK.

EL Mansouri Moulay Hassan is a doctoral student in the laboratory of science of management, University Hassan 1st of Settat, Morocco.

Meryem Makoudi is Professor at the Faculty of Juridical, Economic and Social Laboratory CRIMAD, Fez, Morocco.

Mazen F. Rasheed is Director of the Centre for Corporate Social Responsibility, King Saud University, Riyadh, Saudi Arabia.

Boubker Regragui is Professor at the National School of Computer Science and Systems Analysis, Rabat, Morocco.

Shahla Seifi lives in the UK and is a doctoral research student at Universiti Putra Malaysia.

Evans Sokro lectures in the Department of Human Resource Management, Central Business School, Central University College, Tema, Ghana.

CHAPTER ONE

DEVELOPING A GLOBAL PERSPECTIVE

DAVID CROWTHER, SARA ABDALESS,
MOURAD OUBRICH AND REDOUANE BARZI

Introduction

It seems to have become generally accepted by businesses and their managers, by governments and their agencies, and by the general public that there is considerable benefit in engaging in CSR. Consequently, every organisation will place increasing importance on its CSR policy, which will have been translated into activity. Despite the fact that many people remain cynical about the genuineness of such corporate activity, the evidence continues to mount that corporations are actually engaging in socially responsible activities, not least because they recognise the benefits which accrue. It seems, therefore, that the battle is won and that everyone accepts the need for CSR activity – all that remains for discussion is how exactly to engage in such activity, and how to report upon that activity. Even this has been largely addressed through such vehicles as GRI and ISO 26000.

There has also been a considerable change in the emphasis of corporations reporting on their CSR activities, which has taken place in recent years. This change is not just in terms of the extent of such reporting, which has become more or less ubiquitous throughout the world, but also in terms of style and content. When researching into corporate activity and the reporting of that activity in the 1990s, it was necessary to acknowledge (Crowther 2012) that no measures of social or environmental performance existed which had gained universal acceptability. Good social or environmental performance was subjectively based upon the perspective of the evaluator and the mores of the temporal horizon of reporting. Consequently any reporting concerning such performance could not easily be made, which would allow a comparative evaluation between corporations to be undertaken. This was regarded as helpful to the image creation activity of the corporate reporting, as the authors of the script were therefore able to create an image which could not be refuted through quantificatory comparative evaluation. Instead such images could be created through the use of linguistic and non-linguistic means. Thus, each company was able to select measures which created the semiotic of social concern and environmental responsibility and of continual progress, through the selective use of measures which support these myths. As a consequence of the individual selection of measures to be reported upon, a spatial evaluation of performance, through a comparison of the performance with other companies, was not possible and a temporal evaluation was all that remained.

While this research was being undertaken, steps were being taken to change this and to develop some kind of standards for reporting. Thus, in 1999, the Institute of Social and Ethical Accountability[1] published the AA1000 Assurance Standard with the aim of fostering greater transparency in corporate reporting.

At the same time the Global Reporting Initiative (GRI) produced its Sustainability Reporting Guidelines, which have been developed through multi-stakeholder dialogue. The guidelines are claimed to be closely aligned to AA1000, but focus on a specific part of the social and environmental accounting and reporting process, namely reporting. The GRI aims to cover a full range of economic issues, although these are currently at different stages of development. The GRI is an initiative that develops and disseminates voluntary Sustainability Reporting Guidelines. These Guidelines are for voluntary use by organisations for reporting on the economic, environmental, and social dimensions of their activities, products, and services. Although originally started by an NGO, GRI has become accepted as a leading model for how social, environmental and economic reporting should take place. It aims to provide a framework that allows comparability between different companies' reports whilst being sufficiently flexible to reflect the different impacts of different business sectors.

The GRI incorporates the active participation of representatives from business, accountancy, investment, environmental, human rights, research and labour organisations from around the world. Started in 1997, GRI became independent in 2002, and is an official collaborating centre of the United Nations Environment Programme (UNEP) and works in cooperation

---

[1] The Institute of Social and Ethical Accountability is probably better known as AccountAbility.

with the Global Compact. The guidelines are under continual development, and in January 2006 the draft version of its new Sustainability Reporting Guidelines, named the G3, was produced and made open for feedback. The GRI pursues its mission through the development and continuous improvement of a reporting framework that can be used by any organisation to report on its economic, environmental and social performance. The GRI has become the popular framework for reporting, on a voluntary basis, for several hundred organizations, mostly for-profit corporations. It claims to be the result of a permanent interaction with many people that supposedly represents a wide variety of stakeholders relative to the impact of the activity of businesses around the world.

GRI and AA1000 provide a set of tools to help organisations manage, measure and communicate their overall sustainability performance, including social, environmental and economic factors. Together, they draw on a wide range of stakeholders and interests to increase the legitimacy of decision-making and improve performance. Individually, each initiative supports the application of the other – at least this is the claim of both organisations concerned; AA1000 provides a rigorous process of stakeholder engagement in support of sustainable development, while GRI provides globally applicable guidelines for reporting on sustainable development that stresses stakeholder engagement in both its development and content. Part of the purpose of this chapter, however, is to question the need for these standards as all the evidence concerning standard-setting here suggests that these standards are derived by consensual agreement rather than by the actions of a third party.

The EC approach

The European Union, through its Commission, has concentrated on the enaction of corporate social responsibility (CSR) as an expression of European cohesion. The Green Papers *Promoting a European framework for Corporate Social Responsibility* (EC, 2001) and *Corporate Social Responsibility: A business contribution to Sustainable Development* (EC, 2002) define the pressure from the European institutions for corporations to recognise and accommodate their responsibilities to their internal and external stakeholder community. The first document (EC, 2001: 8) described CSR as:

> "… a concept whereby companies integrate social and environmental concerns in their business operations and in their interaction with their stakeholders on a voluntary basis."

The essential point is that compliance is voluntary rather than mandatory and this voluntary approach to CSR expresses the reality of enterprises in beginning to take responsibility for their true social impact, and recognises the existence of a larger pressure exercised by various stakeholder groupings in addition to the traditional ones of shareholders and investors.[2] Moreover it reflects the different traditions of business and the differing stages of development throughout the community. Nevertheless the need for social responsibility is by no means universally accepted, although evidence shows that ethical and socially responsible behaviour is being engaged in successfully by a number of large corporations – and this number is increasing all the time. Additionally, there is no evidence that corporations which engage in socially responsible behaviour perform, in terms of profitability and the creation of shareholder value, any worse than any other corporations. Indeed there is a growing body of evidence[3] suggesting that socially responsible behaviour leads to increased economic performance – at least in the longer term – and consequentially greater welfare and wealth for all involved.

All of this means that a wide variety of activities have been classed as representing CSR, ranging from altruism to triple bottom line reporting, and different approaches have been adopted in different countries, in different industries and even in different but similar corporations.

Defining CSR

The broadest definition of corporate social responsibility (see Aras & Crowther 2009) is concerned with what is – or should be – the relationship between global corporations, governments of countries and individual citizens. More locally the definition is concerned with the relationship between a corporation and the local society in which it resides or operates. Another definition is concerned with the relationship between a corporation and its stakeholders. All of these definitions are pertinent and each represents a dimension of the issue. A parallel debate is taking place in the arena of ethics,[4] concerning whether corporations should be controlled through increased regulation or whether the ethical base of citizenship has been lost and needs replacing before socially responsible behaviour can ensue. However this debate is represented, it seems that it is

---

[2] We recognise however that an alternative interpretation that this voluntary approach can enable firms and governments to escape their responsibilities.
[3] See Crowther 2002 for detailed evidence
[4] We acknowledge, of course, that ISO 26000 includes ethics as a part of social responsibility.

concerned with some sort of social contract between corporations and society.

This social contract implies some form of altruistic behaviour – the converse of selfishness (Crowther & Caliyurt 2004) – whereas the self-interest of Classical Liberalism connotes selfishness. Self-interest is central to the utilitarian perspective championed by such people as Bentham, Locke and J. S. Mill. The latter, for example, advocated as morally right the pursuit of the greatest happiness for the greatest number. Similarly, Adam Smith's free-market economics is predicated on competing self-interest – recognising what he regarded as inevitable, despite his personal concern for ethical behaviour. These influential ideas put the interest of the individual above the interest of the collective. The central tenet of social responsibility, however, is the social contract between all the stakeholders of society, which is an essential requirement of civil society. This is alternatively described as citizenship, but for either term, it is important to remember that social responsibility needs to extend beyond present members of society. Social responsibility also requires a responsibility towards the future and towards future members of society. Subsumed within this is, of course, a responsibility towards the environment because of implications for other members of society both now and in the future.

Regulation of standards

Much of the broader debate about corporate social responsibility can be interpreted, however, as an argument between two positions: greater corporate autonomy and the free market economic model versus greater societal intervention and government control of corporate action. There is clear evidence that the free market proponents are winning the argument. They point to the global spread of capitalism, arguing that this reflects recognition that social wellbeing is dependent on economic growth. Opponents concede this hegemony but see the balance shifting in their favour, through, for example, greater accountability and reporting. Some opponents, however, suspect that the corporate team is cheating on its obligations to both the ecological and social dimensions of behaviour, while others object fundamentally to the idea that a free market economy is beneficial to society.

Resolving these arguments seems intractable, if not impossible, because they assume divergent philosophical positions in the ethics v. regulation debate, as well as in more fundamental understandings of human nature. We do not propose to offer any definitive answers since any attempt to do so would itself involve making value judgements. We can, however, examine the debated territory. Moreover, we can look for evidence of the relationship between economic growth, as manifest through corporate profitability, and socially responsible behaviour in an effort to resolve this seemingly dichotomous position. It has been argued elsewhere (e.g. Crowther & Jatana, 2005) that the creation of shareholder value is often not through the operational activities of the firm but rather through the externalisation of costs, which are passed on to customers, employees and other stakeholders, including society at large. Examples of this practice are evidenced elsewhere and it seems that companies adopt a philosophy that no stakeholder matters in isolation.

There is, however, a growing body of evidence (e.g. Crowther & Caliyurt, 2004) which shows a link between socially responsible corporate behaviour and economic profitability which is reinforced by much of the research into socially responsible investment funds. This evidence, however, suggests that there is a positive relationship between the two if a longer term view of corporate performance is recognised.

Similarly there have been many claims (see Crowther 2000) that the quantification of environmental costs and the inclusion of such costs into business strategies can significantly reduce the operating costs of firms; indeed this was one of the main themes of the 1996 Global Environmental Management Initiative Conference. Little evidence exists that this is the case, but Pava and Krausz (1996) demonstrate empirically that companies which they define as 'socially responsible' perform in financial terms at least as well as companies which are not socially responsible. It is accepted, however, that different definitions of socially responsible organisations exist and that different definitions lead to different evaluations of performance between those deemed responsible and others. Similarly, in other countries, efforts are being made to provide a framework for the certification of accountants who wish to be considered as environmental practitioners and auditors. For example, the Canadian Institute of Chartered Accountants is heavily involved in the creation of such a national framework. Azzone, Manzini and Noel (1996), however, suggest that despite the lack of any regulatory framework in this area, a degree of standardisation, at least as far as reporting is concerned, is beginning to emerge at an international level, one of the central arguments of this chapter.

Growth in the techniques offered for measuring social impact, and reporting thereon, has continued throughout the last twenty-five years, during which time the concept of this form of accounting has existed. However, the ability to discuss the fact that firms, through their actions, affect their external environment and that this should be accounted for has often exceeded within the discourse any practical suggestions for measuring such impact. At the same time as the technical implementation of social accounting and reporting has been developing, the philosophical basis for such accounting – predicated in the transparency and accountability principles – has also been developed. Thus, some people consider the extent to which accountants should be involved in this accounting and argue that such accounting can be justified by means of the Social Contract as benefiting society at large. Others have argued that sustainability is the cornerstone of social and environmental accounting and that auditing should be given prominence.

An examination of the external reporting of organisations gives an indication of the extent of socially responsible activity. Such an examination does indeed demonstrate an increasing recognition of the need to include information about this, and an increasing number of annual reports of companies include some information in this respect. This trend is gathering momentum as more organisations perceive the importance of providing such information to external stakeholders. It has been suggested however that the inclusion of such information does not demonstrate an increasing concern with the environment, but, rather, some benefits – for example, tax breaks – to the company itself. One trend which is also apparent in many parts of the world, however, is the tendency of companies to produce separate social and environmental reports. In this context, such reports are generally termed CSR reports or Sustainability Reports, depending upon the development of the corporation concerned. This trend is gathering momentum as more organisations realise that stakeholders are both demanding more information and are also demanding accountability for actions undertaken. Equally, the more enlightened of these corporations are realising that socially responsible activity makes good business sense and actually assists in improving economic performance.

This realisation obviates any need for regulation and calls into question the standards suggested by such bodies as accountability. The more progressive corporations have made considerable progress in what they often describe as their journey towards being fully socially responsible. In doing so, they have developed an understanding of the priorities for their own business – recognising that CSR has many facets and needs to be interpreted differently for each organisation – and made significant steps towards both appropriate activity and appropriate reporting of such activity. The steps towards CSR can be likened to increasing maturity as all organisations progress towards that maturity by passing through the same stages (see below), although at different paces. The most mature are indeed recognising the nature of globalisation by recognising that the organisational boundary is permeable (see Crowther & Duty, 2002) and that they are accountable also for the behaviour of other organisations in their value chain.

Developing a typology of CSR activity

The preceding analysis makes possible the development of a typology of CSR maturity. It would be relatively easy to develop a typology of CSR activity based upon the treatment of the various stakeholders to an organisation but, as Cooper et al. (2001) show, all corporations are concerned with their important stakeholders and make efforts to satisfy their expectations. Thus, a concern with employees and customers is apparent in all corporations, being merely a reflection of the power of those stakeholder groupings rather than any expression of social responsibility. Similarly, in some organisations, a concern for the environment is less a representation of social responsibility and more a concern for avoiding legislation or possibly a reflection of customer concern. Such factors also apply to some expressions of concern for local communities and society at large. It is, therefore, inappropriate to base any typology of CSR activity upon the treatment of stakeholders, as this is often based upon power relationships rather than a concern for social responsibility, and it is not realistic to distinguish between the motivations.

A different typology is therefore proposed – one which is based upon the three principles of social responsibility outlined earlier. Moreover, it shows the way in which CSR develops in organisations as they become more experienced and more convinced of the benefits of a commitment to this form of corporate activity. The development of this typology is based upon research and interviews with CSR directors and concerned managers in a considerable number of large corporations, many of which are committed to increasing social responsibility. It demonstrates stages of increasing maturity.

Stage of development	Dominant feature	Typical activity	Examples
1	Window dressing	Redesigning corporate reporting	Changed wording and sections to reflect CSR language (see Crowther, 2004)
2	Cost containment	Re-engineering business processes	Energy efficiency programmes
3	Stakeholder engagement	Balanced scorecard development	Customer / employee satisfaction surveys (See Cooper et al., 2001)
4	Measurement and reporting	Sophisticated tailored measures	CSR reports
5	Sustainability	Defining sustainability: re-engineering processes	Sustainability reporting
6	Transparency	Concern for the supply chain: requiring CSR from suppliers	Human rights enforcement: e.g. child labour
7	Accountability	Reconfiguration of the value chain	Relocating high value added activity in developing countries

Fig 1.1: Stages of Maturity of CSR activity. From Crowther, 2008

This can be explained as stages of growth reflecting increased maturity. The stages can be elaborated as follows:

Stage 1 Window dressing

The initial engagement with CSR was to change corporate reporting to indicate a concern for CSR without any actual change in corporate behaviour. This is the stage which led to accusations of green-washing. It is also the stage which most observers of corporate activity continue to see, even though, in reality, probably every organisation has progressed to a stage of greater maturity

Stage 2 Cost containment

Corporations are always of course looking at their processes and seeking to operate more efficiently, thereby reducing costs. Organisations have realised that some of these can be represented as CSR activity – with things like energy efficiency or water efficiency being obvious examples. So there is a double imperative for this kind of activity – to improve financial performance and also improve their socially responsible image. Not surprisingly, therefore, corporations quickly moved from stage 1 to this stage – where action has been taken even though it is not necessarily motivated by a sense of social responsibility.

Much of this kind of activity is easy to undertake and requires very little in the way of capital investment. Naturally, this activity has been undertaken first. Activities requiring capital investment have a longer payback period and tend to be undertaken more cautiously, with the threat of regulation often being needed to encourage organisations to adopt such activities. All organisations have also progressed through this stage, although it must be recognised that the possible actions available at this stage will probably never be completed by most organisations. Cost containment remains ongoing even when the easier targets have been addressed.

Stage 3 Stakeholder engagement

As stated earlier, all corporations are concerned with their important stakeholders and make efforts to satisfy their expectations. Thus, a concern with employees and customers is apparent in all corporations, being merely a reflection of the power of those stakeholder groupings rather than any expression of social responsibility. Similarly, in some organisations, a concern for the environment is less a representation of social responsibility and more a concern for avoiding legislation or possibly a reflection of customer concern. Such factors also apply to some expressions of concern for local communities and society at large. For CSR, though, this concern has become formalised, often through the development of a balanced scorecard and such things as customer or employee satisfaction surveys. Most organisations have also progressed through this stage, with such activity being embedded into normal ongoing business practice.

Stage 4 Measurement and reporting

Some companies have been practicing social and environmental reporting for 15 years, but for many, such behaviours are more recent. Now most companies – certainly most large companies – provide this information in the form of a report. Over time, these reports have become more extensive and more detailed with a broader range of measures of social and environmental performance being included. As such, most organisations have reached this stage of maturity. The problem with this stage, however, is that at the moment there are no standards of what to report and so organisations tend to report different things, thereby hindering comparability. Organisations such as AccountAbility, with its AA1000 standard, and the Global Compact have sought to redress this through the introduction of standards, but none have gained universal acceptance. Consequently, it is probably true to state that this is the current stage of development for most organisations.

Stage 5 Sustainability

The discourse of sustainability has become as ubiquitous as the discourse of CSR, and Aras & Crowther (2007a) report that every firm in the FTSE100, for example, mention sustainability, with 70% of them focusing upon this. Any analysis of these statements regarding sustainability, however, quickly reveals the uncertainty regarding what is meant by this sustainability. Clearly, the vast majority do not mean sustainability as defined by Aras & Crowther (2007b), or as defined by the Brundtland Report. Often, it appears to mean little more than that the corporation will continue to exist in the future. A full understanding of sustainability would imply radical changes to business practice and a significant amount of process re-engineering, and there is little evidence that this is happening. So we argue that most companies are only starting to reach this stage of maturity and to grapple with the issues involved.

Stage 6 Transparency

One of the biggest issues of the moment – certainly in Europe – is the question of firms accepting responsibility for what happens further along their supply chain. This is something that has been brought about largely because of customer pressure and has come about because of the revelations made about such things as child labour, slavery and other human rights abuses. So it is no longer acceptable for a firm to say that what happens in a supplying firm – or even the supplier of a supplier – is not their responsibility. Popular opinion says for companies that the firm is responsible for ensuring socially responsible behaviour among their suppliers as well as in their own company. Thus there have been examples of some very large companies – such as Gap or Nike – acknowledging responsibility and taking appropriate action to ensure change.

This is an issue which is growing in importance and is being addressed by the more mature (in CSR terms) companies. Thus it is claimed that some companies are at this stage in their maturation, although this is still only a minority of companies.

Stage 7 Accountability

The final stage represents our wishes rather than actuality – at least so far! It is based upon the fact that multinational organisations can decide where to locate their operations and that all high value added operations are located in developed countries. For many it would be relatively easy to transfer to less developed countries, and if that happened then the company would be making a real contribution towards effecting change. We argue that there is no real cost involved – just that corporations should seek to do this to benefit society rather than simply for cost minimisation.

Essentially the argument being made here is that CSR must be considered as a process of development for every organisation – a process which is still taking place. Furthermore, every organisation goes through the same stages in the same chronological order[5]. Thus, the leading exponents of CSR are only now beginning to address stage 6 and possibly consider stage 7. Less developed corporations are at lower stages of development. What is significant about this, however, is that our argument is that sustainability only starts to be recognised once a company has reached stage 5 of its development. More significantly, stages 6 and 7 are essential for true sustainability, as it is only then that an organisation recognises – and acts upon the recognition – that it is an integral part of a value chain and that sustainability depends upon the actions of the complete value chain. In others words, an organisation cannot be sustainable without its suppliers and customers. At the moment, it is doubtful if organisations recognise this and whether any organisation is (yet) truly sustainable.

---

[5] This can be likened to Erikson's stages of growth for human beings, of which (coincidentally) there are also 7.

Crisis and accountability

The events that marked 2011[6], from the Arab Spring revolutions to the different collapses in the financial markets in the western world and the Euro Debt Crisis in Europe, all have in common the issue of governance. The numerous different types of media, especially social media, have contributed to the rapid spread of the awareness of governance issues and enabled unprecedented numbers of people to manifest their fury about the lack of governance in the management of not only firms and markets, but whole countries and regions.

Governance crises were originally known mainly in the corporate world, where scandals such as Enron and News International have captured the attention of the media and have been the number one subject of discussion for many; now, however, they have been transferred to entire nations, where citizens claim the right to change things the better and to have the last say. The main claims that the people have been making are centred around the establishment of accountability mechanisms that were absent, as well as real governance reforms that will lead to democracy. The causes of the problems that happened in both the Arab and Western worlds have been divergent; however, the consequences were similar: street protests and a lack of confidence by citizens, investors, rating agencies and international organisations. This shows how much governance is at the heart of a prosperous and durable organisation, whatever size or kind it is, from small and medium companies, multinational corporations, non-governmental organisations, to governments and states.

This led to the 2012 Organisation Governance conference[7] which focused on the importance of accountability, and how it varies from one environment to another, as well as how governance can be practised effectively in the shadow of the turmoil and unrest in the Arab and Western worlds, taking into consideration the specificities of each and every culture. The issue of rules-based or principles-based governance is also still to be discussed, especially as different parts of the world have different cultures and beliefs. The question that could be asked is whether the raising of awareness combined with the stakeholders' power in claiming their rights, is enough to change people's mentalities and behaviours in order to achieve a well-governed organisation, or country.

---

[6] 2011 was just prior to the conference from which this book was the outcome.
[7] Held in Rabat, Morocco in 2012 as the 2nd annual conference of the Research in Organizational Governance Network – see
https://sites.google.com/site/researchogn/home.

This book aims to address these issues and posit answers. So let us turn to the other chapters in this volume.

In the next chapter, Crowther et al. state that business competition comes in many different forms and includes a great variety of competitors. Successfully positioning the enterprise, properly deciding on the correct allocation of resources, and deciding what an acceptable level of performance might be in such a competitive environment are key tasks of decision makers. This article attempts to shed light on the extent to which competitive intelligence (CI) impacts on corporate governance, that is, how competitive intelligence allows company to compete and deliver value to its stakeholders. This issue is worthwhile insofar as it provides a new way for companies to develop new frameworks that hold together competitive intelligence and corporate governance. The approach taken by the authors is to obtain insight and views on how competitive intelligence influences corporate governance. To that end, a range of recent research literature publications on competitive intelligence, and governance within organizations is reviewed to explore the link between competitive intelligence and corporate governance. Findings reveal the representation of cross-disciplinary literature which emphasises the multi-faceted role which competitive intelligence plays in a modern organisation. The chapter identifies the extent to which competitive intelligence is utilised within organisations, as tool to enhance corporate governance, and identifies the benefits or problems that are experienced by implementing and using competitive intelligence as an input to corporate governance and what value competitive intelligence adds in the decision-making process.

In the following chapter, Gulliver commences by stating that Organisational Governance is a term used to describe a field of academic research that focuses on the way organisations are governed. It includes a wide range of issues relating to all aspects of "management", particularly the management of companies or corporations in the private sector. The term management can be applied equally to other types of groups of people, apart from corporations, such as public sector organisations and even individuals, so their governance issues are also discussed. The organisational governance mechanisms in place today are inadequate. Too many issues are not addressed at all and many others need improvement. Her chapter explores some of the possible meanings of the terms organisational, governance and organisational governance, leading to some useful insights and more precise descriptions of some of the issues that are being addressed. These 3 propositions are developed and discussed in detail.

Crowther and Seifi, in chapter 4, begin from the premise that, as the world moves into an era of depleted environmental resources coupled with global warming, accounting seeks to adapt to address the needs of businesses in this new environment. Thus, the discourse becomes one of accounting for sustainability. In this chapter, they argue that sustainability cannot be achieved through accounting until the notion of equity is included and accounting adapts from a focus upon efficiency to a focus upon equity. In doing so, they highlight the various problems which they consider need to be addressed. Following this, Elachgar et al. deal with the 4th wave of the Information Security as a new approach to the governance of information security. After introducing the four waves of information security, the writers focus on the most recent part. In addition, following the PDCA approach (Plan, Do Check, Act), they then establish an inventory of information systems with the SoM (Statement of Maturity), a risk assessment of assets, a business continuity plan to ensure a resumption of IT.

In the first part of the book, we have considered theoretical aspects of the relevant issues. In the second part we turn to an examination of different sectors, starting with a chapter by Efiong and Crowther considering accountability in public government in Africa. They start from the position that, all over the world, governance crises have become a recurrent decimal in recent times, arguing that these crises are traceable to a lack of accountability in governance. Although accountability is a concept that is difficult to define in precise terms, it exists where there is the demand for the justification for a function or task that is performed by an individual or body for another individual or body. The available literature distinguishes between two major stages of accountability; namely 'answerability' and 'enforcement'. While the answerability stage involves the responsibility of the government, its agencies or public office holders to provide information concerning their actions and the justification for taking such actions to the public or any other institutions that provide them with oversight functions, enforcement on the other hand is the stage where the public or institutions with oversight functions seek ways to correct the infringement or sanction the offending party. It has been observed that, many times, human beings have to be 'pushed' to do what they are supposed to do. This chapter, therefore, examines the theoretical perspectives of accountability in public governance with an emphasis on enforcement. It is the authors' view that the enforcement of accountability in governance will ultimately assist in correcting the behaviours of those in public governance, thereby resulting in good governance.

In the next chapter, Farooq and Aguenaou consider web traffic and firm performance to decide whether the traffic generated by websites of firms signals anything to stock market participants. This chapter aims to answer these questions by documenting a positive relationship between the extent of web-traffic and firm performance in the MENA region during 2010. They argue that higher web-traffic lowers the agency problems in firms by disseminating more information to stock market participants. Consequently, lower agency problems translate into better performance. Furthermore, they also show that the agency-reducing role of web-traffic is more pronounced in regimes where the information environment is already bad. For example, the results show the stronger impact of web-traffic on firm performance in civil law countries, firms with concentrated ownership, and firms with more intangible assets. All of these groups are characterized by higher agency problems. Their results, therefore, indicate that web-traffic can play a substitute role for traditional governance mechanisms in the MENA region.

In the subsequent chapter, Seifi and Crowther consider the governance of domestic energy consumption. They commence by stating that, in the ever-increasing worldwide attention to the concept of sustainable development, the pillars of which are economic, social and environmental development, industrial engineering as the champion of productivity has not really received major attention. This is unfortunate as one can see it as the toolkit to attain sustainable development because industrial engineering is concerned with productivity as the measure for production and service efficiency. Without this, it would be difficult to quantify the quality aspects of sustainable development, including, for example, those related to the environment. And without this there would be a difficulty in evaluating the integrated systems of man, money, materials, energy, knowledge, information and equipment, which are all instances of these three pillars. Energy efficiency is one route towards minimising environmental impact. Minimising such impact is one important factor in achieving sustainability and therefore making sustainable development possible. In this chapter, they show the use of industrial engineering tools like risk analysis to assess how sustainable our current energy consumption is, and so refrigerators are taken as the sample for such analysis. This is due to the general usage of refrigerators by all people everywhere and due to its major role in worldwide energy consumption. Energy labels are nowadays a common feature of refrigerators put into the market for sale, although this trend is diverse in different parts of the world, which signals non-harmonized comprehension of sustainable development in the world. This is explored in this contribution at a theoretical level to show that industrial engineering tools and techniques have a contribution to make to sustainability.

In the next chapter, the final in Part 2, Rasheed and Gagern consider Saudi Arabia, starting from the premise that, by the year 2030, the likelihood of Saudi Arabia needing all the oil they produce for internal use is very high. They then consider how Saudi Arabia can make sure that it will continue to have something to sell in the global market. Possibilities considered include solar technology, infrastructure management, E-government, E-learning and education, date products, perfume, gold and zinc, as well as tourism. The authors examine issues, including whether this will all be enough to safeguard a decent standard of living and whether self-reliance is an alternative path towards sustainable development. This scenario is particularly interesting as, contrary to many other Arab states, Saudi Arabia seems to still have the time and resources to contemplate and experiment with alternative developmental strategies. And the discussion is particularly interesting in the context of conflicting interests between global governance and local government issues.

The final part of the book looks at regional issues and understandings, starting naturally with Morocco. In the first chapter of this part, Hassan proposes an approach to set up a relevant and simple methodology to improve the capacity of management to manage the new practices of organizational sustainable development, to federate the actions and to strengthen the governance and the piloting of the company. The purpose of this methodology is to bring to managers a real strategic decision-making support, allowing them to act on all the levels of improvement of the company performance.

This is followed in the next chapter by Agbola and Sokro's concern with judgement debt in Ghana. The purpose of their research was to analyse the issues related to the recent scandals over government accountability in payments of the judgement debt in Ghana. The study investigates the extent to which the public institutions of accountability and mechanisms of control operate effectively to ensure that those who exercise power account for their stewardship in the use of public funds. The research procedure applied was mainly the careful analysis of source materials, including newspaper articles, parliamentary proceedings, government documents and public reports, as well as radio and television reports. A 6-item survey questionnaire was also administered to the general public to ascertain public opinion on the issues. Their findings reveal that blatant disregard for the public procurement laws, illicit abrogation of contracts, weak institutions of accountability, a catalogue of errors, negligence, and the sometimes deliberate corruption of government, private and corporate officials resulted in the fraudulent payment of colossal sums of money to the judgement debt. The study is particularly significant to international and corporate bodies doing business with the Republic of Ghana in that it alerts these institutions of the importance of ensuring that all the stipulations of the country's financial and procurement laws are carefully observed when entering into a contract with the government to avoid future abrogation and ensure restitution in the event of government default.

In the final chapter in this part, Abdaless and colleagues investigate risk management in UK city councils. The financial crisis had a knock out effect on the economy of the UK as it affected businesses as well as the public and not-for-profit sector. The lack of research regarding governance in the public sector and its importance in the global economy and the wider stakeholders it affects, was the main driver in carrying out this study. The chapter studies the implication of the global financial crisis translated into budget cuts within the public sector in the UK on governance in local councils, focusing on risk management and accountability. The chapter begins by highlighting the stakeholder theory and governance in the public sector, before emphasising the methodology adopted in this research, and analysing the data collected. The last part of this article is devoted to discussing the findings and conclusions. This research explored the gap in the literature regarding governance in the public sector. The findings of this research proved that there is a direct impact of the crisis on the general management of people and resources in local government. The risk management ability of these councils has been affected and a range of stakeholders have been directly impacted by the crisis, whether these are employees of the council or the communities in which the councils are operating.

This is followed by the final concluding chapter in the book, in which the editors try to bring this together and summarise with the aim of moving towards the development of a theoretical basis of governance, which was the intended outcome of the conference from which these chapters ensue. The authors and editor hope that you find them stimulating.

References

Aras G & Crowther D (2007a); What level of trust is needed for sustainability?; *Social Responsibility Journal* 3 (3), 60-68

Aras G & Crowther D (2007b); The Development of Corporate Social Responsibility; *Effective Executive*; Vol. X No 9, September 2007 pp. 18-21

Aras G & Crowther D (2009); The Durable Corporation: strategies for sustainable development; Farnham; Gower

Azzone G, Manzini R & Noel G (1996); Evolutionary trends in environmental reporting; *Business Strategy and Environment*, 5 (4), 219-230

Cooper S, Crowther D, Davies M & Davis E W (2001); *Shareholder or Stakeholder Value? The development of indicators for the control and measurement of performance*; London; CIMA

Crowther D (2000); *Social and Environmental Accounting*; London; Financial Times prentice Hall

Crowther D (2008); The Maturing of Corporate Social Responsibility: A Developmental Process; in D Crowther & N Capaldi (eds.), *Research Companion to Corporate Social Responsibility*; pp. 19-30; Aldershot; Ashgate

Crowther D (2012); *A Social Critique of Corporate Reporting; Semiotics and web-based integrated reporting*; Farnham; Gower

Crowther D & Caliyurt K T (2004); Corporate social responsibility improves profitability; in D Crowther & K T Caliyurt (eds.), *Stakeholders and Social Responsibility*, Penang; Ansted University Press; pp. 243-266

Crowther D & Duty D J (2002); Operational performance in post-modern organisations - towards a framework for including time in the evaluation of performance; *Journal of Applied Finance*, May, 23-46

Crowther D & Jatana R (2005); Modern epics and corporate well-being; in D Crowther & R Jatana (eds.), *Representations of Social Responsibility*; Hyderabad; ICFAI University Press; pp. 125-165

European Commission (EC, 2001), *Green Paper – Promoting a European framework for Corporate Social Responsibility,* COM (2001) 366 final, Brussels: Official publications of the European Commission, July 18.

European Commission (EC, 2002), *Corporate Social Responsibility: A business contribution to Sustainable Development*, COM (2002) 347 final, Brussels: Official publications of the European Commission, July 2.

McLuhan, M & Fiore, Q (1968). *War and Peace in the Global Village.* San Francisco: Hardwired.

Pava M L & Krausz J (1996); The association between corporate social responsibility and financial performance: the paradox of social cost; *Journal of Business Ethics*, 15 (3), 321-357

PART I:

THEORETICAL UNDERSTANDINGS

CHAPTER TWO

LINKING COMPETITIVE INTELLIGENCE TO CORPORATE GOVERNANCE: INSIGHT FROM A STAKEHOLDER PERSPECTIVE

DAVID CROWTHER, MOURAD OUBRICH, REDOUANE BARZI AND SARA ABDALESS

> "In business, the competition will bite you if you keep running,
> if you stand still, they will swallow you."
> —William Knudsen Jr

Introduction

It is generally acknowledged that, as a concept, governance has existed as long as any form of human organisation has existed. The concept itself is merely one to encapsulate the means by which that organisation conducts itself. Recently, however, the term has come to the forefront of public attention, and this is probably because of the problems of governance which have been revealed at both a national level and in the economic sphere at the level of the corporation. These problems have caused there to be a concern with a re-examination of what exactly is meant by governance, and more specifically the definition of the features of good governance. It is here, therefore, that we must start our examination. When considering national governance, then, this has been defined by the World Bank as the exercise of political authority and the use of institutional resources to manage society's problems and affairs.

In today's society, knowledge is the primary resource for individuals and for the economy. Land, labor, capital and entrepreneurship, the economist's traditional factors of production, have not disappeared, but the first three have declined in importance. They can be easily obtained and provided (Drucker, 1992). Interest in a new economic world order based upon intellectual capital has grown exponentially in both industrialized nations and developing countries around the world. The need for fast and reliable information exchange came as a response to rapidly changing markets, products and services.

By consulting the literature, a tentative conclusion may be that companies do not necessarily need more information; what they need is useful and relevant information in time (Frishammar, 2002). The reason for this is that there are a lot of different terms used to describe how useful and relevant information might be collected, interpreted, analysed, distributed and so forth.

Sometimes competitive intelligence (CI) is confused with business intelligence (BI). The difference between business intelligence and competitive intelligence is that business intelligence is internal intelligence about and within one's own company, whereas competitive intelligence is external intelligence about the firm's competitors (Bose, 2008).

Competitive intelligence is a business tool that can make a significant contribution to the strategic management process in modern business organizations, driving business performance and change by increasing knowledge (Priporas, Gatsoris & Zacharis, 2005). In the strategy literature, corporate governance is an important factor affecting a firm's performance and long-term survival (Filatotchev, Toms & Wright, 2006). If competitive intelligence and corporate governance influence how firms compete, it will be of interest to see how competitive intelligence influences the various aspects of corporate governance. With regard to this point, it will be interesting to study the impact of competitive intelligence within a stakeholder approach to corporate governance.

The purpose of this research is twofold: first, to study the relationship between competitive intelligence and corporate governance; and second, to provide an insight into how competitive intelligence influences corporate governance. The rest of the chapter is organized as follows. The first part focuses on corporate governance and its relationship to risk management. The second part presents a brief overview of the literature on competitive intelligence, and its processes and tools. The third part presents the link between competitive intelligence and corporate governance.

Good governance and corporate behaviour

Good governance is of course important in every sphere of society, whether it be the corporate environment, general society or the political environment. Good governance levels can, for example, improve public faith and confidence in the political environment. When resources are too limited to meet the minimum expectations of the people, a good governance level can help to promote the welfare of society. And of course, a concern with governance is at least as prevalent in the corporate world.

Good governance is essential for good corporate performance. One view of good corporate performance is connected with the concept of stewardship, and thus, just as the management of an organisation is concerned with the stewardship of the financial resources of the organisation, so too would management of the organisation be concerned with the stewardship of environmental resources. The difference, however, is that environmental resources are mostly located externally to the organisation. Stewardship in this context therefore is concerned with the resources of society, as well as with the resources of the organisation. As far as stewardship of external environmental resources is concerned, the central tenet of such stewardship is that of ensuring sustainability. Sustainability is focused on the future and is concerned with ensuring that the choices of resource utilisation in the future are not constrained by decisions taken in the present. This necessarily implies such concepts as generating and utilising renewable resources, minimising pollution, and using new techniques of manufacture and distribution. It also implies the acceptance of any costs involved in the present as an investment for the future.

A great deal of concern has been expressed all over the world about shortcomings in the systems of corporate governance in operation, and its organisation has been exercising the minds of business managers, academics and government officials all over the world. The main target of companies is often to become global – while at the same time remaining sustainable – as a means to gain competitive power. But the most important question is concerned with what will be a firm's route to becoming global, and what will be necessary in order to gain global competitive power. There is more than one answer to this question and there are a variety of routes for a company to achieve this. Corporate governance can be considered as an environment of trust, ethics, moral values and confidence – as a synergic effort of all the constituents of society - that is, the stakeholders, including the government, the general public, and professional/service providers - and the corporate sector.

Of equal concern is the question of corporate social responsibility – what this means and how it can be operationalised. Although there is an accepted link between good corporate governance and corporate social responsibility, the relationship between the two is not clearly defined and understood. Thus, many firms consider that their governance is adequate because they comply with the Combined Code on Corporate Governance, which came into effect in 2003. Of course, all firms reporting on the London Stock Exchange are required to comply with this code, and so these firms are doing no more than meeting their regulatory obligations. Many companies regard corporate governance as simply a part of investor relationships and do nothing more regarding such governance except to identify that it is important to investors / potential investors and to flag up that they have such governance policies. The more enlightened recognise that there is a clear link between governance and corporate social responsibility, and make efforts to link the two. Often this is no more than making a claim that good governance is a part of their CSR policy as well as a part of their relationship with shareholders.

One of the consequences of a concern with the actions of an organisation, and the outcomes of those actions, has been an increasing concern with corporate governance. Corporate governance is therefore a current buzzword the world over. It has gained tremendous importance in recent years.

Since the mid-1980s, corporate governance has attracted a great deal of attention. Early impetus was provided by Anglo-American codes of good corporate governance[1]. Stimulated by institutional investors, other countries in the developed world, as well as those in emerging markets, established an adapted version of these codes for their own companies. Supra-national authorities like the OECD and the World Bank did not remain passive and developed their own set of standard principles and recommendations. This type of self-regulation was chosen above a set of legal standards (Van den Barghe, 2001). After big corporate scandals, corporate governance has become central to most companies. It is understandable that investors' protection has become a much more important issue for all financial markets after tremendous recent firm failures and scandals. Investors are demanding that companies implement rigorous corporate governance principles in order to achieve better returns on their investment and to reduce agency costs. Most of the time, investors are ready to pay more for companies to have good governance standards. Similarly a company's corporate governance report is one of the main tools for investors' decisions. Because of these reasons, companies cannot ignore the pressure for good governance from shareholders, potential investors and other market actors.

Nevertheless, it is certain that the link between corporate governance and actual performance is still open for discussion. In the literature, a

---

[1] An example is the Cadbury Report.

number of studies have investigated the relation between corporate governance mechanisms and performance (such as Agrawal and Knoeber, 1996, and Millstein and MacAvoy, 2003). Most of these studies have shown mixed results without a clear-cut relationship. Based on these results, we can say that corporate governance matters to a company's performance, market value and credibility, and, therefore, that the company has to apply corporate governance principles. However, the most important point is that corporate governance is the only means for companies to achieve corporate goals and strategies. Therefore, companies have to improve their strategy, and find an effective route to the implementation of governance principles. As such, companies have to investigate what their corporate governance policy and practice needs to be.

Corporate governance can be highly influential for firm performance, and firms must know what corporate governance is. There are four principles of good corporate governance, which are:

- Transparency;
- Accountability;
- Responsibility;
- Fairness.

All these principles are related to the firm's corporate social responsibility. Corporate governance principles, therefore, are important for a firm, but the real issue is concerned with what corporate governance actually is.

Good Governance and Sustainability

It is clear that all these long term benefits are also directly related to the sustainability of a firm and that firm's success. We can evaluate corporate governance from different perspectives, such as those of the general economy, the company itself, private and institutional investors, and banking and other financial institutions. Some research results show that the quality of the corporate governance system of an economy may be an important determinant of its competitive conditions (Fulghieri and Suominen, 2005). Some authors suggest the existence of a reverse causality between corporate governance and competition, and also examine the role of competition in the production of good corporate governance. Van de Berghe and Levrau (2003), on the other hand, investigated corporate governance from the perspective of companies, investors and banks. From the company's perspective, the pressure for good corporate governance from the investor community can no longer be ignored. Installing proper governance mechanisms may provide a company with a competitive advantage in attracting investors who are prepared to pay a premium for well-governed companies. From an investor's perspective, corporate governance has become an important factor in investment decisions as it is recognized to have an impact on the financial risks of their portfolios. Institutional investors put issues of corporate governance on a par with financial indicators when evaluating investment decisions.

Bøhren, and Ødegaard (2004) also showed that corporate governance matters for economic performance; insider ownership matters the most, while outside ownership concentration destroys market value; direct ownership is superior to indirect; and that performance decreases with increasing board size, leverage, dividend payout, and the fraction of non-voting shares. Black et al. (2005) investigated the relationship between governance and firm value. They found evidence that better-governed firms pay higher dividends, but found no evidence that they report higher accounting profits.

Governance and performance

The relationship between good governance and business performance is clear, and investors are increasingly willing to pay a premium for good governance in a business because of the expected improvements in sustainable performance, which will, over time, be reflected in future dividend streams (Crowther & Seifi 2010). The relationship between social responsibility and governance is similarly clear (see Aras & Crowther, 2007, 2008). In an attempt to satisfy the necessities of the stakeholders, other conflicts between the interests of the different groups included in the wider concept of stakeholders may emerge.

An important component of sustainability is risk management. This too provides an intersection with operational requirements, as minimising exposure to risk both makes a company more socially responsible and more sustainable, but also reduces cost in the longer term (Crowther & Seifi, 2010). Often, however, the methodologies for the evaluation of risk are deficient in their effectiveness of evaluating environmental risk in particular.

Obviously, there is an element of risk attached to any operational decision, and this risk arises because we are attempting to predict future outcomes of decisions made now (Crowther 2004). Various techniques

exist which can help a manager to understand the nature of the risk
associated with any decision, and to quantify the effects of that risk. One
such technique is Risk Analysis, which is based on clearly distinguishing
risk from uncertainty and then treating risk probabilistically in order to
make the best decisions. In all cases of strategy development, the selection
of an appropriate strategy depends upon a realistic assessment of the risk
and a quantification of possible effects through analysis. It is to Risk
Analysis, therefore, that we now turn.

When a range of possible outcomes for an event exists, then obviously
the sum of the probabilities for all possible outcomes must equal 1 – as
one of the outcomes must occur. The assignment of probabilities to each
of the outcomes, however, enables us to construct a probability
distribution showing the range of possible outcomes and their respective
probabilities. Such a distribution may well be important to the analysis,
because merely selecting the most likely outcome may well not reflect the
level of risk involved.

For example, in the two projects shown below the best estimate of
profitability for each of the projects is identical, but it can be seen from the

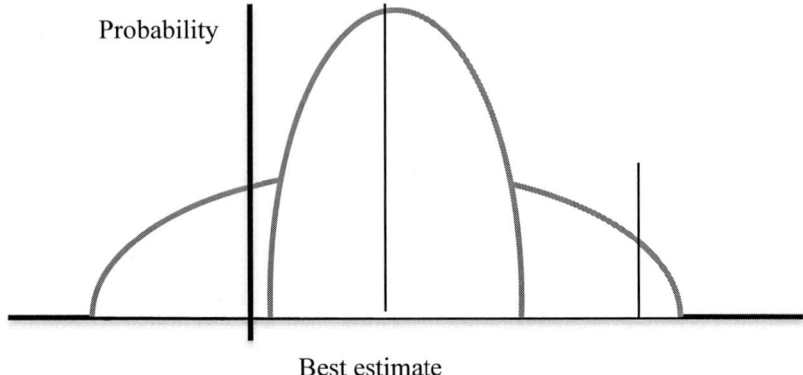

Best estimate

Figure 2.1: Differing probability profiles

probability distributions (figure 2.1) that the risk associated with them is
quite different, with one of the projects having a risk of incurring a loss
(project B). Without the probability distributions, therefore, a firm would
be indifferent as to which project was chosen, but with an understanding
of the distribution of risk then it can be seen that project A is the
preferable project, providing always that the expected returns for the two
projects are similar. Risk Analysis can be used to quantify the expected

values of the return from each project, but assessing the relative relationship between risk and rewards inevitably relies upon managerial judgement and a person's attitude to risk.

Risk Analysis as a technique is based upon probability theory (Crowther, 2004) and upon the ability to construct probability distributions. It is a technique which is designed to enable individual risks associated with a project to be combined and totalled to find the overall risk for the project. It is based upon assigning a probability distribution for each risk factor, rather than merely assigning a best estimate. These probability distributions are then combined using Monte Carlo Simulation techniques to arrive at an overall assessment of risk (Crowther, 1996).

This kind of analysis can lead to a very different assessment of risk for a particular decision than would our assessment if we based our quantification solely upon mean values from our understanding of the probability of particular outcomes. In complex problems with a range of possible outcomes and a variety of factors to be included, this technique, therefore, can help in our understanding of the risks involved, and hence can affect our decision-making in such cases.

Although Risk Analysis can be a useful tool when it comes to making strategic decisions, the most useful tool is Games Theory. This is particularly helpful when deciding about refrigerator labelling because, just as in making many engineering and management decisions, it is important to recognise that the decision is not made in isolation, and that the effects of the decision cannot be realistically quantified as if that was the case. This is particularly true when the external environment is affected by the decision, such as when a firm is considering the launch of a new product, a change to its prices, or the conduct of an advertising campaign. In such circumstances it is not sufficient to consider how the decision might affect the firm itself or how it might be received by its customers. It is also necessary to recognise that the firm's competitors will be affected by the decision and may very well decide to respond to the actions of the firm. In such a situation, the firm and its decision makers can be regarded as either in competition with another firm and its decision makers or in conflict, and the generic term to describe this kind of situation is that of a game. As such, Games Theory can help to model this kind of situation (Crowther, 2004), and therefore improve the decisions which are made.

In games, the participants are competitors and the success of one is usually at the expense of the other, such as when one firm gains market share through the use of an advertising campaign – or through its labelling strategy – at the expense of the other firms in the industry. For the purposes of Games Theory, in such a situation, the number of players can very often be simplified to two players – the firm and the competition, with all competitors being regarded as a single player. It is possible to model the actions and reactions of all competitors separately through Games Theory, but this makes the mathematics very complicated, often without significantly changing the analysis. Games Theory provides a method of formulating a business situation in terms of strategies – the strategy of the decision maker and the strategy of his / her opponent – and in terms of outcomes. Each player in the game selects and executes those strategies which (s) he believes will result in 'winning the game', that is, will result in the most favourable outcome to the problem situation. In determining this strategy for winning, each player makes use of both deductive and inductive logic and attempts quantification of the outcomes.

Stakeholder management

The 1980s' economic environment was the reason for the proliferation of the stakeholder theory (Donaldson & Peterson, 1995), which was a response to the lack of opportunities available to managers to explore, given their focus on the traditional, sole stockholders. The stakeholder theory has broken the borders, and made every individual or group of individuals that may have an interest in and can affect, or be affected by, the firm, be classified as a stakeholder; and therefore, be considered by the management when making decisions (Freeman, 1984; Freeman & McVea, 2001).

In this regard, stakeholder theory has been subject to a wide range of investigations (Freeman & McVea 2001, Donaldson & Peterson, 1995), and many authors have attempted to classify stakeholders according to different criteria. However, in the context of Competitive Intelligence and Governance, the focus will be on one particular group: competition.

Part of the stakeholder management suggested by Freeman and McVea (2001) is to identify the stakeholders, then make sure that the interests and need of all these stakeholders are balanced. Therefore, the key to good management is in taking into consideration the interests of the relevant stakeholders identified, and then balancing the actions taken by management in order to fulfil the needs of these stakeholders.

Good governance procedures enable the identification of risks and therefore also aid their management and reduction. Equally competitive intelligence is enabled through good governance, and it is to this that we now turn.

Competitive intelligence: Definition

According to Beatty and Ulrich (1991), novel ways to beat the competition may arise from the ability of an organization to conceptualize and manage change. Competitive intelligence can help an organization to achieve this objective.

A lot of people think that competitive intelligence is similar to corporate spying (Marin and Poulter, 2004). However, much of this work consists of finding interesting available data from public sources (including government filings, news clippings, surveys, press releases and industry journals) or from the organization itself (Lackman et al., 2000). Diverse sources of competitive intelligence can be used, such as customers, competitors, associations, employees and company records.

There are many definitions of competitive intelligence. The Society of Competitive Intelligence Professionals (SCIP, 2008) defines competitive intelligence as "a systematic and ethical process for gathering, analysing and managing external information that can affect the company's plans, decisions and operations". Dishman and Calof (2007) define competitive intelligence as "actionable recommendations arising from a systematic process, involving planning, gathering, analysing and disseminating information on the external environment, for opportunities or developments that have the potential to affect a company or a country's competitive situation". Indeed, another definition of competitive intelligence is the use of public sources to develop information about the competition, competitors, and market environment (McGonagle and Vella, 1990). Competitive intelligence includes competitor intelligence as well as intelligence collected on customers, suppliers, technologies, environments, or potential business relationships (Saayman, et al, 2008).

Lackman et al. (2000) define an effective competitive intelligence function by its emphasis on users, total commitment to competitive intelligence by the company's top leadership, and effective methods of disseminating the gathered intelligence within the organization. Powell and Allgaier (1998) stress that competitive intelligence staff need to make available the results of their intelligence analysis to decision-makers both quickly and effectively.

Importance of competitive intelligence

Dishman and Calof (2007) believed that competitive intelligence may imply the true purpose of intelligence, that is, to gain strategic advantage.

According to Strauss and Du Toit (2010), organisations are paying attention to competitive intelligence, because it supports organisational needs in terms of gathering, interpreting and disseminating external information. Therefore, the primary output from competitive intelligence is the ability to make forward-looking decisions (Bose, 2008). Johns and Van Doren (2010) pointed out four major benefits: 1) Differentiation, 2) Cohesive marketing communication plans, 3) Pre-selling an idea to the target audience, and 4) Building credibility with the customer.

Kahaner (1996) states that companies need competitive intelligence in the global economy for the following reasons:

- The pace of business is increasing rapidly and businesses are required to handle more projects and make more decisions more quickly than before;
- Technological development resulted in the introduction of wireless communication, personal computers, the internet and biotechnology. This has increased the speed and availability of communication and companies are experiencing an information overload;
- Increased access to resources, increased number of global competitors and decreased importance of close physical proximity;
- Existing competition is becoming more aggressive. Many market places are maturing, resulting in companies increasing their market share at the expense of their competitors;
- Political changes affect companies quickly and forcefully. Many countries have moved from communism or socialism to capitalism in the last decade.

According to Prescott (2001), three functions within an organization are mainly concerned with competitive intelligence programs: marketing, planning and R&D. As a result, and for a good understanding of the change in dynamics, competitive intelligence programs should allow a better understanding of the industry and competitors, a better identification of areas of vulnerability, and an evaluation of the possible moves of competitors (Prescott, 1995).

Pole et al. (2000) stress that competitive intelligence has a determining effect on the development of five selected characteristics, which are involved in organizational learning:

1. **Question the Status Quo:** Competitive intelligence methods unfreeze attitudes and make the organization comfortable with exploring other

solutions than only conventional ones. Sharing information enhances trust, encourages mental risk-taking and tends to equalize power.

2. **Reduction of Complacency:** Some organizations consider the absence of dramatic events as the absence of competitive threats. This attitude of complacency might be dangerous because it may lead to negative organizational issues, which can create strategic blind spots. Competitive intelligence recognizes that slow but cumulative threats can be perilous for an organization. It provides tools to identify and deal with such threats.

3. **Challenge Existing Assumptions:** It is common for organizations to have some shared assumptions, known in the management field as "dominant logic". These institutionalized assumptions can exclude other perspectives, consequently limiting an organization's vision in its current markets because of a tendency towards myopia. Picken and Dess (1998) claim here that competitive intelligence participates in challenging habitual assumptions for a different and new interpretation of a competitor's strategy.

4. **Reduction of Arrogance:** Market awareness uncovers changes in the environment that dispel the basis for arrogance due to entrenched cultures or histories of financial success.

5. **Patterns of Collaboration:** Teamwork leads to the discovery of other processes, and can lead to a wider view of a company's challenges. Also, it encourages effective actions with deadlines and evaluation. 22/11/15

Competitive intelligence process

According to Bose (2008) competitive intelligence is both a process and a product (intelligence). The process of competitive intelligence is the action of "gathering, analysing, and applying information about products, competitors, suppliers, regulators, partners, and customers for the short- and long-term planning needs of an organization".

Many departments are involved in competitive intelligence processes, but Lackman et al. (2000) have found in their study that nearly half of the companies examined indicated that the competitive intelligence function was housed in the marketing/market research department, followed by the sales department and accounting with 14 per cent of the responses.

The SCIP describes the competitive intelligence cycle as the process by which raw information is acquired, gathered, transmitted, evaluated, analyzed and made available as finished intelligence for policymakers to use in decision-making and action. There are five phases which constitute this cycle: planning and direction, collection, analysis, dissemination, and feedback (Bose, 2008).

In their empirical research based on 1025 executives surveyed about their companies' usage of competitive intelligence, Dishman and Calof (2008) have found that competitive intelligence process is constituted of five steps: planning and focus, collection, analysis, communication, and decision, although this process is affected by certain contextual influences, namely the organizational culture and awareness, and the available formal infrastructure, as well as employee involvement (Saayman, et al, 2008).

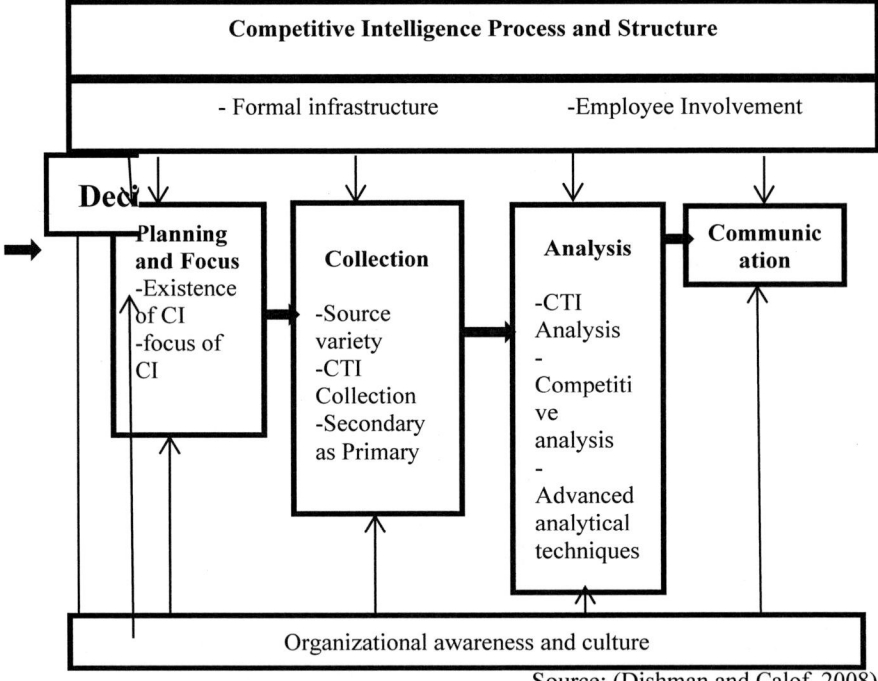

Source: (Dishman and Calof, 2008)

Figure 2.2: Model of Competitive Intelligence

In this study, we attempt to provide a better understanding of competitive intelligence, and its role in a firm's success. Specifically, we examine the competitive intelligence process with a view to discerning its impact on organizational governance. A model of the competitive intelligence process is thus proposed. This provides additional insight as to significant factors related to the various phases, which may impact on organizational governance. In order for the competitive intelligence process to have an impact on organizational governance, the information must be disseminated to decision-makers within the firm. Greater dissemination and faster feedback enable the managers to enhance the way in which they manage their company, and allow them to make better decisions that respond to, and sometimes anticipate, competitors' moves.

Competitive intelligence tools

Senior managers within certain organizations are demanding informed and accurate intelligence, and are requesting that it is made available at the earliest opportunity.

For a good study of competitive intelligence, competitive intelligence staff need to evaluate the various tools and techniques that are available for studying evolving intelligence problems and situations. They need to think "outside the box" and become abstract thinkers. By thinking "outside the box", they update their skills, become more knowledgeable and can solve various problems, even those with no apparent immediate solution (Trim, 2004).

Johnson and Scholes (1997) claim that an organization is forced to respond to the competitive situation and to retaliate accordingly. As such, competitive intelligence should be clearly defined and corporate intelligence staff have to consider the various organizational barriers that exist (Breeding, 2000). With respect to this, Porter's (1980, 1985) work is valuable. Other companies use scenario work or role-playing to identify and analyse competitors' strategic intent (Gieskes, 2000).

To disseminate information, most common methods use technology, and direct (such as presentations) or indirect (such as emails) exchange, because of the time-sensitive-nature of competitive intelligence products and the speedy delivery afforded by technology tools (Marin and Poulter, 2004).

For a good dissemination of competitive intelligence, companies should have the necessary hardware, software and user accounts to access email and/or the intranet. With respect to this, newsletters, alerts and competitor profiles can be attached and distributed from a generic email account or uploaded onto an intelligence-related intranet site (Hohhof, 2000). For example, Microsoft uses a combination of web and email based communication methods to receive potentially useful information from its sales division or partner companies (Rosen, 1998). A group like Lexis-Nexis has many central competitive intelligence units, with full-time employees in touch with over 1000 people from sales and marketing departments in order to gather and share data via an email hotline (Gieskes, 2000). The group uses also a mechanism called "Smart Tools" which tracks mentions of competitors and of the company itself in the press or in trade journals, on a daily basis. Many other companies use these web tools, which are automatically updated to provide fresh data.

In addition, online discussion or news groups can be used for sharing information and knowledge with employees or researchers working in a specific sector or industry.

Companies use many tools to collect and share information. However, competitive intelligence work has to be measured and competitive intelligence data evaluated to provide efficient competitive intelligence. Empirically, the evaluation of competitive intelligence usage is not a straightforward activity because it is difficult to quantify. Some companies exploit intranet usage statistics, while others try to measure the value of competitive intelligence, but these efforts remain insufficient (Marin and Poulter, 2004).

Link between competitive intelligence and corporate governance

Nowadays, organizations are facing significant changes. Corporate governance is one of the most important dimensions impacted by these changes and, as such, has evolved over time. It is the focus of attention of many actors in this environment, like directors, investors, stakeholders, regulators, in order to provide better efficiency, effectiveness and ethical management (Demirbas and Yukhanaev, 2011).

Good corporate governance involves a set of relationships between a company's management, its board, its shareholders and other stakeholders, with increasingly accepted "good" corporate governance practices (Solomon et al., 2003), in order to maximize its residuals (Pistor, 2006; Meharey, 2006), meaning profits. In order to ensure effective decision-making and the success of marketing or planning processes, organizations need to have timely and relevant information (Brod, 1999). The previous custom of waiting weeks for a comprehensive competitor analysis is no longer acceptable if a company wishes to be competitive (Gallagher, 2001). Therefore, how can competitive intelligence impact corporate governance? Does competitive intelligence encourage good corporate governance or, in contrast, does it create bad conditions for wealth generation?

Laidroo (2009) states that information is more readily available in larger firms with concentrated ownership, lower leverage and higher market-to-book ratios. His empirical tests reveal the importance of the ownership structure in providing information. The lack of sharing information can be harmful. Mueller and Peev (2007) stress that an asymmetry of information between managers and external investors may result in underinvestment by external firms, while companies with high managerial discretion tend to overinvest.

Hussey (1998) thinks that competitive intelligence staff need to communicate with various stakeholders. He stresses that top management has to define what exactly competitive intelligence involves.

From a marketing point of view, competitive intelligence allows the identification of security related threats (such as the acts of counterfeiters, fraudsters and terrorists), in order to ensure that the impact of both predicted and unpredicted events and their consequences are neutralized or at least reduced (Trim, 2004).

Some organizations, such as Motorola and 3M, not only use competitive intelligence to become better acquainted with their environment, but also take counterintelligence measures (Prescott, 1995). Trim (1999) has highlighted that senior managers have to stay within the law in their organizational policy and security measures.

Pole et al. (2000) explain that competitive intelligence is expanding, and identify three dimensions which indicate this:

- Institutionalized watchfulness: Organizations with competitive intelligence teams pay more attention to their external environment, such as to key competitors, relevant industries, and target customers. Francis (1997) talks about a state of watchfulness when competitive intelligence teams provide the framework to institutionalize this alertness to the external environment. Therefore, alertness to external stakeholders increases the understanding of unexpected developments which can provide opportunities to explore and prevent potential threats.
- Shared information: A competitive intelligence team legitimizes the sharing of information and offers a model for desired behaviour across competitive intelligence team boundaries. As a result, participation in the organization's intelligence process can be enhanced.
- Development of enabling structures: The organization enhances its learning capability not only from the information collected but also from internal interactions with employees and external interactions with customers, vendors, and competitors.

Competitive intelligence creates an ongoing link with stakeholders. It becomes a forum both for the exchange of ideas inside and outside the organization and for the evaluation of new partnerships and synergies (Bonthous, 1996). In essence, competitive intelligence helps strategists to understand the forces that influence the business environment and which should be an important responsibility of top management (Priporas et al., 2005).

Conclusion

Governance is about providing transparent and fair information on the organization and holding the managers accountable, which can enable a quick and effective intervention by different stakeholders when all or some of their interests are in danger. However, being an open and transparent company may lead to disclosing valuable information to competitors, and threatening the competitiveness of the organisation. Competitive intelligence can be requested easily, using the freedom of information as a right.

Good governance leads to sustainability and better performance, as discussed earlier in this chapter, but over-disclosing core and vital information related to the activity of the organisation can be more harmful than helpful.

Therefore, in a transparent world where information is disclosed and available, organisations will attempt to get their competitors to provide them with as much information as possible, while at the same time being vigilant in disclosing theirs. This leads to a vicious circle and could be dangerous for the companies involved and may lead to bad governance practices.

Competition is a stakeholder of any organisation, and, as such, managers have to take it into consideration when making decisions not only through competitive intelligence. but also by getting as much information as possible on other organisations, and then protecting the survival and interests of their own institution.

Moreover, governance and competitive intelligence can be contradictory in some ways and complementary in others, depending on where the organisation stands and how developed and established it is. In a competitive environment where transparency is a requirement, organisations face the dilemma of how much information to disclose to have good governance without harming its competitiveness. This is the balance that organisations will have to maintain for their sustainability.

References

Agrawal, A & Knoeber C R (1996), Firm Performance and Mechanisms to Control Agency Problems between Managers and Shareholders, *Journal of Financial and Quantitative Analysis*, 31(3) pp.377–398.

Aras G & Crowther D (2007), What level of trust is needed for sustainability? *Social Responsibility Journal* 3 (3), 60-68

Aras. G & Crowther D (2008), Corporate sustainability reporting: a study in disingenuity?, *Journal of Business Ethics* 87 (supp 1), 279-288

Bonthous, J.-M (1996), Intelligence as learning, *Competitive Intelligence Review*, 7(Supp.), S49–S59.

Brod, S (1999), Competitive Intelligence: harvesting information to compete and market intelligently, Camares Communications, New Jersey.

Black et al (2005), Does Corporate Governance Predict Firms' Market Values? Time Series Evidence from Korea, Working Paper, Downloadable at: http:// ssrn.com/abstract=844744

Bøhren, Ø & B. A. Ødegaard (2004), Governance and Performance Revisited, 2003 Meetings of the European Finance Association.

Beatty, R.W., & Ulrich, D.O (1991), Re-Energizing the Mature Organization. *Organizational Dynamics*, American Management Association, 16-30.

Bose, R. (2008), Competitive intelligence process and tools for intelligence analysis, *Industrial management & data system*, 108(4), pp. 510-528.

Breeding, B. (2000), Competitive intelligence and HM convergence: a case study at Shell Services International, *Competitive Intelligence Review*, Vol. 11 No. 4, pp. 12-24.

Crowther D (1996), *Management Accounting for Business*, Cheltenham; Stanley Thornes

—. (2004), *Managing finance – a socially responsible approach*, London; Elsevier

Crowther D & Seifi S (2010), *Corporate Governance and Risk Management*; Copenhagen; Ventus

Drucker, P. F. (1992), The new society of organizations. *Harvard Business Review*, 70(5).

Donaldson, T., and L. E. Preston (1995), The stakeholder theory of the corporation: Concepts, evidence, and implications, *Academy of Management Review*, 20: 65-91.

Dishman P. & Calof J. (2007), Competitive intelligence: a multiphasic precedent to marketing strategy, *European Journal of Marketing*, Vol. 42 N°. 7/8, pp. 766-785.

Du Toit, A.S.A. & Strauss, A.C (2010), Competitive intelligence and Africa's competitiveness: what's happening in South Africa? *Mousaion*, 28(2):17-32.

Demirbas D., Yukhanaev A. (2011), Independence of board of directors, employee relation and harmonisation of corporate governance: Empirical evidence from Russian listed Companies, *Employee Relations*, Vol. 33 No. 4, pp. 444-471.

Filatotchev I, Toms S, Wright M (2006), The firm's strategic dynamics and corporate governance lifecycle, *International Journal of Managerial Finance*, 2(4): 256-279.

Frishammar, J (2002), Characteristics in information processing approaches. *International Journal of Information Management* 22

Fulghieri, Paolo and Matti Suominen (2005), Does Bad Corporate Governance Lead to too Little Competition? Corporate Governance, Capital Structure and Industry Concentration, *ECGI Working Paper Series in Finance*, No.74.

Freeman, R.E (1984), *Strategic Management : A stakeholder Approach.* Boston, MA: Pitman.

Freeman, R.E. & McVea, J. (2001), A Stakeholder approach to strategic management, in Hitt, M. A., Freeman, R. E. and Harrison, J. S. (eds), *The Blackwell Handbook of Strategic Management*, Blackwell Business, Oxford, 189- 207.

Francis, D.B. (1997)., Your competitors: Who will they be? Competitive Intelligence Review, 8(1), 16–23.

Gieskes H. (2000)., Competitive intelligence at Lexis-Nexis, Competitive Intelligence Review 11(2), 4–11.

Hohhof, B. (2000), The information technology marketplace. In: J.P. Miller (ed.), Millennium Intelligence, (Cyber Age Books, Medford) 133–153.

Hussey, D. (1998)., Sources of information for competitor analysis, Strategic Change, Vol. 7, No. 6, pp. 343-56.

Johns, P & Van Doren, D.C. (2010)., Competitive intelligence in service marketing : A new approach with practical application, Marketing Intelligence & Planning Vol. 28, No. 5, pp. 551-570.

Johnson, G. & Scholes, K. (1997)., Exploring Corporate Strategy. Pearson Education.

Kahaner, L. (1996)., Competitive intelligence from black ops to boardrooms-how businesses gather, analyze, and use information to succeed in the global marketplace, New York : Simon and Schuster.

Lackman C.L., Saban K., and J.M. Lanasa, (2000)., Organizing the competitive intelligence function: a benchmarking study, Competitive Intelligence Review, 11(1), 17–27.

Laidroo, L. (2009)., Association between ownership structure and public announcements' disclosures, Corporate Governance : The International Review, Vol. 17 No. 1, pp. 13-34.

Marin, J., Poulter, A. (2004)., Dissemination of Competitive Intelligence, Journal of Information Science, Vol. 30, No. 2, pp165-180.

Millstein. I.M. and MacAvoy. P.W.(2003)., The Active Board of Directors and Performance of the Large Publicly Traded Corporation, Columbia Law Review, Vol. 8, No. 5, 1998, pp. 1283-1322

McGonagle, J.J. & Vella, C.M. (1990)., Outsmarting the Competition: Practical Approaches to Finding and Using Competitive Information. Naperville, IL: Sourcebooks

Marin J. and Poulter A., (2004)., Dissemination of competitive intelligence, Journal of Information Science, 30 (2), pp. 165–180

Meharey, P.G. (2006), The common law and economic growth: Hayek might be right, in Fox, M.

Mueller, D.C. and E. Peev (2007)., Corporate governance and investment in Central and Eastern Europe, Journal of Comparative Economics, Vol. 35, pp. 414-437.

Priporas, C-V., Gatsoris, L. & Zacharis, V. (2005). Competitive Intelligence Activity: Evidence from Greece. Marketing Intelligence & Planning, 23(7), 659-669

Powell, T, & Allgaier, C (1998)., Enhancing Sales and Marketing Effectiveness Through Competitive Intelligence, Competitive Intelligence Review, vol. 9, n° 4, p. 29-41.

Prescott J.E. (2001), Introduction: Competitive Intelligence. Lessons from the Trenches, in Prescott J.E. & Miller S.H. (eds), Proven Strategies in Competitive Intelligence, New York, NY: John Wiley & Sons, pp.1-22.

—. (1995), The Evolution of Competitive Intelligence, International Review of Strategic Management, vol. 6, pp.71-90.

Picken, J & Dess, G (1998), Right strategy – wrong problem, Organizational Dynamics, vol. 27, no. 1, pp. 35-49

Pole, J.G., Madsen, E. and Dishman, P. (2000)., Competitive intelligence as a construct for organizational change, Competitive Intelligence Review, Vol. 11 No. 4, pp. 25-31.

Porter, M. (1980), Competitive Strategy: Techniques for Analyzing Industries and Competitors, The Free Press, New York, NY.

—. (1985), Competitive Advantage: Creating and Sustaining Superior Performance, The Free Press, New York, NY.

Pistor, K. (2006), Patterns of legal change: shareholder and creditor rights in transition economies", in Fox, M.B. and Heller, M.A. (Eds), Corporate Governance Lessons from Transition Economy Reforms, Princeton University Press, Princeton, NJ, pp. 35-84.

Prescott, J.E. (1995), The evolution of competitive intelligence, in Hussey, D.E. (Ed.), International Review of Strategic Management, Wiley, Chichester, pp. 71-90.

Priporas, C-V., Gatsoris, L. & Zacharis, V. (2005)., Competitive Intelligence Activity: Evidence from Greece, Marketing Intelligence & Planning, 23(7), 659-669

Saayman, A., et al., (2008), Competitive Intelligence: Construct Exploration, Validation and Equivalence, Aslib Proceedings: New Information Perspectives, 60(4), 383-411

Solomon, J.F., Lin, S.W., Norton, S.D. & Solomon, A. (2003), Corporate governance in Taiwan: empirical evidence from Taiwanese company directors", Corporate Governance: An International Review, Vol. 11 No. 3, pp. 235-48.

Trim, P.R.J. (2004), The strategic corporate intelligence and transformational marketing model, Marketing Intelligence & Planning, Vol. 22 No. 2, pp. 240-256

—. (1999), The corporate intelligence information charter: responsibility and accountability in the defense sector, Strategic Change, Vol. 8 No. 6, pp. 359-66.

Van den Berghe, L. (2001), Beyond Corporate Governance, European Business Forum, Issue 5, Spring

Van den Berghe L.A.A. and Abigail Levrau (2003), Measuring the Quality of Corporate Governance: In Search of a Tailormade Approach?, Journal of General Management Vol. 28 No. 3 Spring.

CHAPTER THREE

WHAT IS ORGANISATIONAL GOVERNANCE? AN EXPLORATION OF CONCEPTS AND TERMINOLOGY

SUAN GULLIVER

Introduction

Organisational Governance is a term used to describe a field of academic research that focuses on the way organisations are governed. It includes a wide range of issues relating to all aspects of "management", particularly the management of companies or corporations in the private sector. The term "management" can be applied equally to other types of groups of people, apart from corporations, such as public sector organisations and even individuals, so their governance issues are also discussed. The organisational governance mechanisms in place today are inadequate. Too many issues are not addressed at all and many others need improvement. Proposition 1: This article proposes that conceptual simplification is needed before an effective macro-level solution can emerge.

This article explores some of the possible meanings of the terms "organisational", "governance" and "organisational governance", leading to some useful insights and more precise descriptions of some of the issues that are being addressed. Proposition 2: New definitions of key terms are proposed. Two of those key terms are: "all human organisational behaviour" and "organisational governance mechanisms". Proposition :3 A new macro-level classification framework is proposed, so that all forms of human organisational behaviour can be classified into just four distinct modes of activity, to be called: "Organisationalistic"; "Cooperativistic";[1] "Individualistic"; and "Anti-Social". It is further proposed that each of these four modes of human organisational behaviour has different characteristics that affect the type of governance that will be effective.

What is Organisational Governance? An Exploration of Concepts

Corporate governance emerged from the need to manage companies or corporations. There are currently a wide range of mechanisms that are in place, at local, national and international levels to try to ensure appropriate behaviour. These mechanisms have been added over time from the micro, or bottom, level starting-point in reaction to some problem or need. Two examples of these types of corporate governance mechanisms are: laws and the legal system; and cash, accounting, finance and money (there are others).

There is a wider concept, organisational governance, that takes in the idea that individual people too should also adjust or moderate their behaviour, at least in certain situations. This idea has come about through the history of human behaviour, stretching back into the mists of the past. From the earliest times people have needed to compromise in order to fit into a social group. The idea that the group too can impose restrictions on the freedom of individuals, by force if necessary, undoubtedly has an equally ancient origin. Examples of this behavioural type of adjustment mechanism include peer pressure; religion; and education, both parental and in schools, teaching.

There never was a grand plan to put together a complete and effective network of organisational governance mechanisms; rather, there has just been a reactive process throughout history to provide solutions in order to organise effectively, or at least effectively enough. Not surprisingly, since there was no grand plan, the existing network of organisational governance mechanisms is a random affair, effective in some areas and at some levels, but making overall an ineffective net of ad hoc solutions unfit for the modern world. These mechanisms do not properly integrate and function together to provide comprehensive and effective organisational governance at the macro level that applies to all of us and all of our

---

[1] The terms "cooperativistic" and "organisationalistic" are the copyright of Suan Gulliver, 2012. Please use these two words freely, if you find them useful, whilst acknowledging their source.

organisational behaviour, with disastrous consequences for the planet and for all of us together as its inhabitants, as we can see all around us.

There is a need now, an urgent need in fact, for an effective network of organisational governance mechanisms that applies to all of us and all of our organisational behaviour. To be fair, this need has emerged only over the last few decades, or perhaps the last century or two, as our combined impact on the planet, and consequently on each other, has accelerated beyond the capacity of planet Earth to absorb the consequences of our behaviour.

Current Macro Organisational Governance Failings

What is absolutely clear is that the existing network of organisational governance mechanisms is woefully inadequate to effectively adjust all organisational human behaviour so that it is not harmful to others or the planet. There are various reasons for these failings which must be understood if solutions are to be found:

Failing 1: Despite many attempts by several governments, corporate governance mechanisms still fail to successfully moderate all the behaviour of the corporate sector adequately and there is still a need to improve the existing network. This could mean the introduction of additional organisational governance mechanisms to plug gaps in the existing network. It could also mean improving the effectiveness of organisational governance mechanisms already in existence.

Failing 2: The existing network of corporate governance mechanisms does not properly integrate with mechanisms to moderate the behaviour of individuals. Our constantly growing numbers and the growing empowerment of individuals mean that the combined impact of individuals is growing in significance. Changing from corporate to organisational governance will recast corporate behaviour as a sub-set of all human organisational behaviour, so that its relative impact can be understood and managed better. In effect, corporate behaviour may be able to be moderated better by moderating the behaviour of the people involved, in certain circumstances.

Failing 3: Existing governance mechanisms are too clumsy to take account of the rapidly changing work patterns that are emerging, mostly as a consequence of the new information technology revolution. The increasing flexibility and choice for individuals means that they can, and do, move in and out of corporate employment, and combine corporate employment with their own enterprises. The distinction between behaviour relating to the corporation and that relating to the individual is becoming ever more blurred. This can make corporations no more than a screen behind which enterprising individuals can evade not just liabilities, but also responsibilities and certainly detection. There is a need to accommodate the blurring of the edges of organisations and these changing work patterns, a need to deal with the increasing complexity of the behaviour of individuals.

Failing 4: The existing state of the network of organisational governance mechanisms fails to achieve everything that is needed at the macro-level. The macro requirements need to be researched and published widely so that the aims are understandable and widely understood. The macro view must be reconciled with the micro view if the macro theory is then to inform the implementation of change at the micro level. It must all function equally well at both the macro and the micro level.

Effective Macro Organisational Governance

Effective organisational governance must be all-inclusive. What is needed is a new approach to the management of any and all human behaviour leading to impacts on the planet and on other people. The issues of whether the behaviour is motivated by the desire for money or for some other purpose are irrelevant. Whether the behaviour relates to a single individual or to a group of people is irrelevant. What is relevant is that there is a consequence of this behaviour, and an impact on the planet or on others. All behaviours which lead to an impact on the planet or people must be included.

There must be no gaps. Alongside the practical complexity and ineffectiveness of existing organisational governance is a matching theoretical confusion, compounded by the ambiguity of current terms. Conceptual simplification can be initiated by starting not from the historic micro point of view, but from a macro point of view, and by looking at what needs to be achieved. From this bird's-eye overview, the complexity and detail disappear leaving a more simple, broad-brush picture. By identifying a few major over-arching issues and defining them precisely the main concepts can be managed successfully. All human organisational behaviour is classified into these main classifications, and just four are proposed. There are no exceptions.

Proposition 1

The idea is to develop a complete conceptual framework for organisational governance at the macro-level that can be used to develop a vision of a complete and satisfactory network of organisational governance mechanisms that applies equally to all people in the world. This would be a complete solution only in theory. In practice, the implementation of any solution must build up from the current situation piece by piece. The conceptual framework will help, though, to ensure that the design of micro organisational governance solutions will also simultaneously strengthen organisational governance at the macro level. There is no proposition to replace what is already in existence. The proposition is to develop, in an intelligent way, what already exists to achieve more effective macro organisational governance within the shortest possible time-frame.

Managing the Terminology

There are a number of issues to consider:

Organisational Governance Ambiguity: Anything to do with "management", such as Organisational Governance, is going to include a wide range of issues from numerous academic fields, such as sociology, psychology, human behavioural studies, philosophy, ethics, business studies, and finance, with each field of study having its own particular viewpoint. The phrase "Organisational Governance" has a degree of mystery about it, with its several shades of meaning making it useful for a wide range of purposes but perhaps less than effective at transmitting any particular specific concept or idea. This may be because the language in common use around the theme of Organisational Governance is imprecise and often ambiguous in the way that it is used. It may be, though, that the issues themselves are difficult to define precisely, with the borders between different concepts being unclear, fading from one to the other with no clear cut-off point.

Advantages of ambiguity: The phrase "Organisational Governance" is a broad umbrella term that has the advantage of a certain degree of ambiguity and a breadth of meaning that attracts a wide variety of people, providing the opportunity for an interdisciplinary debate with a rich mix of ideas and opinions.

Disadvantages of ambiguity: The disadvantage of the term Organisational Governance is this very same characteristic; that ambiguity may make it difficult to pin down exactly what is meant. Ambiguity is a common problem in social science, perhaps in all science, with new jargon and terminology developing alongside new concepts and theory in order to create a language for deepening levels of understanding.

Need for Transparency: In order to successfully develop the discipline of Organisational Governance, there is a need for less ambiguous language. This will facilitate more meaningful debate and allow the subtlety of new issues to be better understood. This article explores some of the current uses of Organisational Governance related terms. It then proposes more robust definitions for certain terms, some of which are new and some of which refine or redefine the meaning of existing terms.

Defining Organisational: meaning relating to organisations

In its most specific use, the term "organisational" has been adopted to replace the term "corporate". The term "corporate" has been developed from the concept of "incorporation", which is the process by which owners set up their companies to have an independent existence by becoming a "body" in their own right. Owners can then limit their liabilities for the behaviour of the company, which is in effect a headless body. The company then employs directors to govern it and to act as its mind and soul in a way. This process was devised to encourage the wealthy to take on more risky projects than they might otherwise have done. Trade and commerce expanded and the owners of corporations benefited from the resultant easier wealth-generating conditions. Governments benefited because the average quality of life of their citizens improved, meaning that they remained popular—always important in democracies—and they were at the same time able to collect more taxes from both the corporations and the citizens who were earning and spending more money. This is the mechanism at the heart of the runaway "money machine" that currently dominates most of our lives, one way or another.

The term "corporate" excludes the organisations that are set up by governments using the taxes that they are collecting. These organisations, commonly called "not for profit" organisations, have a wide range of purposes, none of which are to do with making money, but are instead about maintaining a socially stable situation in balance with the corporate sector. The not-for-profit sector matches the corporate sector, more or less, in many countries in terms of the number of people employed. These organisations are also run by managers on behalf of their owners, effectively taxpayers. There are also various other types of not-for-profit organisations outside the government sector.

Also excluded by the term "corporate" but included under "organisational" are other profit-focused organisations that are not incorporated. These include privately owned companies, partnerships and perhaps even sole traders, who work within organised frameworks set up by the government, even though they work independently.

The term "organisational" expands from the concept of "corporate" to include all types of organisations, regardless of their ownership and primary purpose. Its scope is far greater than that of the term "corporate", which is necessary because it is not only the corporate sector that impacts on the planet and on people; rather, all types of organisations affect their surroundings. As such, it is essential to manage the total impact caused by all organisations, and not just the corporate sector.

Defining Organisational: meaning a type of human behaviour

The term "organisation" has so far been used in its commonly understood meaning as a description for any group of people that has joined together for a common purpose. Using the word "organisation" in this way implies that organisations are clearly defined entities, though this is not necessarily a robust assumption, as is explored further below. In any case, there is a need to govern all human behaviour, not just the behaviour of people in organisations. As such, the border between organisational human behaviour and all other human behaviour needs clarification.

In its most generic form, "organisational" might mean anything to do with "organisation" in general, that is, getting organised, as well as anything to do with organisations, meaning organised groups of people with a specific purpose. This double meaning of the word organisation, which makes it relate equally to the behaviour of an individual person as well as to the behaviour of groups of people, opens the route to an understanding of the link between people as individuals and people in groups. Humans cooperate with other humans to achieve objectives that they are unable to achieve on their own as individuals. This is the essential social behaviour that characterises all humans. Although there may be some rare exceptions to this general rule and the humanity of any such people who never cooperate is not challenged, social behaviour is probably essential to the survival of each and all of us. In fact, it could be said that our social behaviour has made us such a successful species that our own survival is now under threat from the consequences of our own success.

It is a prerequisite of any social behaviour that a person has a certain degree of organisation. Conventions constrain the individual, limiting their choice of "appropriate behaviour", that is, behaviour appropriate to allow social interactions to take place. Some of what is and is not appropriate is innate, determined by genetic make-up, but much is learned. People start to learn to limit, adjust or govern their behaviour from the day they are born, usually taught by their mother, or, if not, by their mother substitute. This process of getting organised continues through all the stages of childhood, and indeed life, to a greater or lesser extent depending on the individual person's preference for being organised or not. Each individual person has their own distinct mix of genetic and learned organisational behaviour. Furthermore, any individual may engage in different types of organisational behaviour at different times and for different purposes.

The broadest definition is the preferred choice here. The preferred definition of the term "organisational" widens the scope of relevant behaviour from that of corporate behaviour to that of all human organisational behaviour. This is the broadest possible view of the meaning of organisational.

Governance: Government or Governance?

"Governance" is not a word in general use by most people. "Government", however, is a word in common use and is familiar to us all. For this reason, when the word "governance" is used, it is likely to evoke connotations of government and all its associations. There is a clear link between these two words, and their concepts, but they are not equivalent, nor are they always interchangeable. A linguistic approach to investigating these issues can provide insights into new approaches to governance and into how organisational governance might be improved.

"Government" is a noun and can mean the organisation that is governing a country. When the phrase "the government" is used, this is usually what is meant, though the ambiguity of the word and its flexibility in use make it difficult to make definitive generalisations. It is possible that, instead of describing the organisation, the phrase is rather being used to describe the results of what the organisation is doing rather. When "government" is used to mean the results of the actions of a government, the word "governance" can be used in its place. Examples of this include: "The government (the governing organisation of the country) is weak"; "weak government (governance) over many decades has led to the problems"; and "weak government has led to problems" (this is ambiguous as it could mean either the governing organisation of the country or governance).

All organisations need governing (verb), or governance (noun), and even individuals must exhibit good self-governance by governing themselves. The phrase "governing body" means the group of people governing any organisation, which could also be used when speaking of countries. The word "governance" means the results of the activity of governing, regardless of the type of organisation that is being governed. These choices are linguistically unambiguous, and are therefore preferable to the word "government", which is best avoided for our purposes because of its ambiguity.

So far, the discussion of governance has related to the presence of the English language in common use and its weaknesses in this area. This issue is crucial for academics. First, it is important for an agreement to be reached regarding appropriate and unambiguous terminology for any field of research. This will provide a sound language base for researchers and academics in the field. Second, it is important that academics try to make their work as jargon-free as possible so that is accessible to the widest possible readership. Only in this way can their work be applied usefully in society. In our particular field, Organisational Governance, there is a linguistic tightrope that we must successfully negotiate if we are to implement the great solutions that we work so hard to develop.

Governance: the results of governing

What is governing? According to Wiktionary it is the present participle of the verb "to govern". It has a number of meanings: namely, "to make and administer the public policy and affairs of; to exercise sovereign authority in; to control the actions or behaviour of; to keep under control; to restrain; to exercise a deciding or determining influence on; to control the speed, flow etc. of; to regulate; to exercise political authority; to run a government; to have or exercise a determining influence; to require that a certain preposition, grammatical case, etc. be used with a word; sometimes used synonymously with collocate". Related terms include government; governance; governor; governess.[2]

Not all of these fit neatly with the term "Organisational Governance" being used with respect to this field of academic research. Interestingly, governing also relates to machines and language as well as to the behaviour of people. A governor, for example, is "a device, which regulates or controls some action of a machine through automatic feedback"[3] as well as also being a person who governs.

"Regulate" produces a simpler list of definitions: "to dictate policy; to control or direct according to rule, principle, or law; to adjust to a

---

[2] http://en.wiktionary.org/wiki/govern 5 June 2012
[3] http//en.wiktionary.org

particular specification or requirement: regulate temperature; to adjust (a mechanism) for accurate and proper functioning; to put or maintain in order; to regulate one's eating habits".[4]

The introduction of the word "adjusting" is useful with respect to human behaviour. Perhaps "governing" is doing whatever it takes to adjust human behaviour from its current habits to a new and better pattern of behaviour. This definition is neutral in that there is no implication of applying force to achieve the desired adjustment or change. In some cases force may be needed, but the aim of adjusting behaviour by democratic processes and the cooperative choices of individuals fits with the ethos that already underwrites the free world, democracy. Perhaps "governance" means "the results of mechanisms causing adjustment"; if so, organisational governance could mean "the results of mechanisms causing the adjustment of organisational human behaviour".

The broadest definition is again the preferred choice here. The preferred definition of "governance" widens the scope of its meaning from formal systems such as government and the law to include anything that adjusts human behaviour in any way, such as cultural norms and peer pressure. This is the broadest possible view of the meaning of governance.

Proposition 2: Definitions of Main Concepts

The following definitions of "organisational", "governance", "organisational governance" and other related terms are proposed for the main over-arching concepts used in the subsequent discussion.

All Human Organisational Behaviour (HOB): Human behaviour that has no impact on other people and has no impact on the planet is not organisational behaviour. Any behaviour that requires the cooperation of two or more people is organisational behaviour. Any behaviour that requires an interaction with anything that has been made or organised by someone else is also organisational behaviour. Any behaviour that utilises or transforms any natural materials or resources, animal, vegetable or mineral, is organisational behaviour. As such, it can be seen that organisational behaviour involves another person or the use of products or services provided by another person, and makes a change to the physical environment in some way, however small. Following these definitions, organisational behaviour includes the vast majority of human behaviour, but excludes personal activities that have no external consequences, such as playing with your dog in the garden; walking round the block in the

---

[4] http//en.wiktionary.org

evening as long as there is no use of the car, no smoking and no shopping; and skimming stones on the sea as the sun goes down. This is the broadest possible definition of the word "organisational", and means that nothing that causes an impact on the planet or on another person is excluded. The term "all human organisational behaviour" will be used for this concept.

Organisational Governance Mechanism (OGM): The term "governance" is taken to mean adjustment. "Organisational Governance" is therefore taken to mean the adjustment of any and all human organisational behaviour. The means by which any human organisational behaviour is adjusted in any way is an "organisational governance mechanism". This includes any kind of feedback information, personal discipline, reward systems, law, and financial pressures. Any of these organisational governance mechanisms can be used in suitable combinations to provide effective organisational governance for any specific instance of human organisational behaviour.

The Need for New Concept Framework for Organisational Governance: Since we are taking the broadest possible definition of organisational governance to include many additional concepts, there will need to be a new framework for organisational governance which provides an unambiguous method of combining the old and new concepts in a complete but simple structure, discussed further in the following pages.

Human Organisational Behaviour Modes

Proposition 3: HOB Mode and OGM

Four HOB modes: Four modes of human organisational behaviour have been identified in this chapter: organisationalistic, cooperativistic, individualistic, and anti-social. Each one of these modes has very different characteristics and these differences have implications for the choice of appropriate style and type of governance. In order to ensure a complete framework, all human organisational behaviour is classified in one or another of the four modes, with no exceptions. The modes may be further sub-divided into sub-classifications.

Different OGMs for different HOB modes: For any given situation the appropriate mix of organisational governance mechanisms (OGMs) will depend on the characteristics of the target human organisational behaviour. The "mode" of human organisational behaviour (HOB- mode) is one key factor in determining what type of governance mechanisms might be effective.

Summary of the four HOB modes: The use of only four modes of classification provides a simple and robust framework for all types of analysis for both individual human organisational behaviour and the behaviour of groups of people in organisations. Those with business and/or research-type backgrounds should have no difficulties reconciling existing methods of classifying companies with these new all-inclusive classifications. These classifications have been defined to include all companies, but also to include all other types of human organisational behaviour. This is just a taster and more research is needed to refine the definitions of, and borders between, these new HOB-mode classifications. It is important to grasp that both individuals and organisations will mix these modes freely. Different modes of organisational behaviour will be selected for different purposes and at different times. Furthermore, at any one time and for any one purpose the modes may be mixed in any different proportion, depending on the choices made by the person or people involved. This is what makes this four mode framework not only simple and robust but also flexible. It can be applied to any number of people, from one to all the people on the planet. It can be used to gain an understanding of any observed organisational behaviour, whatever its complexity of characteristics.

The table below lays out a simple framework that can be applied at the macro-level to all disciplines and fields of study that relate in any way to Organisational Governance. It compares and contrasts the four human organisational behaviour modes (HOB-modes). Appendix 2 contains some proposed definitions of these and other related terms.

Conclusion

There are more than 7 billion people, (7,000,000,000 +) alive in the world today. A great deal of people currently live in poor conditions, and humans face predicted escalating threats to their future. Every day, there are more people and it is possible that the climate too has deteriorated a little bit more; the forces of the "double squeeze". In order to at least prevent further decline, or, with good luck, improve the position we are in, not only do we have to solve the problems that we see here now, but we have to do even more so that we get ahead of the anticipated problems that will surely come tomorrow. For this reason, it is important to get a better grip on ourselves and manage ourselves better, sooner rather than later.

What is Organisational Governance?

Table 3.1: Four human organisational behaviour modes (HOB modes)

	DESTRUCTIVE		CONSTRUCTIVE	
	Anti-social HOB-mode	Individualistic HOB-mode	Cooperativistic HOB-mode	Organisationalistic HOB-mode
Characteristics	Opposes some or all social organisation passively or actively	Working alone, Living alone	Social groups, Tribes	Employment, Payment, Management, Leading/directing, Contracting
Example	Terrorist activity, Anarchistic behaviour	Sole Trader, Craftsman, Artist, Creative workers	Families, Villages, Close living, Small business sector, Small investors in big business, Consumers	Medium and big business sector (all products and services), Government sector (all levels)
Organisational style	None	Autonomous, Independent	Social, Network	Hierarchical, Systematic
Governance style	None	Self-governing	Democratic	Varies depending on leadership style
Roles	Self-appointed	Multiplicity of roles	Discussion, Voting, Compromising, Agreeing, Committing, Participating	Separation of roles, Leadership, Followership
Power implications	Feels dis-empowered	Sole power over all decisions	Shared power, Individual power often depends on charisma and personal character	Internally - unequal power distribution, often determined by money (A few people with extra, most with restricted power) Externally - combined effect an extraordinary level of power due to scale

Much is being done on a formal level to achieve better international integration through the harmonisation of regulations, and this is all good work in the right direction, but it is too slow-moving. New methods of governance are needed that perhaps exploit our unique electronic information resources and the tools that we have more fully. In addition, we have an ever-growing understanding of our own natures, and, by working with them to find new solutions, both formal and informal, we can enhance and exploit our human propensity to cooperate so that we stand the best chance of successfully regulating our behaviour.

This chapter makes three propositions: firstly, a conceptual framework is needed for better macro-organisational governance; secondly, key terms need to be defined for an effective and complete framework for macro-organisational governance; thirdly, there are just four "modes" of human organisational behaviour and each of the four modes needs different governance mechanisms in order to be effective.

Organisational governance is the aspect of management that is concerned with the way we govern ourselves, which effectively means our ability to adjust our behaviour. Organisational human behaviour throughout the world manifests itself in a myriad of ways. If we define the term "organisational" in the widest possible sense as a type of human behaviour, then we can also consider "governance" in its widest possible form, matching appropriate types and styles of governance mechanisms to all of the myriad aspects of organisational human behaviour in a rich mix of solutions. There are many factors that will determine exactly what type and style of organisational governance mechanisms might be effective in any given situation. The aim, then, is to develop a rich mix of organisational governance mechanisms to provide a complete and effective network to govern all organisational human behaviour whatever its mode. There promises to be plenty of surprises ahead, and the possibility of discoveries of new democratic and cooperative ways to achieve better solutions to both old and new problems.

Appendix 1

Proposed Definitions of Organisational Governance Terms

organisational	relating to organisation	
organisational human behaviour	getting organised, behaviour leading to organisation, work related behaviour	behaviour that is planned to contribute towards a purpose and is not reactive, random or spontaneous
human behaviour	all human behaviour including both non-organisational and organisational human behaviour	
organised	ordered, prepared for a purpose	not natural, random
organisation (i)	the results of organisational behaviour	
organisation/s (ii)	a group of people working together towards a particular purpose	not recommended due to ambiguity – use "organisational enterprise" instead
organisational enterprise	an individual or group of people working together towards a specific purpose	
governance	the results of governing	
government (i)	the results of governing	not recommended due to ambiguity – use "governance" instead
government (ii)	the group of people responsible for governing a nation or country	due to ambiguity – use the phrases "national government" or "national governing body" instead
governing body	a group of people responsible for implementing governance mechanisms for adjusting the human behaviour for an enterprise, nation or country	
governance mechanism	anything, any system, any behaviour that leads to the adjustment of an action or behaviour of a human or a machine	
organisational governance	the results of governing organisational human behaviour	
organisational governance mechanism/s	actions, systems, rules, regulations, enforcement processes, anything that leads the adjustment of organisational human behaviour	

Appendix 2

Proposed definitions of terms relating to the four human organisational behaviour modes (HOB-modes)

HOB-modes	classifications of the type of human organisational behaviour leading to results, changes, effects or impact on people or the planet
anti-social HOB-mode	human organisational behaviour that has the purpose of disrupting or disorganising the organisational activities of others
individualistic HOB-mode	human organisational behaviour that is carried out in isolation by an individual
cooperativistic HOB-mode	human organisational behaviour that is carried out by groups of people working together cooperatively
organisationalistic HOB-mode	human organisational behaviour that is carried out by groups of people who contract or promise to behave in a restricted way to fulfil pre-determined roles within the group
anti-social enterprise	an individual or group of people putting in effort to disrupt the achievement of the purposes of others
individualistic enterprise	an individual putting in effort to achieve their own purposes
cooperativistic enterprise	a group of people putting in effort to achieve an agreed purpose
organisationalistic enterprise	a group of people putting in effort to achieve the purpose of the owners of the enterprise
Organisational Governance (OG) sectors	the new OG sectors divide up the results of organisational human behaviour in a different way than the traditional sectors which are: corporate sector, government sector, not-for-profit sector, small and medium business sector, clubs, other. Traditional sectors are defined by their financial purpose. OG sectors are defined by their HOB-mode
individualistic sector	the collective impact of all individualistic enterprise
cooperativistic sector	the collective impact of all cooperativistic enterprise
organisationalistic sector	the collective impact of all organisationalistic enterprise
anti-social sector	the collective impact of all anti-social enterprise

CHAPTER FOUR

NO ACCOUNTING FOR INEQUITY: ACCOUNTING'S OPPOSITION TO SUSTAINABILITY

DAVID CROWTHER AND SHAHLA SEIFI

Introduction

The social responsibility of organisations – commonly known as Corporate Social Responsibility (CSR) or Corporate Responsibility – has become an important issue in contemporary international debates (see Aras & Crowther, 2007a). More recently, however, the discourse has changed to that of sustainability and many corporate reports which used to be designated as environmental reports, and subsequently as CSR reports, have now been repackaged as sustainability reports. CSR, however, is more problematic as it is often perceived that there is a dichotomy between CSR activity and financial performance, with one being deleterious to the other and corporations having an imperative to pursue shareholder value. Moreover, there is no agreed-upon definition of exactly what constitutes CSR (Ortiz Martinez & Crowther, 2005) and therefore no agreed-upon basis for measuring that activity and relating it to the various dimensions of corporate performance. Consequently, much of the previous research regarding CSR deals with this issue and the problems in the development of standards for the definition and reporting of such an indeterminate activity (see Crowther 2006).

Although this problem is widely recognised, it is equally widely accepted that the impact of corporate activity upon society and its citizens – as well as all stakeholders including the environment – is considerable and has an impact not just upon the present but also upon the future. Moreover these stakeholders are increasingly exercising their power not just in their own interests but also in the interests of long-term sustainability. As such, it is necessary to develop some methods of analysing and measuring sustainable CSR activity (see Aras & Crowther, 2007b) in such a way that it is universally understood, and can be evaluated by interested parties. It will therefore become of assistance to societal decision making.

It is fairly obvious that the resources of the planet are finite and that this is a limiting factor to growth and development. The depletion of the resources of the planet, however, is one of the factors which have helped create the current interest in sustainability. Of particular concern are the extractive industries, and such things as aluminium are becoming in short supply. In the UK, mineral resources such as tin and lead were fully extracted long ago and the thriving industries based around them are long gone. As other resources – such as coal – become exhausted, the companies based upon them disappear, as do the jobs in those industries. This is an obvious source of concern for people.

Probably most concerning is the extinguishing of supplies of oil, because much economic activity is only possible because of the energy created by the use of oil. Indeed, many would argue that the wars in the Middle East[1], particularly the problems in Iraq and Iran, are caused by oil shortages, actual or impending, and the troubles thereby caused, rather than by any concern for political issues. Most people have now heard of Hubbert's Peak,[2] and engaged with the debate as to whether or not it has been reached (Deffeyes 2004; Bower 2009). Certainly it has in parts of the world, such as the USA and the North Sea, but it is less certain if it has been reached for the world as a whole. Nevertheless the whole crux of sustainability – and sustainable development – is based upon the need for energy and there are insufficient alternative sources of energy to compensate for the elimination of oil as a source of fuel. Consequently, resource depletion, real or imagined, and particularly that of energy resources, is one of the most significant causes of the current interest in sustainability.

---

[1] And most probably any other parts of the world also – it would be instructive to correlate the presence of oil with conflicts.
[2] In 1956, M. King Hubbert developed a model of oil production which showed that, when the mid-point of oil reserves was reached, then future production would slow down and less would be available. Although originally developed for US oil production, it has been shown to be equally valid globally. This mid-point is known as Hubbert's Peak and has arrived, or soon will arrive; at that point oil supplies start to decrease, with obvious implications in an environment in which demand continues to increase.

The efficiency of accounting

Accounting, from its inception, has been harnessed generally to dominant political interests and ideological views. It has been part of hegemonic discourses and has aroused controversy and public debate. The development of accounting in the early twentieth century worked hand in glove with early management theory, designed to order the workplace in such a way as to maximise management control and to minimise the power of the workforce, both in terms of decision-making and expertise and discretion regarding the work. Accounting has also been used to legitimate the corporate values of performance over other values such as truth and ethics, and has been co-opted to manipulate figures in favour of large-scale fraud, as has been revealed in recent years.

Management accounting principles and techniques support Frederick Taylor's ideas of scientific job design (specialisation) and productivity in terms of reducing work criteria to those that could be measured and that would produce higher productivity in terms of profit and/or cost, thereby dispensing with unwanted humanistic considerations altogether. Similarly, classical management's emphasis on hierarchical chains of command and rules and procedures was supported by kindred ideas regarding the practice of management accounting (Covaleski & Aiken 1986). Concepts of discipline and surveillance, taken much further by Foucault in his analysis of organisations, are also made more acceptable through reference to accounting techniques. Accounting has been used as a form of control, through its emphasis on precision, rules, measurement, and on material, as opposed to psychological or humanistic, outcomes (Jackson & Carter 1998) to legitimate the increasing control exerted particularly over employees in the workplace.

Accounting techniques have been used 'efficiently' in bringing about structural and cultural change in industries undergoing privatisation. Thus, Ogden and Anderson (1999) have shown how the delegation of work was introduced into newly-privatised water companies in such a way as to make new managers strictly accountable, while at the same time suggesting that they were being 'empowered'. Some managers accepted this as part of the corporate values, while others realized that their newly-gained power was limited to operational boundaries and was being subjected to tight financial constraints. Accounting was also used in the privatisation of the electricity industry as a means of shifting power and status from professional electricians to managers (Carter and Crowther (2000). In both cases, values changed from those of professional standards of maintenance and safety to market criteria of high profits and low costs.

One of the roles of accounting is, of course, to exercise control through the measurement of performance. The inadequacy of accounting has been recognised by many, such as Johnson and Kaplan (1987) who argue that the role of accounting has changed so much it is no longer relevant to managerial needs. It has also been argued (Crowther, 2002) that, although one aspect of managerial need is the internal control of organisational activity and resource allocation, this is not in fact the prime need for accounting information which is used for the semiotic purpose of creating the desired impression of an organisation.

The ability to measure efficiency was predicated in the confidence arising from the Cartesian view of the world with its essential and measurable certainties. This point was argued by Sombert (1915), who stated:

> "Thought in economic activities then becomes more definite and conscious, in other words, more rational, and modern science has tended to make it so. But it has also helped to make it more exact and punctual, by providing the necessary machinery for measuring time."

This was of particular importance for the development of management accounting as early cost management systems emphasised the need to control the level of input resources consumed per output unit. This was particularly true of labour, as a unit of resource consumed, because labour normally comprised the greatest factor cost of production in any nineteenth century industrial organisation. Different industries developed different control measures to serve their own particular requirements and the exacting temporal practices of Scientific Management (see Clark, 1987) were resonant with the key features of management accounting, and the natural evolution of this concept was to ascertain the standard cost of a process and the concomitant comparison of variances between actual and standard performance. Organisational changes in the form of vertically integrated, and later divisionalised, businesses also led to the development of innovative forms of accounting. Thus, for example, return on investment (ROI) was developed in order to be used centrally in vertically integrated firms to guide decisions on capital allocation between various activities. At a later date, when divisionalised businesses delegated the responsibility for using capital efficiently to managers, ROI also came to be used to judge local performance. Similarly flexible budgets were developed to assess and control business units subject to variations in output.

Every business will develop a number of performance measures that it considers to be key indicators of operational success and these tend to be tailored to the particular firm. Accordingly, each firm will develop various performance metrics targeted at the perceived critical variables. Whilst there is a degree of variability in these operational measures there is far more uniformity in the use of financial performance metrics. Most companies, and, where appropriate, their divisions, use the level of profits earned as a measure of performance. Whilst the level of profit is important, on its own it is a poor indicator of performance. Instead, profit adequacy requires expression in relation to the amount of capital resource utilised in the generation of that profit. The most common method of achieving this evaluation is through the measure of return on capital employed (ROCE). This is determined by the result of the firm's or division's net earnings before tax (NEBT) divided by the capital employed in the economic unit. The widespread use of ROCE reflects the fact that the measure has many positive features. Specifically, it uses routinely collected accounting data, and, as such, it benefits from having a low data collection cost and having the objectivity that is inherent in financial accounting numbers. In addition, ROCE makes possible performance comparisons across divisions of different size and business activity.

One of the purposes of accounting, therefore, is to enable the evaluation of performance and thereby allow decisions to be made regarding the future of the business. Thus. measures such as ROI and ROCE have been developed for this purpose. Sadly, though. these accounting measures equate efficiency with effectiveness and ally them to cost reduction – something to which we will return later in the chapter. So producing for lower cost is considered to be desirable and is assumed to lead to sustainable competitive advantage. The prime ways of reducing costs include both their externalisation and reducing the variable cost of labour by getting rid of people.

The evaluation of performance is partly concerned with the measurement of performance and partly with the reporting of that performance, and, with the greater importance being given to social accountability, the changing reporting needs of an organisation are also being recognised. Thus Birnbeg (1980) states that accounting is attempting to supply various diverse groups, with different needs for information, and that there is a need for several distinct types of accounting to perform such a function. Similarly, Gray (1992) considers the limitations of the traditional economic base for accounting and questions some of its premises, such as the desirability of growth; the existence of rational economic man; the exclusion of altruism; and the ignoring of the way in which wealth is distributed. He argues that there is a need for a new paradigm which considers the environment as part of the firm rather than as an externality, and giving sustainability and the use of primary resources increased importance. Rubenstein (1992) goes further and argues that there is a need for a new social contract between a business and the stakeholders to which it is accountable, and a business mission which recognises that some things go beyond accounting.

Introduction to sustainability

One of the most frequently used words relating to corporate activity at present is "sustainability". Indeed, it can be argued that it has been so heavily overused, and with so many different meanings applied to it, that it is effectively meaningless. For example, according to Marrewijk & Were (2003), there is no specific definition of corporate sustainability and each organisation needs to devise its own definition to suit its purpose and objectives, although they seem to assume that corporate sustainability and corporate social responsibility are synonymous and based upon voluntary activities including environmental and social concerns, implicitly thereby adopting the EU approach.

Thus, the term "sustainability" currently has a high profile within the lexicon of corporate endeavour (Aras & Crowther, 2008a). Indeed, it is frequently mentioned as being central to corporate activity without any attempt to define exactly what sustainable activity entails. This is understandable as the concept is problematic and subject to many varying definitions – ranging from platitudes concerning sustainable development to the deep green concept of returning to the 'golden era' before industrialisation – although often it is used by corporations merely to signify that they intend to continue their existence into the future. Indeed, their accounting leads them to the assumption that cost reduction equates to efficiency and therefore continued existence. This is true even when cost reduction sacrifices future capability at the expense of present cash flow through the elimination of technical experience and expertise in the manner categorised by many people (see for example Carter & Crowther, 2000). This represents a misunderstanding of the meaning of sustainability as mere continued existence (Aras & Crowther, 2008b).

Sustainability discourse is of course significantly different and has implications in terms of managing corporate behaviour. Sustainability implies that society must use no more of a resource than can be regenerated. This can be defined in terms of the carrying capacity of the ecosystem (Hawken 1993) and described with input–output models of resource consumption. Viewing an organisation as part of a wider social and economic system implies that these effects must be taken into account, not just for the measurement of costs and value created in the present, but also for the future of the business itself. This approach to sustainability is based upon the Gaia theory (Lovelock 1979) – a model in which the whole of the ecosphere, and all living matter therein, is co-dependent upon its various facets, forming a complete system. According to this hypothesis, this complete system and all the components of it are interdependent and equally necessary for maintaining the Earth as a planet capable of sustaining life.

Such concerns are pertinent at the macro level of society as a whole, or at the level of the nation state, but are equally relevant at the micro level of the corporation, the aspect of sustainability with which we are concerned in this chapter. At this level, measures of sustainability would consider the rate at which resources are consumed by the organisation in relation to the rate at which resources can be regenerated. Unsustainable operations can be accommodated for either by developing sustainable operations or by planning for a future lacking in resources currently required. In practice, organisations mostly tend to aim towards less unsustainability by increasing efficiency in the way in which resources are utilised. An example of this would be an energy efficiency programme.

Sustainability is a controversial topic because it means different things to different people. Nevertheless there is a growing awareness (or diminishing naivety) that one is, indeed, involved in a topical debate about what sustainability means and, crucially, the extent to which (if at all) it can be delivered by corporations in the simple manner that they promise (United Nations Commission on Environment and Development (Schmidheiny, 1992)) and others assume.

There is further confusion surrounding the concept of sustainability: for the purist, sustainability implies nothing more than stasis – the ability to continue in an unchanged manner – but often it is taken to imply development in a sustainable manner (Marsden 2000; Hart & Milstein 2003) and the terms "sustainability" and "sustainable development" are for many viewed as synonymous.

As far as corporate sustainability is concerned, the confusion is exacerbated by the fact that the term "sustainable" has been used in the management literature during the last 30 years (see for example Reed & DeFillippi, 1990) to merely imply continuity. Thus, Zwetsloot (2003) is able to conflate corporate social responsibility with the techniques of continuous improvement and innovation to imply that sustainability is thereby ensured.

An almost unquestioned assumption, however, is that growth remains possible (Elliott 2005) and that sustainability and sustainable development are therefore synonymous[3]. Indeed the economic perspective of post-Cartesian ontologies continues to predominate, and growth is considered to be not just possible but also desirable – even essential (see for example Spangenberg, 2004). So it is possible therefore for Daly (1992) to argue that the economics of development is all that needs to be addressed and that this can be dealt with through the market with the clear separation of the three basic economic goals of efficient allocation, equitable distribution, and sustainable scale. Hart (1997) goes further and regards the concept of sustainable development merely as a business opportunity, arguing that once a company identifies its environmental strategy then opportunities for new products and services become apparent.

There seem therefore to be two commonly-held assumptions which permeate the discourse of corporate sustainability. The first is that sustainability is synonymous with sustainable development. The second is that a sustainable company will exist merely by recognising environmental and social issues and incorporating them into its strategic planning. We reject both of these assumptions – both are based upon an unquestioning acceptance of market economics predicated in the need for growth. While we do not necessarily reject such market economics, we argue that its acceptance has led to these assumptions about sustainability which have confused the debate. Thus we consider it imperative at this point to reiterate the basic tenet of sustainability: that sustainable activity is an activity in which decisions made in the present do not restrict the choices available in the future. If this tenet of sustainability is accepted then it follows that development is neither a necessary nor desirable aspect of sustainability. Sustainable development may well be possible, and even desirable in some circumstances, but it is not an integral aspect of sustainability.

Our second point is that corporate sustainability is not necessarily about continuing into the future with little change except to incorporate environmental and social issues – all firms are doing this in some way. Nor is "corporate sustainability" a term which is interchangeable with the term "corporate social responsibility". Furthermore, environmental sustainability – the context in which the term is generally used – is not the same as corporate sustainability.

---

[3] In other words, the assumption which was prevalent 30 years ago continues to be widely-used today – that corporations need to develop and grow in order to continue to exist.

Corporate sustainability

Sustainability is a fashionable concept for corporations, often being discussed on corporate websites. It is, however, apparent that sustainability and sustainable development are used as interchangeable terms. It is equally apparent that all corporations claim to have engaged with sustainability and solved the attendant problems[4]. It is apparent, therefore, that a very powerful semiotic (Guiraud 1975; Kim 1996) of sustainable activity has been created – conveniently, as Fish (1985) shows, truth and belief are synonymous for all practical purposes. It has been argued elsewhere (Aras & Crowther, 2008b) that this is a deliberate ploy, as one of the effects of persuading people that corporate activity is sustainable is that the cost of capital for the firm is reduced because investors are misled into thinking that the level of risk involved in their investment is lower than it actually is.

Traditional accounting theory and practice assumes that value is created in the business through the transformation process and that distribution is merely concerned with how much of the resultant profit is given to the investors in the business now and how much is retained in order to generate future profits and, hence, future returns to investors. This is, of course, overly simplistic for a number of reasons. Even in traditional accounting theory it is recognised that some of the retained profit is needed merely to replace worn-out capital – and hence to ensure sustainability in its narrowest sense. Accounting, of course, only attempts to record actions taking place within this transformational process, and even in doing so regards all costs as things leading to profit for distribution.

This traditional view of accounting is that the only activities with which the organisation should be concerned are those which take place within the organisation;[5] consequently it is considered that these are the only activities for which a role for accounting exists. Here, therefore, is located the essential dialectic of accounting – that some results of actions taken are significant and need to be recorded, while others are irrelevant and need to be ignored. This view of accounting places the organisation at the centre of its world, with the only interfaces with the external world taking place at the beginning and end of its value chain. It is apparent, however, that any actions which an organisation undertakes will have an

---

[4] See Aras & Crowther 2008a. The claim regarding all corporations engaging with sustainability is based on their research regarding all firms in the FTSE100.

[5] Essentially, the only purpose of traditional accounting is to record the effects of actions upon the organisation itself.

effect not just upon itself, but also upon the external environment within which that organisation resides. In considering the effect of an organisation upon its external environment, it must be recognised that this environment includes both the business environment in which the firm is operating, the local societal environment in which the organisation is located and the wider global environment.

The discourse of accounting can therefore be seen to be concerned solely with the operational performance of the organisation. Contrasting views of the role of accounting in the production process might therefore be epitomised either as providing a system of measurement to enable a reasonable market mediation in the resource allocation problem or as providing a mechanism for the expropriation of surplus value from the labour component of the transformational process. Both strands of the discourse, however, tend to view that labour as a homogeneous entity and consider the effect of organisational activity upon that entity. Labour is, of course, composed of individual people; moreover, these individual people have a lifetime of availability for employment and different needs at different points during their life cycle. The depersonalisation of people through the use of the term "labour", however, provides a mechanism for the treatment of labour as an entity without any recognition of these personal needs. Thus, it is possible to restrict the discourse to that of the organisation and its components – such as labour capital – and to theorise accordingly. The use of the term "labour" is a convenient euphemism which disguises the fact that labour consists of people, while the treatment of people as a variable cost effectively commodifies these people in the production process. In order to create value in the transformational process of an organisation, commodities need to be used efficiently, and this efficient use of such commodities is measured through the accounting of the organisation. When such a commodity consists of people, this implies using them in such a way that the maximum surplus value can be extracted from them. The way in which this can be achieved is through the employment of young, fit people who can work hard and then be replaced by more young, fit people. In this way, surplus value (in Marxian terms) can be transferred from the future of the person and extracted in the present. As people have been constituted as a commodified variable cost, they have become merely a factor of production which can be exchanged for another factor of production, as the costs determined through the use of accounting legitimate. Thus, it is reasonable, through an accounting analysis, to replace people with machinery if more value (profit) can be extracted in doing so. This provided the imperative for the industrial revolution, which has continued up until the present. Accounting is only concerned with the effect of the actions of an organisation upon itself, and so the effect of mechanisation upon people is not taken into account. Thus, if mechanisation results in people becoming unemployed (or possibly unemployable), this is of no concern – except to the people themselves. This, of course, is also an inevitable outcome of any system which is predicated in Utilitarian theory, as the present economic system undoubtedly is. Arguably, this is the root cause of many of the problems of overproduction and overconsumption existing alongside the commodification and exploitation of people – but this is another story which will be told elsewhere…

Developing a full discourse of sustainability

In this chapter, we have sought to show that the accounting discourse of operational performance is predicated in cost reduction as a means of achieving efficiency, while sustainability discourse is predicated in other factors, such as, for example, the environmental sustainability discourse epitomised by the work of Jacobs (1991), Welford (1997) and Gray & Bebbington (2001), or the going concern principle of accounting as epitomised by the corporate reporting described earlier. Thus, the two discourses tend to run in parallel without actually communicating. Corporate sustainability requires this communication. Although seemingly incompatible, both discourses are actually based on an acceptance of a conventional view of the transformational process, as shown in Figure 1:

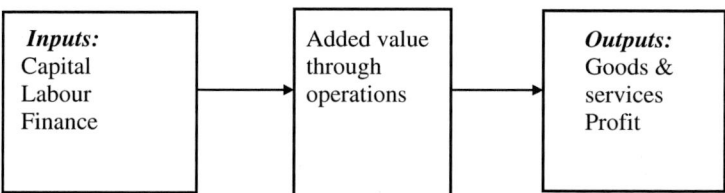

Fig 4.1: The Conventional Transformational Process

This model assumes that inputs (of capital, labour and finance) are used to make goods and services through the employment of the operational factors of production (such as employees and suppliers) in order to make goods and services with a resultant profit. The implications of this conventional view of the transformational process are that the inputs can be freely acquired in desired quantities and that the operational factors of production are commodified. This view of the process enables mediation through the market and is legitimated by the views of such theorists as Spangenberg (2004).

There are, however, two fundamental flaws with this form of analysis, from a sustainability perspective:

1. The input referred to as capital actually represents environmental resources, and these are quite definitely finite in quantity (Daly, 1996). Thus, the market cannot mediate adequately as the ensuing competitive bidding will raise the price but will not bring more of the resource into the market because there is no more in existence. Substitution can compensate for shortages only to a limited extent: it is difficult, for example, to see the extent to which more finance or labour can compensate for the absence of oil or any other fuel.

2. The factors of production are not actually commodities; rather, they are stakeholders of the organisation. It may aid analysis to commodify them, but they require benefits from the organisational activity. In particular, when resources are recognised to be finite, market mediation in this way does not satisfactorily accommodate the requirements of all stakeholders to the organisation. Thus, these stakeholders need to become a part of the output section of the transformational process.

As far as inputs to the transformational process are concerned, it is apparent that environmental resources are finite and effectively fixed. Currently, all the resources of the planet are in use (some would say overuse), and the resources for one corporation can only be increased by taking them from another through the process of competition in the market place. This highlights two alternative routes to development. The first is through the substitution of environmental resources with other inputs – namely, with labour or finance. The second is through making better use of the available environmental resources – effectively doing more with less. Both require technological development in order to be brought into effect, and so sustainable development essentially requires technological development – also known as research and development – in order to be tenable. This is the first point of intersection whereby sustainability comes into conflict with organisational accounting. Technological development for sustainability requires the more efficient use of environmental resources, whereas accounting efficiency requires the more effective use of financial resources. Sustainable development, therefore, requires greater use of human resources, particularly highly skilled people, in order to develop that technology, and this of course will incur additional cost. Accounting efficiency requires the replacement of people – particularly skilled and, therefore expensive, people – with relatively low-cost techniques such as programmed change initiatives (such as business process re-engineering) and computer-based management systems. We therefore argue that the use of conventional accounting is, to a large extent, in direct opposition to the concept of sustainability.

Introducing equitable sustainability

A further problem with the conflict between accounting and sustainability derives from the output part of the transformational process. Accounting assumes that the corporation is run on behalf of its shareholders and investors and that outputs therefore consist only of goods or services for sale and profit for distribution. Additionally, however, there are a wide variety of other stakeholders who justifiably have a concern with those activities, and are affected by those activities. Those other stakeholders have not just an interest in the activities of the firm, but also a degree of influence over the shaping of those activities. This influence is so significant that it can be argued that the power and influence of these stakeholders is such that it amounts to quasi-ownership of the organisation. It therefore follows that these stakeholders are more than a part of the transformational process, and that how the effects of the actions of the corporation – both positive and negative – are distributed is an essential part of sustainability. Our argument, therefore, is that sustainability can only exist if equity also exists.

Hence we introduce the term "equitable sustainability" (Aras & Crowther, 2008c) to reflect this argument that sustainability cannot exist without equity in the distributional process. It is our argument that sustainability is presently not really either understood by theorists or addressed by corporations, despite the many claims that are being made. Indeed we regard much analysis – based on the notion of mediation through the market – as being both complacent and obfuscatory concerning the issues which need to be addressed. It is only by introducing the concept of equity into the analysis that we can start to address the question of sustainability.

The environmental strand of sustainability discourse extends this by recognising a wider set of inputs and outputs in the form of the triple bottom line approach to performance measurement. Essentially, this is, however, an acceptance of the traditional model of the transformational process with more effects recorded. Our argument is that this does not actually lead to corporate sustainability without a consideration of the distributional impact of corporate activity. Thus, in our model, none of the stakeholders are merely factors of production, but are also affected by— and hence concerned with—the results of corporate activity, as described through the transformational process.

This is essentially a balancing model of corporate activity. In other words, we are stating, for example, that the conventional view of sustainability in terms of either using no more of a resource than can be regenerated or not limiting the choices of future generations[6] – in other words stasis (Aras & Crowther 2009b) – is neither a realistic nor an ethical model of sustainability. An ethical view of sustainability, predicated in a Utilitarian philosophy, would allow action, as long as a full evaluation of the consequences is made and as long as all stakeholders understand and accept the implications. This would then be ethical behaviour if the net effect of the summation of effects was positive. Thus, it could be acceptable to affect the environment, and hence the possibilities for future generations, if this condition was met. Part of our argument is that there are inevitable conflicts between the requirements and expectations of different stakeholders[7], but that these conflicts will be exacerbated as the implications of finite environmental resources become more overt. It is therefore apparent that the expectations of all stakeholders must be addressed and outcomes must be deemed acceptable – in other words satisficed (Simon 1981) – by all in order to avoid these conflicts. Accounting, however, assumes that these stakeholders are merely resources to be utilised in the seeking of returns to investors – the second source of conflict between accounting and sustainability.

A traditional view of organisational accounting

Thus, although risk management, efficient management, regulation, international standards and corporate governance are all necessary for sustainability and for sustainable business (Aras & Crowther, 2009c), there

---

[6] As defined in the Brundtland Report (WCED 1987) and used as the standard definition of sustainability. This report is also used as the standard work to justify that sustainable development is possible without significant change – a flawed argument as is shown in this chapter.

[7] Balancing these conflicting requirements and expectation has, of course, always been one of the tasks of the managers of a corporation. Until recently, however, the environment has not been treated as one of these stakeholders and future generations are still not taken into account in this balancing, except in very rare circumstances.

are actually two discrete discourses concerning corporate sustainability which are operating in parallel with each other, as described earlier. Although seemingly incompatible, both are actually based on an acceptance of a conventional view of the transformational process (see Figure 4.1).

The transformational process revisited

In order to explain our alternative approach to developing sustainable practice, we need to go back to the transformational process which describes corporate activity.

As mentioned earlier, the use of conventional accounting is, to a large extent, in direct opposition to the concept of sustainability. Our model of sustainable corporate activity seeks to resolve this into a model which recognises both the transformational process within a corporation but also the distribution of the benefits as being equally significant to sustainability.

There are a number of problems with this economic view of corporate activity, encapsulated in the way that accounting for corporate activity has evolved.

- Firstly, the economic view of corporate activity is that efficiency is all that matters.
- Secondly, efficiency is always equated as cost reduction – organisations produce at a lower financial cost because finance is a scarce resource
- Thirdly, cost reduction is sustainable, meaning businesses have migrated around the world in search of ever lower costs of production, such as cheap labour and cheap raw materials
- Finally, substitution is always possible, whether labour by technology, or one source of energy by another.

These are all incorrect.

The other main problem with the traditional economic view of corporate activity is the assumption that stakeholders are a part of the factors of production – to be used to provide the surplus which is distributed to the owners and investors of the corporation. As such, in this traditional way of thinking, employees and suppliers are regarded as merely a part of the production process; the effects of corporate activity are externalised to society at large with impunity; and the environment is viewed as a free resource to be used for financial gain. This view of corporate activity additionally regards the future – an important stakeholder – as something that can be neglected, while also audaciously venturing to speak of sustainable corporate activity!

Let us return to the transformational process and redefine the key terms. When we talk about "Capital", what we really mean is natural resources. "Labour" means people, while the meaning of "Finance" is unchanged.

We accept that value is created through corporate activity, but a crucial part of this is the distribution of the effects – both positive and negative – to all stakeholders, including society, the environment and the future. Our argument is that corporate sustainability is impossible without a consideration of the distributional impact of the corporate activity. Thus, in our model, none of the stakeholders are merely factors of production but are also affected by, and hence concerned, with the results of corporate activity, as described through the transformational process. A reconsideration of sustainability shows that, when resources are limited, the way to manage sustainable development is through the more efficient use of those resources. Consequently, all corporations must practice cost management and efficient operational management as a matter of course but also as a means of achieving sustainability.

Conventionally, corporations grow by consuming more resources. Redefining the problem, however, shows us that natural resources are finite and are being fully committed at present – if not actually being over committed. So growth through the use of more natural resources is not possible. Natural resources are the most important scarce resource – not finance.

Consequently, efficiency must be redefined away from financial efficiency and applied to the use of natural resources. Growth requires us to do more with less. As such, innovation, technology and R&D become more important, meaning we must redefine the transformational process to provide a more realistic description of the input resources used – and the potential for substitution – and highlight that growth must come through technological improvement rather than through the use of more resources. The sustainable transformational process therefore is:

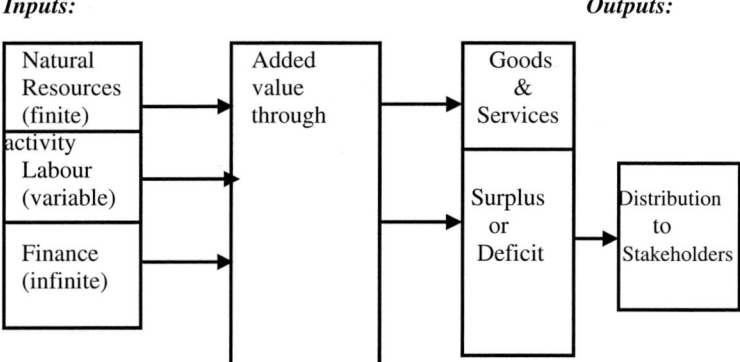

Fig 4.2: The Sustainable Transformational Process

Moreover, in our model, none of the stakeholders are merely factors of production but are also affected by, and hence concerned with, the results of corporate activity, as described through the transformational process.

We deliberately use the term "distributable sustainability" in order to reflect one of the key components of this argument, namely that true sustainability depends not just upon how actions affect choices in the future but also upon how the effects of those actions – both positive and negative – are distributed among the stakeholders involved. A central tenet of our argument is that corporate activity, to be sustainable, must not simply utilise resources to benefit owners, but must recognise all effects upon all stakeholders and distribute these in a manner which is acceptable to all concerned – both in the present and in the future. This is, in effect, a radical reinterpretation of corporate activity.

It is necessary to consider the operationalization of this view of sustainability. Our argument has been that sustainability must involve greater efficiency in the use of resources and greater equity in the distribution of the effects of corporate activity. To be operationalised, the effects must be measurable and the combination must, of course, be manageable.

This can be depicted as a model of sustainability.

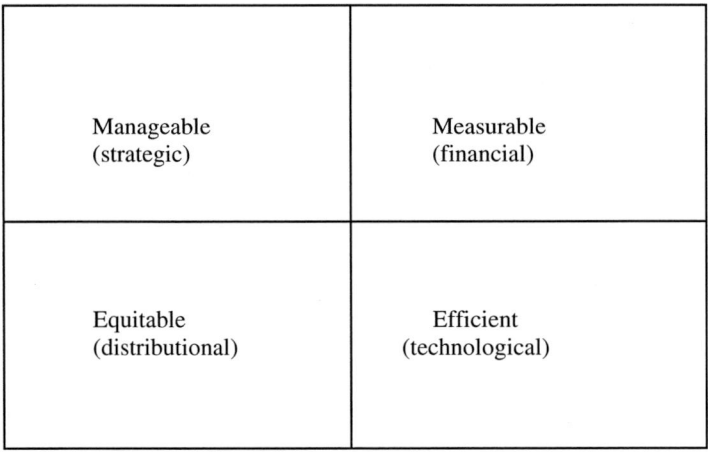

Fig 4.3: The facets of sustainability

This acts as a form of balanced scorecard to provide a form of evaluation for the operation of sustainability within an organisation. It concentrates upon the 4 key aspects, namely:

- Strategy
- Finance
- Distribution
- Technological development

Moreover, it recognises that it is the balance between these factors which is the most significant aspect of sustainability. From this, it is possible to draw a plan of action for an organisation which will recognise priorities and provide a basis for performance evaluation.

To summarise, sustainability requires a radical rethink and a move away from the cosy security of the Brundtland definition. We therefore reject the accepted terms of "sustainability" and "sustainable development", preferring instead to use the term "durability" to emphasise the change in focus.

The essential features of durability can be described as follows:

- Efficiency is concerned with the best use of scarce resources. This requires a redefinition of inputs to the transformational process and a focus upon environmental resources as the most important scarce resources.

- Efficiency is concerned with optimising the use of scarce resources (namely environmental resources), rather than with cost reduction
- Value is added through technology and innovation rather than through expropriation
- Outputs are redefined to include distributional effects on all stakeholders

Conclusions

An accounting view of corporations is that they are able to grow by acquiring more resources. Moreover, they are able to shed costs (and people) at will in order to conserve their capability in difficult times for future growth and development. In this chapter, we have contrasted this view of corporations with the needs of sustainable development. In doing so, we have developed a model outlining the circumstances in which such development is both possible and acceptable to all parties. In doing this, we are not arguing for, or against, sustainable development (as others do), but merely acknowledging that it can be accommodated. Our central argument is that a radical rethinking of corporate accounting is essential in order to prioritise the key features of sustainability which are in conflict with the central tenets of accounting.

References

Aras G & Crowther D (2007a); Sustainable corporate social responsibility and the value chain; in D Crowther & M M Zain (eds), *New Perspectives on Corporate Social Responsibility*, pp 119-140; Shah Alam, Malaysia; MARA University Press

Aras G & Crowther D (2007b); Is the global economy sustainable?; in S Barber (ed), *The Geopolitics of the City*; London; Forum Press pp 165-194

Aras G & Crowther D (2008a); Governance and sustainability: An investigation into the relationship between corporate governance and corporate sustainability; *Management Decision*, 46 (3) (forthcoming)

Aras G & Crowther D (2008b); Corporate sustainability reporting: a study in disingenuity?; *Journal of Business Ethics* 87 (supp 1), 279-288

Aras G & Crowther D (2008c); Towards Equitable Sustainability; *Ivey Business Review* Jan/Feb 2008;
http://www.iveybusinessjournal.com/article.asp?intArticle_ID=734

Aras G & Crowther D (2009a); Making sustainable development sustainable; *Management Decision* 47 (6), 975-988

Aras G & Crowther D (2009b); *The Durable Corporation: strategies for sustainable development*; Farnham; Gower

Birnbeg J G (1980); The role of accounting in financial disclosure; *Accounting, Organizations & Society*, 5 (1), 71-80

Carter C & Crowther D (2000); Unravelling a Profession: the case of engineers in a British regional electricity company; *Critical Perspectives on Accounting*, 11, 23- 49.

Clark P (1987); Anglo-American Innovation; Berlin; Du Gruyter

Covaleski M & Aiken M (1986); Accounting and Theories of Organizations: some preliminary considerations; *Accounting, Organizations & Society*, 11 (4/5), 297-319

Crowther D (2002); A Social Critique of Corporate Reporting; Aldershot; Ashgate

—. (2006); Standards of Corporate Social Responsibility: Convergence within the European Union; in D Njavro & K Krkac (eds), *Business Ethics and Corporate Social Responsibility*; Zagreb; MATE; pp 17-34

Daly H E (1996); Beyond Growth; Boston, Ma; Beacon Press

Elliott S R (2005); Sustainability: an economic perspective; *Resources Conservations and Recycling*, 44, 263-277

Fish S (1989); *Is there a text in this class? The authority to interpret communities*; Cambridge, Mass; Harvard University Press.

Gray R (1992); Accounting and environmentalism: an exploration of the challenge of gently accounting for accountability, transparency and sustainability; *Accounting, Organizations & Society*, 17 (5), 399-425

Gray, R. & Bebbington, J. (2001); *Accounting for the environment*; London; Sage

Guiraud P (1975); *Semiology*; London; Routledge & Kegan Paul.

Hart S L (1997); Beyond greening: Strategies for a sustainable world; Harvard Business Review, Jan / Feb 1997, 75 (1), 66-76

Hart S L & Milstein M B (2003); Creating sustainable value; *Academy of Management Executive*, 17 (2), 56-67

Hawken P (1993); *The Ecology of Commerce*; London; Weidenfeld & Nicholson.

Jackson N & Carter P (1998); Labour as Dressage, in A McKinlay & K Starkey (eds.); *Foucault, Management and Organization Theory*, London, Sage.

Jacobs, M. (1991); *The green economy – environment, sustainable development and the politics of the future*; Pluto Press: London

Johnson H T and Kaplan R S (1987); *Relevance Lost: The Rise and Fall of Management Accounting*; Boston, Mass; Harvard Business School Press

Kim K L (1996); *Caged in our own signs: a book about semiotics*; Norwood, N J; Ablex Publishing.

Lovelock J (1979); *Gaia*; Oxford; Oxford University Press.

Marrewijk M van & Werre M (2003); Multiple levels of corporate sustainability; *Journal of Business Ethics,* 44 (2/3), 107-119

Marsden C (2000); The new corporate citizenship of big business: part of the solution to sustainability; *Business & Society Review*, 105 (1), 9-25

Ogden S G & Anderson F (1999); The Role of Accounting in Organisational Change: promoting performance improvements in the privatised water industry; *Critical Perspectives on Accounting*, 10, 91-124.

Ortiz Martinez E & Crowther D (2005); Corporate Social Responsibility creates an environment for business success; in D Crowther & R Jatana (eds), *Representations of Social Responsibility Vol 1*; Hyderabad; ICFAI University Press, pp 125-140

Reed R & DeFillippi R J (1990); Causal ambiguity, barriers to imitation, and sustainable competitive advantage; *Academy of Management Review*, 15 (1), 88-102

Rubenstein D B (1992); Bridging the gap between green accounting and black ink; *Accounting, Organizations & Society*, 17 (5), 501-508

Schmidheiny S. (1992); *Changing Course;* New York; MIT Press.

Simon H (1981); The Science of the Artificial (2nd edition); Cambridge, Ma; MIT Press

Sombert W (1915); *The Quintessence of Modern Capitalism*; New York; E P Dutton & Co

Spangenberg J H (2004); Reconciling sustainability and growth: criteria, indicators, policies; *Sustainable Development*, 12, 74-86

WCED (World Commission on Environment and Development) (1987); *Our Common Future* (The Brundtland Report); Oxford University Press; Oxford.

Welford, R. (1997); *Hijacking environmentalism – corporate responses to sustainable development*; London: Earthscan

Zwetsloot G I J M (2003), From management systems to corporate social responsibility; *Journal of Business Ethics,* 44 (2/3), 201-207

CHAPTER FIVE

A NEW APPROACH TO INFORMATION SECURITY GOVERNANCE

HICHAM ELACHGAR, BRAHIM BOULAFDOUR, MERYEM MAKOUDI AND BOUBKER REGRAGUI

Introduction

Today, information can be viewed as a commodity, like electricity, without which many companies and organizations cannot function. However, in the interconnected world we live in, information is much more vulnerable than other commodities. While it is highly unlikely that the actions of a disgruntled teenager on another continent affect the electricity supply company, it is easy to envisage that the actions of this youth can ruin the system information of prestigious organizations.

It is therefore essential for organizations to ensure continued access to information while protecting their information assets. Many organizations will not do business without access to their information resources. However, the protection of information resources often has no direct return on investment. The security of information resources as a rule does not generate revenue for an organization. Therefore, investors are rarely interested in how their information resources are protected. From a business perspective, information security is not an axis of development for organizations, which are more likely to be concerned about the profitability of investment, which considerably slows down investment in information security.

In this regard, the information security has gone through several stages:

The first wave was characterized by the reduction of information security to a technical problem left in the hands of technical experts.

The second wave was marked by the passage of information security from a technical dimension to a dimension of management by including policies and procedures.

The third wave was characterized by the need to adopt some form of standardization of information security and integration of aspects of best practices, certification, and integration of culture and information security of the measurement and monitoring.

The fourth wave is the development of the Governance of Information Security. The origins of this wave are closely linked to developments made in the areas of corporate governance and especially in legal and regulatory requirements. The Board felt the need to secure information systems because they started to become personally responsible for the security of their information systems [SOX, BASEL II, ACT 0908].

This chapter addresses this wave, and highlights the relationship between corporate governance and the governance of information security.

Corporate Governance and Information Security

Several documents related to corporate governance have emerged in recent years; the importance of governance in general is now internationally established. Corporate governance is defined as "all taken responsibilities and practices implemented by a general direction in order to provide a strategic direction, to ensure objectives are met, to ensure that risks are managed appropriately, and to ensure that organizational resources are used responsibly." Corporate governance makes it clear that the board of administration is responsible for ensuring information integrity of accounting and financial reporting, and compliance with laws.

Several legal and regulatory developments related to corporate governance have focused on the role and responsibility of the board, including the Sarbanes - Oxley (SOX, 2002) which also requires putting in place a system control related to operational risks that often results in the establishment of measures to manage risks related to the security of information systems. It is therefore clear that, although not directly mentioned, there is a significant relationship between corporate governance and information security. The following diagram helps illustrate the relationship between corporate governance and information security.

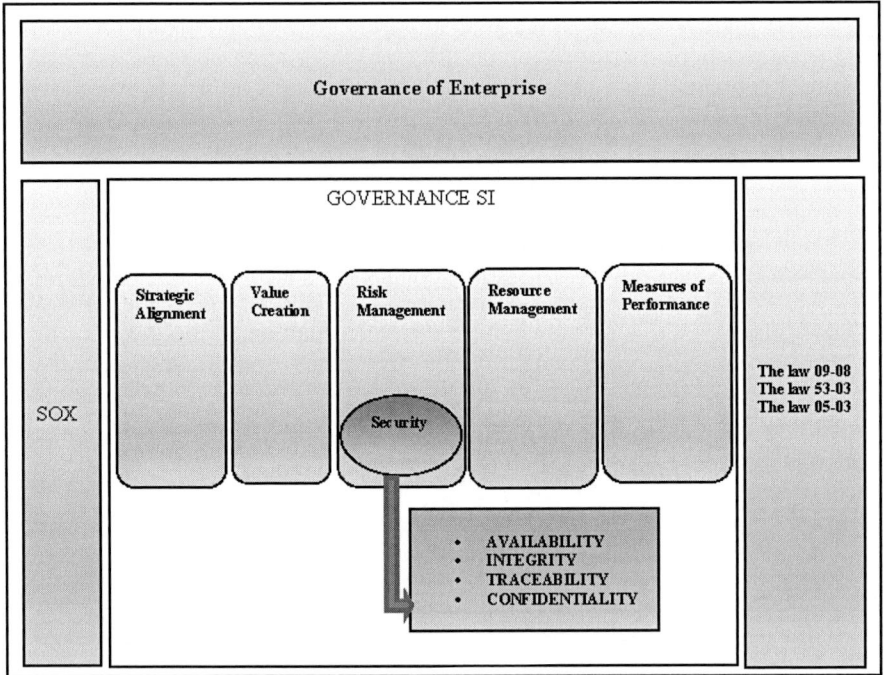

Fig 5.1 Corporate governance and information security

The governance of information security: the 4th wave

ISACA defines the governance of information security as a kind of strategic alignment, value creation, risk management, performance management, and also the management of resources against requirements for the company's business. It is part of the axis of risk management and top management must assure the availability, confidentiality, traceability, and integrity of information, as well as compliance with laws and procedures when handling and storing information.

From this perspective, the governance of information security aims to ensure that the availability, integrity, confidentiality, and traceability of information (DICT) are assured.

• Availability of information: ownership of information to be accessible and usable upon demand by an authorized entity, when it needs it.

- Integrity of information: ownership of information to be accurate, complete and unaltered.
- Confidentiality of information: information ownership that is made available or disclosed to any persons, entities or processes allowed.
- Traceability of information: ownership of information to be reviewed and audited. It is especially possible to track all events related to information during a certain period.

The governance of Information Security is reflected in the establishment of a set of structures and measures that ensure:

- The management commitment and leadership to secure information systems: this commitment is reflected in the establishment of a security policy based on risk analysis, a classification of information assets by adopting methods analysis of risk such as: MEHARI EBIOS, ISO 27005, RISK IT etc..
- The adoption of standards for information security, in this case: ISO 27002, ITIL, COBIT.
- The establishment of an organization and structures in charge of information security with a clear definition of the roles and responsibilities of different actors (such as the committee of information security, the security official of the information, process owners (business managers), the local correspondents of security, IT professionals, and auditors).
- User awareness of the issues, threats and best practices in information security. They must thus be able to support the security policy information. This awareness may relate to topics concerning information security: security issues, threats and vulnerability, risk management, authorization management, password management, information classification, access control, continuity of activity, and compliance.
- The implementation of policies, processes and procedures to secure the information system
- The introduction of technology adequate to secure the information system by setting up according to the risks and needs of firewalls, proxies, antivirus, the IDS, the IPS, certificates, and the SSO.
- Compliance with regulatory requirements regarding the information security information. These regulatory requirements may concern the protection of personal data and respect for intellectual property
- The establishment of a dashboard of measurement and control of the security information to be able to supervise and control the evolution of

information security. This process necessarily requires the establishment of indicators and measures of security management. These indicators should accurately reflect the levels of security in terms of availability, confidentiality, integrity and traceability of information.

How to ensure good governance of information security

Surf the 4th wave; it is important to go through the third wave. Indeed, the adoption of standard reference is an interesting and rewarding step that allows preparation for the 4th wave "Governance Information System". The establishment of good governance of information systems should follow the Deming cycle of quality. This is the application, the area of security, of the cycle in four points:

- Plan: Security is planning to move from a reactive posture to a proactive posture;
- Develop: Security is a set of processes to be developed following a security benchmark.
- Check: Security is controlled through audits and penetration tests, and most common methods;
- Act: All control activities carried out during phase "Check" are likely to highlight a number of malfunctions that need to provide for corrective actions, preventive actions and improvement actions.

Our approach to ensure the governance of the security of information systems is based on five principals, namely:

- ✓ P1. Commitment of top management
- ✓ P2. Risk Analysis
- ✓ P3. Measure of maturity with regard to repositories of information security
- ✓ P4. Development of action plans
- ✓ P5. Definition of indicators measuring

P1. Commitment of top management

Governance and management of information security within the organization requires that senior management actively support the security policy within the organization through clear direction, a commitment to honest, allocation functions, and explicit recognition of responsibilities for information security.

ISO 27001 [2] recommends that the branch ensure that the objectives for information security are identified, meet the needs of the organization, and are integrated into processes adapted.

In addition, senior management must formulate, approve and return policy information security to monitor the effectiveness of its implementation.

The formulation of clear guidelines clearly manifests its support with the initiatives taken to strengthen security.

P2. Risk Analysis

MEHARI (a harmonized method of risk analysis) for risk analysis is proposed by CLUSIF, and is based on a top-down approach.

MEHARI is intended to enable risk assessment and control of security management information systems in the short, medium and long term.

The essence of this approach, allowing the risk assessment, is to analyse, for a representative set of risk scenarios, the actual state of the risk level, depending on the status of security measures. This analysis will help to optimize the choice of complementary measures to be implemented.

MEHARI addresses the following areas:

1. Organization
2. Site Safety and Buildings
3. Security of premises
4. WAN between sites
5. Local Area Network
6. Network Operations
7. Architecture and Systems Security
8. Production Computer
9. Application security
10. Safety of projects and application development
11. Protecting the working environment
12. Legal and regulatory

As a simplified version of MEHARI, we advocate that a rosette can generate summary and prioritize actions to ensure information security:

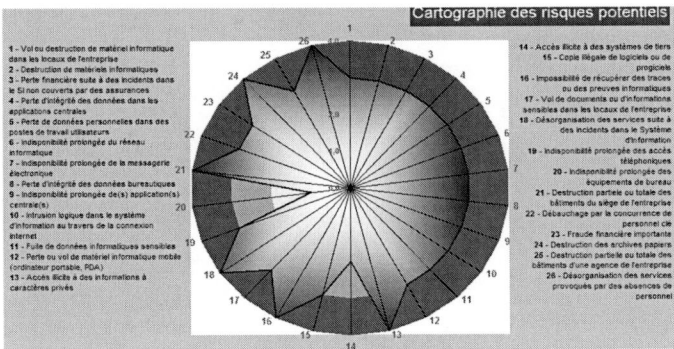

Fig 5.2 Map of potential risks

P3. Measure of maturity with regard to repositories of information security

The body of ISO 27002 identifies the best practices related to information security, but does not mention the process of their implementation. Organizations can use ISO 27002 as a template to create rules and procedures regarding information security. It can be a tool to assign roles and responsibilities.

ISO 27002 therefore meets the needs of organizations that want to establish the objectives in terms of information security, through a series of practical recommendations, addressing both technical aspects and organization. The standard covers eleven chapters:

· Security Policy
· Security Organization
· Asset Classification and Control
· Security Personnel
· Physical Security and Environment
· Operation and Networks
· Incident Management
· Development and Maintenance of Systems
· Logical Access Control
· Business Continuity
· Compliance

Below is an example of synthesis that can be developed to measure the maturity of the security in relation to different chapters of the standard.

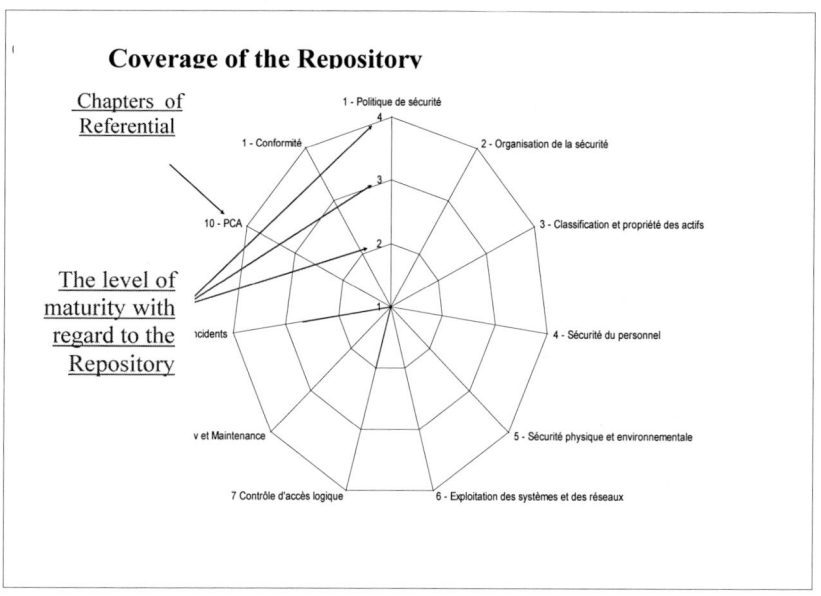

Fig 5.3 Coverage of the Repository

P4. Development of action plans

The development of an action plan for describing security or updating tasks for the year related to the implementation of information security within the company is necessary. This is proof of the diligence of the company to implement its security policy in practice.

- It will be used for recording the activity of the company in favour of an alignment of security on its economic goals.
- The security action plan is sequenced according to priorities, i.e. according to the needs of safety calculated during the risk analysis. It is a kind of operational implementation of security blueprint.

To this end, the action plan is a tool that describes:

- The key priorities from these two steps in implementing security measures,
- Actions to take,
- Managers and internal resources and external support,

- The overall planning and detailed task,
- Funding of this plan,
- Monitoring its implementation (including its progress and what remains to be done).

P5. Definition of indicators measuring

The use of indicators in the field of information security is a new concept. It was imposed by ISO / IEC 27001 in the MSIS without specifying how and where to use which aims to identify points of WSIS that need improvement or correction.

All indicators in IS Security provide a very active area of discussion. However, there are two large families of indicators, namely performance indicators, which verify the effectiveness of security measures, and compliance indicators, which monitor compliance with its specifications WSIS.

D1. Development of security policy information

Security policy ensures an acceptable level of risk for the company, by implementing a security architecture, taking into account the technical, human, organizational and regulatory business.

The parameters of risk analysis, when it comes to computer security, are many and of a very different nature.

Confidentiality, integrity and availability of means of communication will be dependent on continued vigilance with regards to the elements of:

- Physical Security: buildings, access, control, fluids, fire;
- Logical Security: computer backup, access, authentication, and encryption.

Computer security is a broad concept that encompasses application security, system security and operational safety, which also includes logical security, physical security, and the Communications Security Establishment.

However, the policy implementation of information security according to ISO 27001 should consider the following:

- a definition of information security, the general objectives sought and the scope chosen, and the importance of security as a necessary mechanism to share information;

- a statement of management's intentions supporting the goals and principles of information security, in accordance with the strategy and objectives of the organization;
- an approach to defining security objectives and measures, including the assessment and risk management;
- A brief explanation of policies, principles, standards and compliance requirements that are of particular importance for the organism, namely the following:
- compliance with legal, regulatory and contractual requirements;
- requirements in terms of training and safety awareness;
- management of business continuity;
- the consequences of breaches of information security;
- The definition of general and specific responsibilities in the management of information security, addressing in particular the rise of security incidents;
- References to documentation that will support policy and which are to be respected, including policies and procedures for more detailed safety or security rules to be followed by users.

D2. Design of procedures

In most cases, safety procedures should be supplemented by a description of the security process. These processes specify the rules through a vision of "organizational" roles and responsibilities. The bottom line is that all components of the WSIS are clearly identified. If some documents apply only partially to the WSIS, this should be stated explicitly.

This is the role of the Declaration of Applicability (SoA) which, although it is not binding outside of official certification, is a highly relevant document to build the MSIS.

D3. Execution of the action plan

After determining the overall security policy of the company, it should define the actions and measures to be taken in environmental, human and technical terms.

- **Environmental Dimension:** This concerns the physical infrastructure, insurance coverage, and redundancy of sites.

- **Human Dimension:** This involves all stakeholders of the company. Awareness and support are the best assets to avoid, often involuntary, malicious behavior.

The Internet offers many professional services useful to businesses, though there are a number of disadvantages associated with it.

The risks associated with Internet use are also a loss of productivity in the company, a saturation of the bonds, a lack of confidentiality, information leakage, and unauthorized downloading applications.

All these types of connections in many cases provide important information to hackers penetrating the enterprise system.

- **Technical dimension:** It must be adapted and consistent with the other two dimensions. Technical solutions are plentiful, and their vendors are full of good points. Nevertheless, and because no one should be judge and jury, nothing replaces a real security audit to qualify the solution. The recipe of computer equipment must include safety testing, and induce rules and procedures for verifying that the security level can be maintained.

C1. Measure

The security measures include a set of provisions to implement. These are the steps that should be followed to provide a good security policy.

133 measures have been defined for security information, and each was accompanied by several checkpoints that must be addressed in the implementation of ISMS.

These actions occur in several areas such as asset management, physical security, and compliance.

In MEHARI, security measures are chosen for their efficiency and robustness with respect to the severity of the disaster scenarios for the company. Four levels of severity of damage are distinguished by dysfunction (4: Vital, 3: Severe, 2: Important, 1: Not significant) to develop security measures. These malfunctions can happen because of the lack of confidentiality and integrity, or the availability of resources and data.

C2. Analysis of measures

The evaluation of computer security results from the analysis of protective measures in place to ensure information security.

These analyses identify and take specific decisions and are situation-specific, with the strong involvement of the Directorate General in managing risks.

A1. Corrective actions

It becomes "corrective" when a malfunction or a deviation is detected. The first of the effects is to correct this discrepancy or malfunction, then the causes to prevent their repetition.

A2. Preventive action

These are launched when a situation is detected that may cause actual harm or an incident if nothing is done. Preventive actions act on the causes before the deviation occurs.

A3. Improvement actions

Their goal is not to correct or prevent a gap, but to improve the performance of the MSIS process.

Conclusion

The concept of SSI is a set of methods, techniques and tools responsible for protecting the resources of a computer system to ensure service availability, confidentiality and integrity of information.

The security of information systems (IMS) is emerging as a critical component of protecting the company in its own interests and those related to external issues.

Given the risks involved and the functional and organizational context specific to the organization, it should identify what needs to be protected, to quantify the corresponding issue, formulate security, goals and to identify, arbitrate and implement appropriate countermeasures so that the correct level is maintained.

In general, the safety of SI has several objectives: safety, then, must protect information such as company assets against data loss, disclosure or alteration to ensure the continuity of business operations. In addition, IS security preserves the image of the company and the trust of others.

References

Basie Von Solms, Information Sécurity- the fourth Wave, computers & security 25 (2006) 165-166.

Technologies de l'information —Techniques de sécurité — Code de bonne pratique pour la gestion de la sécurité de l'information, Première édition, 2005, page 8.

Abdelhaq Elbekkali, Eric Lachapelle, René St-Germain, Gouvernance, audit et sécurité des TI, édition CCH, Québec, 2008, page 336. http://www.ssi-conseil.com/content/view/124/159/

Thierry Boileau, Mise en oeuvre de la SSI (Sécurité du Système d'information) de SUSS MicroOptics par l'approche processus ISO/CEI 2700, page 43

Michel Kamel, Patrons organisationnels et techniques pour la sécurisation des Organisations Virtuelles. the first word in a paper title, except for proper nouns and element symbols.

PART II:

SECTORAL UNDERSTANDINGS

CHAPTER SIX

THE ENFORCEMENT OF ACCOUNTABILITY
IN PUBLIC GOVERNANCE IN AFRICA

EME JOEL EFIONG AND DAVID CROWTHER

Introduction

Globally, governance crises have become a recurrent decimal in recent times. Most of these crises occur within the African continent; countries like Egypt, Tunica, and Libya have been swallowed by these crises and are yet to fully recover. These crises can be traceable to a lack of accountability in governance. It is widely recognized that there is a need for state authorities to report and explain to their citizens the use and management of public resources, and for the development of a framework of how citizens could demand and enforce accountability from those in power

Unethical behaviour, corrupt practices and the absence of accountability have apparently become erosive and 'normal' ways of life in most African countries. This has resulted in a number of uprisings in which citizens demand good governance from their leaders. Countries like Libya, Tunisia and Egypt are very recent examples of this. In the Nigerian public services, the extent of unethical behaviour and the lack of accountability has reached a crisis. Unethical practices have contributed to the economic difficulties that most African countries are currently facing. The truth is that there is a dire need for accountability in the public services of African countries.

The Concept of Accountability

Accountability is a concept with several meanings when applied to ethics and governance. According to Oluwu (1993), "it is the requirement that those who hold public trust should account for the use of the trust to citizens or their representatives". This indicates that the public will is superior to personal interests, and endeavours to ensure that the former should be supreme in every conduct and activity of the public official. In the same way, Laleye (1993) sees public accountability as the sanctions and procedures by which public officials may be held to account for their actions. Basically, accountability is a term that is often associated with the expectation of giving an account. Governance is frequently described as an account-giving relationship between individuals (Mulgan, 2000); where an individual, group or organisation is accountable to another individual, group or organisation and is obliged to inform the individual, group or organisation about its actions and decisions (past, present and future) to justify them, and to suffer punishment in the case of eventual misconduct. In view of the foregoing, accountability refers to the idea that public officials should be held responsible for their actions and/or inactions while in office. To McKinney (1979), accountability is a greater commitment to values and a higher standard of morality. However, for this to be effective, there must be certain norms and values that public officials should be required to observe (Odhiambo –Mbai, 2003).

Accountability can be viewed as the fundamental requirement for preventing the abuse of power and for ensuring that power is aimed towards the achievement of transparency, efficiency, effectiveness, and responsiveness (Raga and Taylor). The efficiency of such accountability is therefore imperative in any given society.

Interestingly, the concept of accountability has a long tradition in both political and financial accounting (Lindberg, 2010). The central idea has been that when decision-making power is transferred from a principal (such as the citizens) to an agent (such as government), there must be a mechanism in place for holding the agent to account for their decisions and, if necessary, for imposing sanctions. In accounting, the concept's long tradition refers to financial prudence and accounting in accordance with regulations and instructions (Barton, 2006).

The concept of accountability can be classified based on the type of accountability that is being exercised and/or the person, group or institution that the public official is answerable to. On a basic level,, we have the concepts of horizontal and vertical accountability. The capacity of an institution of accountability, such as parliament and the judiciary or other institutions of relatively autonomous powers, to call into question, and eventually punish, the unethical conduct of a given official, is commonly termed horizontal accountability. Invariably, horizontal accountability is the capacity of state institutions to check abuse by other public agencies and units of government, and to appropriate sanctions where necessary.

On the other hand, the means through which citizens, mass media and civil society seek to enforce ethical standards on public officials is termed vertical accountability. Even though parliament is typically considered as a key institution of horizontal accountability, it is also important in vertical accountability. This is because citizens and civil society groups can seek the support of the parliament in enforcing accountability. As such, the elected representatives can become the public voice and a means through which citizens can question the government and seek parliamentary sanctions where appropriate (Stapenhurst and O'Brien N.D).

Stages in accountability

From the preceding discussions, it can be deciphered that the concept of accountability involves two separate stages. The stages are answerability and enforcement (Stapenhurst and O'Brien N.D). Answerability generally refers to the obligation of the government, its agencies and public officials to provide information about their decisions and actions. It also involves the justification of such decisions and actions to the public and those institutions of accountability responsible for providing oversight.

On the other hand, enforcement gives the idea that the public or institutions responsible for accountability can sanction the offending party or remedy the unethical behaviour. Such institutions may include the legislature, the judiciary or other agencies set up for that purpose.

The concept of governance

It must be acknowledged that the concept of governance has existed as long as any form of human organisation has existed. The concept itself is merely one to encapsulate the means by which that organisation conducts itself. Recently, however, the term has come to the forefront of public attention, probably because of the problems of governance at both a national level and in the economic sphere at the level of the corporation. These problems have caused there to be a concern with a re-examination of what exactly is meant by governance, and more specifically just what the features of good governance are. It is here therefore that we must start our examination.

National governance has been defined by the World Bank as the exercise of political authority and the use of institutional resources to manage society's problems and affairs. This is a currently prevalent view of governance, with its assumption that governance is a top-down process decided by those in power and passed to society at large. In actual fact, the concept is originally democratic and consensual, being the process by which any group of people decide to manage their affairs and relate to each other. Such a consensual approach is, however, problematic for any but the smallest of groups, and no nation has actually managed to institute governance as a consensual process. With the current trend for supra-national organisation[1], this seems even more of a remote possibility; nor is it necessarily desirable. Thus, a coercive top-down form of governance enables a society to accept leadership and to make some difficult decisions which would not otherwise be made[2]. Equally, of course, it enables power to be usurped and used dictatorially, possibly beneficially[3], but most probably in a way in which most members of that society do not wish[4].

This top-down, hierarchical form of governance is the form of governance which normally takes place in large monolithic organisations such as the nation state. Conversely, the consensual form tends to be the norm in small organisations such as local clubs. There are, however, other forms of governance which are commonly found. One of these is governance through the market (see Williamson, 1975). The free market is the dominant ideology of economic activity, and the argument here is that transaction costs are lowered through this form of organisation. From a governance perspective, however, this is problematic as there is no automatic mechanism, and negotiation is used. The effect of this is that governance is decided according to power relationships, which tend to be coercive for the less powerful (such as, for example, consumers). Consequently, there is a need to impose some form of regulation through governments or supra-national organisations such as the World Trade organisation, which thereby re-imposes the eliminated transaction costs. The argument therefore resolves into an ideological argument rather than an economic one.

An increasing number of organisations rely upon informal social systems to govern their relationships with each other, and this is the final form of governance. This form is normally known as network governance

---

[1] Such as, for example, the European Community.

[2] For example the decision to abolish capital punishment in the UK in 1969 could not have been made consensually; nor too could the decision to invade Iraq in 2003.

[3] The ancient Greeks favoured beneficial dictatorship as a means of running their city states.

[4] Few would argue that, for example, power was usurped in the USSR by Stalin because of a centrally imposed governance; equally few would suggest that this power was used beneficially or in a way which most members of the society were happy about.

(Jones, Hesterly & Borgatti 1997). With this form of governance, there are no formal rules – certainly none which are legally binding. Instead, social obligations are recognised and governance exists within the networks because the different organisations continue to engage with each other, most probably in the economic arena. This form of governance can therefore be considered to be predicated in mutual self-interest. Of course, just as with market governance, power relationships are important and this form of governance is most satisfactory when there are no significant power imbalances to distort the governance relationships.

Although in some respects these different forms of governance are interchangeable, they are, in reality, suited to different circumstances. Regardless of the form of governance in existence, however, the most important thing is that it can be regarded as good governance by all parties involved – in other words all stakeholders must be satisfied. For this to be so, it is important that the basic principles of good governance are adhered to.

There are 8 principles which underpin every system of governance:

Transparency

Transparency, as a principle, necessitates that information is freely available and directly accessible to those who will be affected by such decisions and their enforcement. Transparency is of particular importance to external users of such information as these users lack the background details and knowledge available to internal users of such information. Equally, therefore, the decisions which are taken and their enforcement must be done in a manner that follows rules and regulations. Transparency, therefore, can be seen to be a part of the process of the recognition of responsibility on the part of the organisation for the external effects of its actions and equally part of the process of redistributing power more equitably to all stakeholders.

Rule of law

This is a corollary of the transparency principle. It is apparent that good governance requires a fair framework of rules of operation. Moreover, these rules must be enforced impartially, without regard for power relationships. Thus, the rights of minorities must be protected[5].

---

[5] This would imply, of course, the protection of human rights, but could be taken also to imply concern for the environment and its protection.

Additionally there must be appeal to an independent body as a means of conflict resolution, and this right of appeal must be known to all stakeholders.[6]

Participation

Although participation by all stakeholders is of course desirable, this is not an essential principle of good governance. The ability of all to participate if so desired is, however, an essential principle. Participation, of course, includes the freedom of association and of expression that goes along with this. Depending upon the size and structure of the organisation, participation can be either direct or through legitimate intermediate institutions or representatives, as in the case of a national government. Participation, as such, would involve everyone, or at least all adults, both male and female.

Responsiveness

This is a corollary of the participation principle and the transparency principle. Responsiveness implies that the governance regulations enable the institutions and processes of governance to be able to serve all stakeholders within a reasonable timeframe.

Equity

This principle involves ensuring that all members of society feel that they have a stake in it and do not feel excluded from the mainstream. This particularly applies to ensuring that the views of minorities are taken into account and that the voices of the most vulnerable in society are heard in decision-making processes. This requires mechanisms to ensure that all stakeholder groups have the opportunity to maintain or improve their well-being.

---

[6] This can be to national courts, trade associations, supra-national courts such as the European Court of Human Rights, or to an organisation such as the United Nations. Whatever the body, it needs to be appropriate and not just impartial, but also seen to be impartial to all concerned in order to maintain the creditability to adjudicate disputes.

Efficiency and Effectiveness

Efficiency of course implies the transaction cost minimisation referred to earlier, whereas effectiveness must be interpreted in the context of the achievement of the desired purpose. Thus, for effectiveness it is necessary that the processes and institutions produce results that meet the needs of the organisation, while making the best use of resources at their disposal. Naturally this also means the sustainable use of natural resources and the protection of the environment.

Sustainability

This, of course, requires a long-term perspective for sustainable human development and for the achievement of its goals. A growing number of writers over the last quarter of a century have recognised that the activities of an organisation impact upon the external environment. These other stakeholders have not just an interest in the activities of the organisation, but also a degree of influence over the shaping of those activities. This influence is so significant that it can be argued that the power and influence of these stakeholders is such that it amounts to quasi-ownership of the organisation. Central to this is a concern for the future which has become manifest through the term "sustainability". This term has become ubiquitous both within the discourse of globalisation and within the discourse of corporate performance. Sustainability is, of course, a controversial issue and there are many definitions of what is meant by the term. At its broadest definition, sustainability is concerned with the effects which action taken in the present has upon the options available in the future (Crowther, 2002). If resources are utilised in the present, they will no longer be available for use in the future, and this is of particular concern if the resources are finite in quantity. Thus raw materials of an extractive nature, such as coal, iron or oil, which are finite in quantity, will not be available for future use once consumed. At some point in the future, therefore, alternatives will be needed to fulfil the functions currently provided by these resources. This may be at some point in the relatively distant future, but of more immediate concern is the fact that, as resources become depleted, the cost of acquiring the remaining resources tends to increase, and the operational costs of organisations tend to increase as a consequence (Aras & Crowther, 2007a).[7] Sustainability, therefore, implies

---

[7] Similarly, once an animal or plant species becomes extinct, the benefits of that species to the environment can no longer be accrued. In view of the fact that many

that society must use no more of a resource than can be regenerated (Aras & Crowther, 2007b). This can be defined in terms of the carrying capacity of the ecosystem (Hawken, 1993) and described with input–output models of resource consumption.

Accountability

Accountability is concerned with an organisation recognising that its actions affect the external environment, and therefore assuming responsibility for the effects of its actions. This concept therefore implies a recognition that the organisation is part of a wider societal network and has responsibilities to all of that network, rather than just to the owners of the organisation. Alongside this acceptance of responsibility, therefore, must be a recognition that those external stakeholders have the power to affect the way in which those actions of the organisation are taken, and have a role in deciding whether or not such actions can be justified, and, if so, at what cost to the organisation and to other stakeholders. It is inevitable, therefore, that there is a need for some form of mediation of all the different interests in a society in order to be able to reach a broad consensus on what is in the best interests of the whole community and how this can be achieved. As a general statement, we can assert that all organisations and institutions are accountable to all those who will be affected by their decisions or actions, and that this must be recognised within current governance mechanisms. This accountability must of course extend to all organisations – both governmental institutions as well as those in the private sector – and also to civil society organizations, which must all recognise that they are accountable to the public and to their various stakeholders. One significant purpose of such accountability is to ensure that any corruption is eliminated, or at the very least minimised.

All systems of governance are concerned primarily with the management of associations, and therefore with political authority, institutions, and, ultimately, control. Governance in this particular sense denotes formal political institutions that aim to coordinate and control interdependent social relations, and that have the ability to enforce decisions. Increasingly, however, in a globalised world, the concept of governance is being used to describe the regulation of interdependent relations in the absence of an overarching political authority, such as in the international system. Thus, global governance can be considered to be the management

---

pharmaceuticals are currently being developed from plant species still being discovered, this may be significant for the future.

of global processes in the absence of any institutional form of global government. There are some international bodies which seek to address these issues, particularly the United Nations and the World Trade Organisation. Each of these has met with mixed success in instituting some form of governance in international relations, but all such organisations are part of the recognition of the problem and an attempt to address worldwide problems that go beyond the capacity of individual states to solve (Rosenau, 1999).

To use the term "global governance" is not of course to imply that such a system actually exists, let alone to consider the effectiveness of its operations. It is merely to recognise that in this increasingly globalised world there is a need for some form of governance to deal with multinational and global issues. The term "global governance", therefore, is a descriptive term, recognising the issue and referring to concrete cooperative problem-solving arrangements. These may be formal, taking the shape of laws or formally-constituted institutions to manage collective affairs by a variety of actors – including states, intergovernmental organisations, non-governmental organisations (NGOs), other civil society actors, private sector organisations, pressure groups, and individuals. The system also includes, of course, informal mechanisms (as in the case of practices or guidelines) and temporary units (as in the case of coalitions). Thus, global governance can be considered to be a complex of formal and informal institutions, mechanisms, relationships, and processes between and among states, markets, citizens and organizations, both inter- and non-governmental, through which collective interests on the global plane are articulated, rights and obligations are established, and differences are mediated.

Global governance is not of course the same thing as world government; indeed, it can be argued that the former would not actually be necessary if there was such a thing as a world government. Currently, however, the various state governments around the world have a legitimate monopoly on the use of force and on the power of enforcement. Global governance therefore refers to the political interaction that is required to solve problems that affect more than one state or region when there is no power of enforcing compliance. Improved global problem-solving need not of course require the establishment of more powerful formal global institutions, but it could involve the creation of a consensus on norms and practices to be applied. Steps are currently underway to establish these norms; one example of this being the creation and improvement of global accountability mechanisms. In this respect, for example, the United

Nations Global Compact[8] – described as the world's largest voluntary corporate responsibility initiative – brings together companies, national and international agencies, trade unions and other labour organisations and various organs of civil society in order to support universal environmental protection, human rights and social principles. Participation is entirely voluntary, and there is no enforcement of these principles by an outside regulatory body. Companies adhere to these practices both because they make economic sense, and because their stakeholders, including their shareholders (most individual and institutional investors) are concerned with these issues and this provides a mechanism whereby they can monitor the compliance of companies easily. Mechanisms such as the Global Compact can improve the ability of individuals and local communities to hold companies accountable.

Accountability in governance

Governance is simply the exercise of political authority and the use of institutional resources to manage society's problems and affairs. Good governance implies well performing institutions, enabling legal infrastructure, regulatory regimes and consistent enforcement. Good governance is a major contributor to economic growth, prosperity and democracy.

Accountability has been described as one of the cornerstones of good governance (Stapenhurst and O'Brien N.D). This is because it ensures that the actions and decisions taken by public officials are subject to oversight with the view to guaranteeing that the plans of the government for dealing with a particular problem or for achieving a particular purpose meet their stated objectives and respond to the needs of the people they are meant to be benefitting.

Again, accountability is important in governance as it allows for the ongoing evaluation of the effectiveness of public officials and bodies to ensure that they are performing to their full potential. It provides value for money in the provision of public services, the instilling of confidence in the government, and ensures that public officials are responsive to the people they are meant to be serving (Stapenhurst and O'Brien N.D).

---

[8] See www.unglobalcompact.org

Mechanisms for the enforcement of accountability in Africa

Over the years, several mechanisms have been adopted to deal with corrupt practices and unethical behaviours. However, these mechanisms can be generally classified into two groups. These are: those which are associated with norms and values (codes), and those concerned with the establishment of accountability institutions (Rasheed, 1995).

The required norms and values for regulating and monitoring the unethical conduct of public officers are composed of written and unwritten codes of conduct. These codes of conduct, whether written or not, can be classified into four groups. The first category is personal, self-imposed ethics, which stems from personal beliefs and convictions of correct and incorrect behaviour in the conducting of public affairs. The second category is the self-imposed ethics of a group, that is, ethical codes agreed upon by a group which should be adhered to by any member of that group when serving the public. The written ethical rules of conduct for public officials that are enacted by legislation, but without administratively implemented sanctions against offenders and machinery for imposing sanctions, belong to the third category. The enacted statutes, or Acts, of the legislature, or provision, of a country's constitution fall under the fourth category (Barlow, 1993).

Many African countries have adopted these mechanisms in an attempt to enforce accountability in public service. However, due to widespread corruption, abuse of office and the general deterioration of other ethical standards throughout the continent, one can easily conclude that there are no sufficient control mechanisms for the enforcement of accountability. In Nigeria, for example, the Code of Conduct which was enacted in 1975 and subsequently incorporated into the 1979 and 1989 constitutions of the Federal Republic requires that public officials should not:

-   allow personal interests to conflict with their official assignments;
-   operate foreign bank accounts;
-   ask for gifts;
and should
-    declare their assets immediately after taking office, every four years and at the end of their terms in office.

In Kenya, some of the legal and quasi-legal instruments for enforcing accountability in public service include codes of regulations for public servants, the Public Service Commission Act, Cap 185, the Penal Code,

Cap 63, the Prevention of Corruption Act Cap 65, the Election offences Act, Cap 66 and Exchequer and Audit Act, Cap 412. However, despite these provisions, public accountability throughout the constantly deteriorates (Odhiambo-Mbai, 2003).

In addition, numerous different African governments have established accountability institutions to enforce accountability in their respective countries. In Nigeria, the Economic and Financial Crimes Commission (EFCC), the Independent Corrupt Practices and Offences Commission (ICPC) and other similar bodies have been established to combat ethical violations and enforce accountability. In Kenya, the Public Account Committee, Public Investment Committee, the Inspector of State Corporation, and the Public Anti-Corruption Unit were also established for the purposes of enforcing accountability.

Factors that hinder the enforcement of accountability in Africa

The ability to enforce effective accountability faces serious challenges in African countries, though to varying degrees. It should be noted here that, in a few cases, the mechanism for the enforcement of accountability has been partially successful in achieving some of its immediate aims. However, the fact remains that the incidence of unethical behaviours has increased even when a number of violators have been investigated and punished by accountability institutions like the EFCC in the case of Nigeria. While these mechanisms have yielded positive results in the West, the story is somewhat different in Africa. The question is, then, 'why?'

Several reasons for this have been garnered from various relevant studies. They include the lack of an enabling environment; partial enforcement; a lack of resources for enforcement; and a lack of transparency and accountability in public service. Further reasons concern the weak administrative and legislative system, poor political leadership, and malfeasance in government (Gambo, 2011).

Ironically, measures to encourage ethics and accountability often feature prominently as part of the agenda of civil service reforms in African countries. The discourse on the enforcement of accountability and good ethical behaviour in Africa has been intensified primarily due to the following:

1. An increase in the incidence of unethical practices and the lack of accountability.

2. The wave of political liberalization that engulfed most Africa countries since 1989, which has resulted in emboldening civil societies into demanding greater enforcement of ethical codes of conduct and the sanctioning of offenders.
3. The growing recognition that unethical practices have contributed to the economic hardship currently experienced by many African countries
4. The pressure from international donors requiring stricter adherence by African countries to good governance and the curtailment of waste and squandering of resources (Gambo, 2011).

Conclusion

It has been frequently observed that human beings have to be 'pushed' to do what they are supposed to do. This chapter, therefore, examines the theoretical perspectives of accountability in public governance with an emphasis on its enforcement. Our societies operate on the assumption, and often the need, for those who break the rules to be held to account for their actions. Even in a system based on respect, dignity and mutual trust, there will be times when policies and laws will not be adopted, implemented, or will be ignored - by individuals, companies and governments. When this happens, there will need to be ways to enforce the laws, and to hold those responsible to account and enforce necessary sanctions. The proper enforcement of legal instruments, codes of conduct and regulations promoting accountability should therefore be enhanced in the African continent. It is the authors' view that the enforcement of accountability in governance will ultimately assist in correcting the behaviours of those in public governance, thereby resulting in good governance.

References

Aras G & Crowther D (2007a); Is the Global Economy sustainable?; in S Barber (ed.), *The Geopolitics of the City;* London; Forum Press; pp 165-194
Aras G & Crowther D (2007b); Sustainable corporate social responsibility and the value chain; In M M Zain & D Crowther (eds.), *New Perspectives on Corporate Social Responsibility*; Kulala Lumpur; MARA University Press; pp 119-140
Barton, A. D. (2006). Public sector accountability and commercial-in-confidence outsourcing contracts. *Accounting, Auditing and Accountability Journal.* 19 (12): 256 - 271

Gambo, M. (2011). Prospects and challenges of enforcing transparency and accountability in the civil service; Retrieved from: icongfesr2011.tolgaerdogan.net/document

Hawken P (1993); *The Ecology of Commerce*; London; Weidenfeld & Nicholson.

Jones C, Hesterly W S & Borgatti S P (1997); A general theory of network governance: exchange conditions and social mechanisms; *Academy of Management Review*, 22 (4), 911-945

Laleye, M. (19930. "Mechanisms for enhancing ethics and public accountability in francophone Africa". In Rasheed S. and Dele Oluwu, eds. Ethics and Accountability in African Public Services, Addis-Ababa: UNICA and AAPAM

Lindberg, S. I. (2010). Accountability: the core concept and its subtypes. The African Power Politics Programme Discussion Paper series, DFID

McKinney, J. B. (1979). Public administration: balancing power and accountability. Illinois: Moore Publishing Company Inc.

Mulgan, R. (2000). Accountability: an ever expanding concept? Public Administration, 78:555.

Odhiambo-Mbai, C. (2003). Public service accountability and governance in Kenya since independence. African Journal of Political Science. 8 (1): 113 – 145.

Oluwu, D. (1993). "Organizational and institutional Mechanisms for enhancing accountability in Anglophone Africa: A review" In Rasheed S. and Dele Oluwu, eds. Ethics and Accountability in African Public Services, Addis - Ababa: UNICA and AAPAM

Rasheed, S. (1995). Ethics and accountability in African Civil Service. DPMN Bulletin, 3(1): 12 – 14

Rosenau J (1999); Toward an Ontology for Global Governance; in M Hewson & T J Sinclair (eds.), *Approaches to Global Governance Theory*; Albany, NY; State University of New York Press

Williamson O E (1975); *Markets and Hierarchies: Analysis and Anti-trust Implications*; New York; The Free Press.

CHAPTER SEVEN

WEB TRAFFIC AND FIRM PERFORMANCE: EVIDENCE FROM THE MENA REGION

OMAR FAROOQ AND SAMIR AGUENAOU

Introduction

Emerging markets are characterized by weak and ineffective corporate governance mechanisms. For instance, Claessens and Fan (2003) document that corporate governance mechanisms (such as takeovers and boards of directors) are not functioning properly and efficiently in emerging markets. Prior literature shows that the presence of family control, the weak enforcement of investor protection laws, and the lax implementation of anti-director rights contribute to the ineffectiveness of corporate governance mechanisms in emerging markets. One of the implications of weak corporate governance mechanisms is that the culture of information disclosure cannot evolve in these markets. Prior literature documents that managers and insiders do not disclose true information about their firms in emerging markets (Leuz et al., 2003). This results in the exposure of naive investors to an almost impossible task of assessing the true value of firms. Therefore, it becomes hard for these investors to make any informed decision.

This chapter argues that the extent of web traffic is one such publicly available information source that can help investors, especially naive investors, to make value-relevant investment decisions. Using data from the MENA region (Morocco, Egypt, Saudi Arabia, United Arab Emirates, Jordan, Kuwait, and Bahrain), this chapter shows that the extent of web traffic positively affects firm performance. Our results are robust after controlling for several firm-specific characteristics. We argue that web traffic measures investors' access to information regarding firms. Greater access to information can affect firm performance via a number of channels. First, the extent of agency problems is inversely related to the amount of available information. Greater dissemination of information resulting from higher web traffic reduces agency problems and leads to better performance of firms. Second, higher web traffic corresponds to a firm's recognition among investors (Bank et al., 2011). There are a couple of reasons behind considering web traffic as a proxy for a firm's recognition among investors. Anecdotal evidence suggests that the importance of the internet has grown remarkably during recent years. It is not only the source of largest pool of freely available information, but it is also easily accessible by everyone and from everywhere. Therefore, higher web traffic indicates the interest of individuals in accessing information regarding a firm. Bank et al. (2011) complement our arguments by maintaining that web traffic assesses the degree of attention from uninformed investors. We argue that higher recognition spurs interest among investors, increases their appetite to invest in more recognizable firms, and eventually leads to better stock price performance. Our argument is similar to that of Merton (1987) who documents better performance for firms with higher recognition. In addition to affecting stock price performance, a firm's recognition among investors also influences other measures of performance, such as volume (Gervais et al., 2001; Hou et al., 2008). Grullon et al. (2004) document that the investment decisions of both individual and institutional investors are influenced by a firm's reputation among investors. They show that investors' buying decisions are more prone to the firm's reputation than their selling decisions. Consequently, greater buying translates into pushing stock prices high (Barber and Odean, 2008). Consistent with our arguments, Da et al. (2009) also document that the prices of assets are an increasing function of the number of internet enquiries. In another related study, Vlastakis and Markellos (2012) use data generated from a Google search to assess the level of volatility for stocks traded on the NYSE. They find a positive relationship between Internet search volume and trading volume.

Furthermore, we also show that the positive impact of web traffic on firm performance is more pronounced in firms that have higher agency problems. For example, our results show that web traffic is more important in determining firm performance in civil law countries than in common law countries. Civil law countries are characterized by lower investor protection, lower enforcement mechanisms, and lower stock market development. All of these factors lead to more agency problems in civil law countries than in common law countries. We argue that in weak governance regimes, such as civil law countries, stock market participants consider information obtained from websites more value-relevant. As a result, web traffic assumes more importance in civil law countries. Consistent with these findings, we also show that web traffic is more important for firms with concentrated ownership and firms with low fixed assets. Both of these groups represent weak governance regimes. Our results are consistent with those of Da et al. (2009) who show that an increase in internet search volume generates higher returns for small stocks. Small stocks, on average, have higher information asymmetries than large firms. Therefore, investors consider any mechanism, such as information obtained from websites, more value-relevant for these firms (firms where agency problems are high). Our results indicate that, where information asymmetries are high, the extent of web traffic assumes more importance in determining firm performance. Therefore, we can consider web traffic as a substitute for traditional governance mechanisms for firms that do not already have a better governance environment.

It is important to mention here that this is the first study, to the best of our knowledge, which relates web traffic to firm performance in the MENA region. Websites, or information provided on these websites, are not considered to be of prime importance by firms. Our study indicates that firms can use their websites as a strategic tool to attract investors and improve their visibility and recognition among stock market participants. More interest among investors, eventually, will lead to better stock price performance.

Data

This chapter documents the relationship between web-traffic generated by the website of a firm and its stock price performance. The sample consists of firms listed on the MENA (Morocco, Egypt, Saudi Arabia, United Arab Emirates, Jordan, Kuwait, and Bahrain) stock markets during 2010. The following sub-sections will explain the data in greater detail.

Web traffic ranking

We use the web-traffic data provided by Alexa (www.alexa.com) to rank websites. Alexa ranking is a relative measurement on how popular a website is among the Internet community. Alexa ranks web sites according to the Alexa Traffic they get. This means that a site with a rank of 1 gets more traffic than a site with a rank of 2 according to Alexa. Alexa ranking is calculated by considering how many users visited a certain website (known as reach) and how many distinct pages they viewed on that site (known as pageview). The combination of reach and pageview determines the rank of a website. It is important to note that multiple requests for the same website on the same day by the same user are counted as a single pageview. One of the drawbacks of Alexa ranking is that it depends on the data of Alexa Toolbar users. Since Alexa Toolbar is only used by the users of Internet Explorer, it does not count internet traffic generated by other browsers such as Firefox and Chrome. However, there are over 10 million Alexa Toolbar users who make it a worthwhile measurement.

Table 1 documents the Alexa rankings for each country (Panel A) and each industry (Panel B). As was indicated above, a higher value indicates a lower ranking. Our results in Panel A show that firms headquartered in Qatar have the highest ranking, followed by those in Saudi Arabia, United Arab Emirates, Bahrain, Morocco, Egypt, Kuwait, and Jordan. Our results indicate that investors use websites more often to get information about firms in Qatar relative to those in other countries. Panel B indicates that websites of Telecommunication firms generate the highest web traffic, while websites of Oil and Gas firms generate the lowest web traffic. Usually Telecommunication firms have to disseminate information to a vast proportion of the population and websites provide an easy way to do this. Oil and Gas firms, on the other hand, have a very select audience. As such, a personalized way of information disclosure is preferred.

Panel A: Web traffic ranking for firms in different countries

Countries	Mean	Median	Standard Deviation	No. of Firms
Bahrain	293.09	248.50	185.02	32
Egypt	343.41	358.00	203.37	107
Jordan	446.06	517.50	208.41	72
Kuwait	389.69	414.00	181.43	155
Morocco	337.07	340.00	179.53	52
Qatar	252.18	224.00	150.78	43
Saudi Arabia	275.62	275.00	169.23	125
UAE	286.73	257.00	193.70	86

Panel B: Web traffic ranking for firms in different industries

Industries	Mean	Median	Standard Deviation	No. of Firms
Oil and Gas	400.76	430.00	177.27	17
Basic Materials	352.84	326.00	181.70	33
Industrials	394.52	399.50	170.39	106
Consumer Goods	379.06	398.00	166.42	46
Healthcare	393.00	317.00	217.66	11
Consumer Services	267.25	202.00	202.78	43
Telecommunication	39.06	16.00	59.85	15
Utilities	210.85	158.00	144.88	7
Financials	291.80	267.50	185.85	252
Technology	253.83	208.00	248.69	6

Table 7.1: Descriptive statistics of web traffic ranking

Firm performance

Market-adjusted returns (RET) are used as a proxy for firm performance. Market-adjusted returns are the difference between stock returns and market returns. Stock prices and market index are used to calculate market-adjusted returns. We extract the stock price data and the corresponding market index data from DataStream. The stock price data and the market index data were obtained for the first and last days of our sample period in order to compute the market-adjusted returns.

Methodology

The chapter aims to test whether the extent of web traffic generated by a firm is related to its performance or not. In order to answer this question, we estimate a cross-sectional regression with firm performance (RET) as a dependent variable and web-traffic ranking (RANKING) as an independent variable. For the purpose of completeness, we also include industry dummies (IDUM) and country dummies (CDUM) in our regression equation. Our basic regression equation takes the following form.

$$RET = \alpha + \beta_1\left(RANKING\right)$$
$$+ \sum_{Ind} \beta^{Ind}\left(IDUM\right) + \sum_{Ctry} \beta^{Ctry}\left(CDUM\right) + \varepsilon$$

$$(2)$$

Mindful of the effects that firm-specific characteristics may have on firm performance, we also add a couple of firm-specific variables to our regression equation. For example, larger firms and firms paying high dividends generate more interest from stock market participants, and therefore have a better information environment. As a result, they may have better performance. Therefore, we add the log of a firm's market capitalization (SIZE) and dividend payout ratio (PoR) to capture the effect of information environment on performance. We also add total debt to total asset ratio (LEVERAGE) to capture the effect of leverage on firm performance. High leverage firms have higher bankruptcy risk and therefore have lower performance. Similarly, we also include earnings per share (EPS) to control for the effect of profitability on firm performance. Profitable firms tend to have better stock price performance. Our modified regression equation takes the following form.

$$RET = \alpha + \beta_1(MEDIA)$$
$$+ \beta_2(SIZE) + \beta_3(LEVERAGE) + \beta_4(EPS) + \beta_5(PoR)$$
$$+ \sum_{Ind} \beta^{Ind}(IDUM) + \sum_{Ctry} \beta^{Ctry}(CDUM) + \varepsilon$$

$$(3)$$

The results of our analysis are reported in Table 2. Our results show that firms that generate a high amount of web-traffic perform significantly better than firms that generate a low amount of web-traffic. We report a significantly negative coefficient of RANKING for both equations. Given the fact that a higher value of Alexa Rank corresponds to a lower ranking, a negative coefficient of RANKING indicates that firms generating higher web-traffic perform better than firms generating lower web-traffic. We argue that firms generating a high amount of web-traffic are the ones with lower information asymmetries. Since our sample firms do not engage in commerce on their websites, the only purpose of web-traffic is to obtain information. Therefore, high web-traffic means that more individuals are coming to the website to obtain information, thereby lowering the information asymmetry regarding these firms. As a result, we observe the better performance of firms with high web-traffic than otherwise similar firms with low web-traffic.

	Equation (1)	Equation (2)
RANKING	-0.0251***	-0.0214**
SIZE		1.8850
LEVERAGE		-0.2208*
EPS		0.1064
PoR		0.0652
Industry Dummies	Yes	Yes
Country Dummies	Yes	Yes
No. of Observations	580	329
F-Value	4.13	10.11
Adjusted-R^2	0.077	0.191

NOTE: The coefficients that are significant at 10% are followed by *, those at 5% and 1% by ** and *** respectively.

Table 7.2: Relationship between firm performance and web-traffic ranking

Discussion of results

Some of the important questions that arise here are: For which firms is the extent of web-traffic more effective? Is it for firms that already have a better information environment or is it for firms that have higher information asymmetries? Does the extent of web-traffic complement the governance environment or does it substitute for governance environment? We aim to answer these questions by re-estimating Equation (3) for sub-samples representing different governance and information regimes.

Web traffic and firm performance under different legal regimes

For the purpose of this chapter, we characterize legal regimes into common law and civil law. Following La Porta et al. (1999), we classify Bahrain, Saudi Arabia, and United Arab Emirates as common law countries, and Egypt, Jordan, Kuwait, Morocco, and Qatar as civil law countries. Civil law countries, usually, have lower investor protection, lower enforcement mechanisms, and lower stock market development. All of these factors lead to more agency problems in civil law countries relative to common law countries. We argue that any mechanism that can lower the agency problems will be more valued in civil law countries than in common law countries (where agency problems are already low). We consider the extent of web-traffic as one such mechanism that can help reduce agency problems. As a result, we expect a stronger relationship between the extent of web-traffic and firm performance in civil law countries than in common law countries. Our results from a re-estimation of Equation (3) are reported in Table 3. We show that the extent of web-traffic is an important determinant of firm performance in civil as well as common law countries. We report a significantly negative coefficient of RANKING for both groups. However, as expected, our results indicate that the extent of web traffic is more important in civil law countries than in common law countries. The magnitude of the coefficient of RANKING is higher in civil law countries than in common law countries. Our results indicate that, where information asymmetries are high, the extent of web traffic assumes more importance in determining firm performance. Therefore, we can consider web-traffic as a substitute for traditional governance mechanisms for firms that do not already have a better governance environment.

	Common Law Countries	Civil Law Countries
RANKING	-0.0196*	-0.0242*
SIZE	-0.0882	3.1734
LEVERAGE	-0.0630	-0.3273
EPS	-0.2055	0.1010
PoR	0.0621*	0.0710
Industry Dummies	Yes	Yes
Country Dummies	Yes	Yes
No. of Observations	148	181
F-Value	3.33	8.23
Adjusted-R^2	0.121	0.124

NOTE: The results significant at 10% significance level are followed by *, at 5% significance level by **, and at 1% significance level by***.

Table 7.3: Relationship between firm performance and web traffic ranking in different legal regimes

Web traffic and firm performance under different ownership regimes

Prior literature considers the ownership structure as an important governance device. Concentrated ownership structures provide managers and controlling shareholders with a means to evade the effective disclosure of information (Leuz et al., 2003). Poor information disclosure exacerbates information asymmetries between insiders and outsiders, and results in agency problems. Prior literature also suggests that high ownership concentration creates an entrenchment problem that allows controlling shareholders' self-dealings to go unchallenged by boards of directors. On the other hand, dispersed ownership structures reduce some of these agency problems by taking away powers from managers and insiders. In order to test whether ownership structure affects the relationship between the extent of web-traffic and firm performance, we divide our sample into two groups – one with concentrated ownership and the other with dispersed ownership. We define concentrated ownership as the case where insiders hold more than 50% of the shares and dispersed ownership as the case where insiders do not hold absolute majority. We re-estimate Equation (3) for both groups and report our results in Table 4. As was expected, we see a stronger relationship between the extent of web-traffic and firm performance for concentrated ownership firms. Our results show a significantly negative coefficient of RANKING for this group. On the other hand, our results for dispersed ownership firms show an insignificant coefficient of RANKING for this group. As was argued earlier, when information asymmetries are high (concentrated ownership firms), the extent of web-traffic assumes more importance in determining firm performance. Therefore, we can consider web traffic as a substitute for traditional governance mechanisms.

	Concentrated Ownership	Dispersed Ownership
RANKING	-0.0267**	0.0158
SIZE	1.8995	2.7715**
LEVERAGE	-0.2553*	-0.0879
EPS	0.0976	0.2834
PoR	0.0713	-0.0179
Industry Dummies	Yes	Yes
Country Dummies	Yes	Yes
No. of Observations	266	62
F-Value	10.00	6.45
Adjusted-R^2	0.179	0.518

NOTE: The results significant at 10% significance level are followed by *, at 5% significance level by **, and at 1% significance level by***.

Table 7.4: Relationship between firm performance and web traffic ranking in different ownership regimes

Web traffic and firm performance under different tangibility regimes

In the context of agency problems, the kind of assets a firm has is critical in ensuring whether outside investors trust it with their capital. External capital demands a higher proportion of tangibility of assets when financial contractibility is poor and outside financiers are weakly protected. Therefore, tangibility is the measure of investors' interest in a firm. We define tangibility by fixed asset to total asset ratio. As expected, our results show that the extent of web-traffic is a significant determinant of firm performance in a sub-sample of firms with low tangibility. We report a negative and significant coefficient of RANKING for this group of firms. However, our results show that the performance of firms with higher tangibility of assets is unaffected by the extent of web traffic. We report an insignificant coefficient of RANKING for this group. As was argued earlier, when information asymmetries are high (low tangibility), the extent of web-traffic takes on more importance in determining firm performance. Therefore, we can consider web-traffic as a substitute for traditional governance mechanisms.

	High Tangibility	Low Tangibility
RANKING	-0.0074	-0.0442***
SIZE	0.0139	2.1045
LEVERAGE	-0.0610	-0.5000***
EPS	0.1675	0.0490
PoR	0.1200*	0.0193
Industry Dummies	Yes	Yes
Country Dummies	Yes	Yes
No. of Observations	173	156
F-Value	8.70	9.33
Adjusted-R^2	0.174	0.292

NOTE: The results significant at 10% significance level are followed by *, at 5% significance level by **, and at 1% significance level by***.

Table 7.5: Relationship between firm performance and web-traffic ranking in different tangibility regimes

Conclusion

This chapter explores the relationship between the extent of web-traffic generated by a firm and its performance in the MENA (Morocco, Egypt, Saudi Arabia, United Arab Emirates, Jordan, Kuwait, and Bahrain) region during 2010. Our results show that higher web-traffic corresponds to better firm performance. We argue that higher web-traffic on a firm's website relates to more information being disseminated regarding a firm. As a result, information asymmetries and agency problems go down, resulting in better performance. Our results also show that the extent of web-traffic is more important for firms with higher agency problems. For example, we show the stronger impact of web-traffic on firms in civil law countries, firms with concentrated ownership, and firms with a lower amount of tangible assets. It shows that web-traffic can act as a substitute for traditional governance mechanisms in the MENA region.

References

Bank, M., Larch, M., and Peter G., (2011). Google Search Volume and its Influence on Liquidity and Returns of German Stocks. Financial Markets and Portfolio Management, 25, pp. 239-264.

Claessens, S. and Fan, J. P. H., (2003). Corporate Governance in Asia: A Survey. International Review of Finance, 3, pp. 71-103.

Barber, B. M. and Odean, T., (2008). All that Glitters: The Effect of Attention and News on the Buying Behavior of Individual and Institutional Investors. Review of Financial Studies, 21(2), pp. 785–818.

Da, Z., Engelberg, J., and Gao, P., (2009). In Search of Attention. Forthcoming, Journal of Finance.

Gervais, S., Kaniel, R., and Mingelgrin, D. H., (2001). The High-volume Return Premium. Journal of Finance, 56, 877-919.

Grullon, G., Kanatas, G., and Weston, J. P., (2004). Advertising, Breath of Ownership, and Liquidity. Review of Financial Studies, 17, pp. 439-461.

Hou, K., Peng, L., and Xiong, W., (2008). A Tale of Two Anomalies: The Implications of Investor Attention for Price and Earnings Momentum. Working Paper, Ohio State University.

La Porta, R., Lopez-de-Silanes, F. and Vishny, R. (1999). The Quality of Government. Journal of Law, Economics and Organization, 15, pp.222–279.

Leuz, C., Nanda, D., and Wysocki, P., (2003). Earnings Management and Investor Protection: An International Comparison. Journal of Financial Economics, 69, pp. 505-527.

Merton, R., (1987). A Simple Model of Capital Market Equilibrium with Incomplete Information. Journal of Finance, 42, pp. 483-510.

Vlastakis, N. and Markellos, R. N., (2012). Information Demand and Stock Market Volatility. Journal of Banking and Finance, 36(6), pp. 1808-1821.

CHAPTER EIGHT

THE GOVERNANCE OF DOMESTIC ENERGY CONSUMPTION

SHAHLA SEIFI AND DAVID CROWTHER

Introduction

The concept of sustainable development has assumed prominence in the economic world and it is increasingly being based upon a process of interactive, integrative and learnt decision-making by firms through the process of understanding possibilities for common technological futures. In the range of issues that now comprise the soft-technology basket there are the physical environmental issues, social contracts that are mutually suitable to factors of production, and sustainable future of firms that are friendly to physical and human ecology (Hawley 1986; Martinez-Alier 1987; Coombs 1990;Goodland, Daly and El-Serafy 1992). Sustainable development therefore has been extracted from out of the ethical decision-making of corporations and is made to link up with the common interests of ecology and the grassroots for poverty alleviation and gaining human capabilities (Ekins 1992; Daly 1992; Walker and Unterhalter 2010). Korten (1995) refers to such an emergent age of business decision-making as an ecological revolution.

The business world we currently inhabit calls for different kinds of strategies in production, organizational decision-making, and delivery of its social image to the consumer. These dimensions are quite different from those we have learnt and practiced in a conventional neoclassical world.[1] Myrdal (1987) calls upon this kind of challenge to neoclassicism by wondering why the psychologists and philosophers have left the economists alone and undisturbed in their futile exercise of neoclassicism. So we must turn to other disciplines to seek possible answers, and industrial

---

[1] This is the modern world based upon economic growth and rational behaviour.

engineering as the productivity champion has received major attention in other arenas but has not yet engaged with the problems of sustainable development. In this chapter we seek to do so. One can see it as the toolkit to attain sustainable development because industrial engineering is concerned with productivity as the measure for production and service efficiency. Without this it would be difficult to quantify the quality aspects of sustainable development, e.g. those related to environment. And without this there would be difficulty to evaluate the integrated systems of man, money, materials, energy, knowledge, information and equipment, which are all instances of the three pillars. Energy efficiency is one route towards minimising environmental impact which we are investigating.

Sustainability and Industrial Engineering

Industrial engineering (IE) is concerned with the design of processes which will benefit companies and therefore ultimately consumers. This means that they have to be sustainable. Sustainability is a concept which concerns all businesses more than anything else. Sustainability requires R&D and technological development – which is what industrial engineering is concerned with; therefore IE has to be focused upon sustainability to remain relevant. Sustainability is based on the 3 pillars of Brundtland – economic, social and environmental – and these pillars are of importance not just to IE, but also CSR, illustrating that sustainability and CSR are very largely synonymous. In other words – CSR is equivalent to sustainability and sustainability has to be the central focus of IE. Designing anything without considering sustainability is a waste of time.

The current discourse of sustainable development concentrates upon a concern for not limiting the choices available to future generations. This is plainly unrealistic as mankind has been unable to achieve this since he changed from hunter-gatherer to farmer and cut down the forests around the world. In the present, it is not just unrealistic, but is distracting attention from the real issues. Resources are important of course but attention needs to be directed towards the real scarce resources which need to be used efficiently. And those scarce resources are not financial resources as conventional finance theory would have us believe – they are environmental.

Sustainability, or its synonym, sustainable development[2] has so far been referred to in different terms such as durability (Aras & Crowther, 2009), triple bottom line, corporate integrity, etc. The most widely used

---

[2] These are often treated as synonyms although they are in fact different.

definition of sustainable development is the one from the 1987 Report of the United Nations World Commission on Environment and Development (the Brundtland Commission): "*Meeting the needs of the present without compromising the ability of future generations to meet their own needs*".

Sustainability implies *the acceptance of any costs involved in the present as an investment for the future* (Aras & Crowther, 2008a). *Sustainable development is concerned with the effect which action taken in the present has upon the options available in the future* (Crowther & Martinez, 2004). A sustainable society is the society which provides for its needs without impairing the needs of the future generations. Therefore, sustainability implies that society must use no more of a resource than can be regenerated (Crowther & Martinez, 2004). Considering our current consumption, the way we live is not sustainable at all. Hence, sustainability is a matter of international concern which requires the emergence of international standards. This requirement is exacerbated by the recent movement towards globalisation. Indeed, globalisation requires a worldwide integration; therefore countries should adopt international standards and avoid standards as barriers to trade.

> With the increasing globalization of markets, international standards (as opposed to regional or national standards) have become critical to the trading process, ensuring a level playing field for exports, and ensuring imports meet internationally recognized levels of performance and safety. International standards and their use in technical regulations on products, production methods and services play a vital role in sustainable development and trade facilitation– through the promotion of safety, quality and compatibility. The benefits derived are significant. Standardization contributes not only to international trade but also to the basic infrastructure that underpins society, including health and environment, while promoting sustainability and good regulatory practice.
>
> (ISO central secretariat, 2006).

The idea of globalisation encourages countries to adopt harmonised rules; otherwise they will be trapped in diverse and sometimes conflicting rules which would result in unequal trade markets. International standardisation is an ideal opportunity for the countries to raise their voices on the matters which otherwise may become barriers to their trades with the world. So, countries should necessarily participate actively in the process of international standards drafting. This is indeed of vital importance for the developing countries, which could make sure that their national conditions are observed, so that they would willingly meet the international standards formulated through a fair consensus approach. Besides, use of international standards is beneficial in avoiding unnecessary costs to provide national standards which may result in other barriers to trade – spending time and money on already established international standards at national level would be like reinventing the wheel. Therefore, the worldwide trend is to adopt international standards in order to realise the aim of "one standard, one test and one conformity assessment procedure accepted everywhere". However, it is worth mentioning that

> "development is not a one-size-fits-all process. Each country must progress, as ultimately only it can best tell what its ambitions and needs are. However, in a globalization world, sustainable development cannot be achieved in isolation.   (Sudarwo, 2008).

Sustainable development is a concept closely related to social responsibility in that the latter is denoted by WBCSD as the third pillar of sustainable development, the other two pillars being economic growth and ecological balance. Meanwhile, sustainability is referred to as one of the three principles of social responsibility, the other two being accountability and transparency (Crowther, 2002). On the other hand, social responsibility is defined in ISO 26000 (2010) as the responsibility of an organisation for the impacts of its decisions and activities on society and the environment, through transparent and ethical behaviour that contributes to sustainable development, including health and the welfare of society. So here we see that the main focus and final aim of social responsibility is to attain sustainable development. The organisation contributes to sustainable development through social responsibility in its defined borderlines; whereas there is no such a borderline defined for sustainable development, which makes it more comprehensive and belonging to all, not just the organisation.

Pillars of sustainable development

The three pillars of sustainable development are defined as economic growth, ecologic balance and social responsibility. Unlike the sequence mentioned by WBCSD, one can assume that these pillars consist of a circle, all with equal value to create sustainability.

Consider the energy consumption status throughout the world. We waste a good portion of our consumed energy through inefficient methods. This way we ignore the requirements of our children (social irresponsibility). The pollution due to fossil fuel consumption leads to global warming, the consequence of which threatens the environment (ecological imbalance). This demands for investments in limiting damage to the environment (economic pressure). In this example, social irresponsibility leads to ecological imbalance which in turn leads to economic pressure. As a result we may choose to save more fossil fuel for the sake of our children (social responsibility). It results in saving money wasted in removing pollution (economic growth), which could mean switching to a kind of renewable energy such as solar (ecological balance).

In another instance, the government may decide to remove subsidies to fuel in order to make consumers account for externalities. Then people would buy fuel by its virtual price (economic pressure). Such a pressure would necessitate for designing energy-efficient devices to minimise the amount of energy consumed, or people may decide to avoid buying that sort of fuel and instead use a sort of renewable energy for that. The result would be a cleaner atmosphere (ecological balance) and more concern for the future generation (social responsibility).

Figure 8.1 shows that no sequence could be considered for these three pillars. Instead they are interdependent. A shortage in one would result in loss in another.

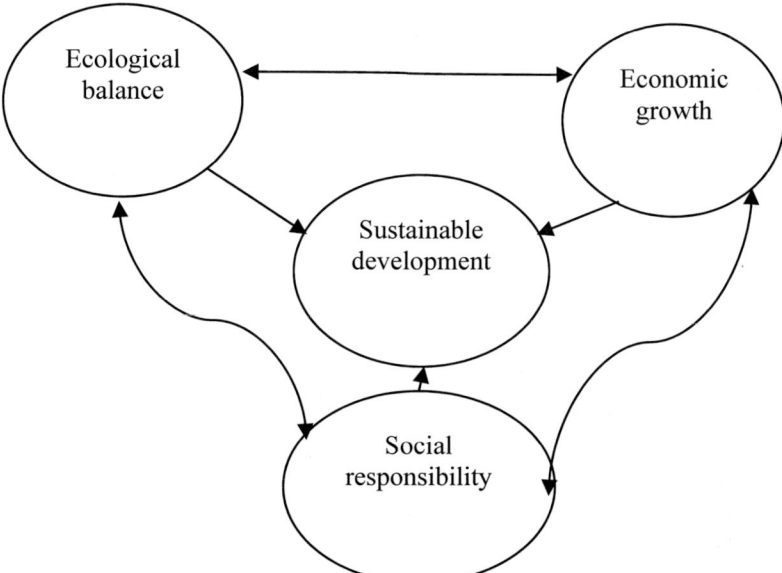

Figure 8.1: The interdependence of sustainable development and its pillars

Energy consumption

The world energy consumption in the residential sector doesn't seem even, and countries use energy according to factors such as their income levels, natural resources, climate, and available energy infrastructure. Therefore, due to a higher income level, typical households in OECD nations generally use more energy than those in non-OECD nations. This is partly because higher income levels allow OECD households to have larger homes and purchase more energy-using equipment. Larger homes generally require more energy to provide heating, air conditioning, and lighting, and they tend to include more energy-using appliances, such as televisions and laundry equipment. Smaller structures usually require less energy, because they contain less space to be heated or cooled, produce less heat transfer with the outdoor environment, and typically have fewer occupants.

A comparison of the United States and China as an example proves this claim. The average residence in China currently has an estimated 300 square feet of living space or less per person, than in the United States, where the average residence has an estimated 680 square feet of living space per person (World Energy and Economic Outlook 2008).

The US GDP per capita and its estimated residential energy use per capita in 2007 were $43,076 and 37.2 million Btu respectively, whereas the same data for China amounted to only $5,162 and 4.0 million Btu, which is only about one-eighth and one-ninth of the U.S. level, respectively (US Department of Energy). It is apparent however that as a country develops, the amount of energy rises in correlation with its per capita income. Its use of ever more sophisticated consumer durables also rises, demanding a corresponding increase in energy availability.

Over the last decade the price of crude oil has varied between $16 per barrel and $150, although it is currently around $100. It is expected however that the price will continue to follow a rising trend as demand continues to increase at a faster rate than supply. This has implications for both energy availability and usage and for sustainable development, which need to be considered.

An increasingly important factor which influences purchasing decisions is that of environmental protection, particularly associated with climate change. This is particularly important as far as the purchase of consumer durables is concerned because of the energy which they consume; energy efficiency is one route towards minimising environmental impact. Minimising such impact is one factor towards achieving sustainability and therefore making possible sustainable development. The central argument of this chapter is that the desire to make sustainable purchasing decisions necessitates better information to make decisions according to this criterion. This in turn requires manufacturers to provide better information through their labelling. This research extends our knowledge of the components of sustainability and requirements for sustainable development, particularly as far as consumer purchasing decisions are concerned. It also has potentially important implications for manufacturers and shows for them too an important route towards achieving sustainable development for themselves and for the global economy.

Risk Reducing

An important component of sustainability is that of risk management. This too provides an intersection with operational requirements as minimising exposure to risk both makes a company more socially responsible and more sustainable, and it also reduces cost in the longer term (Crowther & Seifi 2010). Often, however, the methodologies for the evaluation of risk are deficient in their effectiveness of evaluating – particularly of environmental risk. So we will demonstrate how some IE techniques can be used to address the problem.

It is accepted that design, and specifically energy labelling, influences the consumer purchasing decision (Seifi, Zulkifli & Crowther 2010; Seifi & Crowther 2010). This is an important area for manufacturers to be concerned with as it has crucial effects upon the design of products. Consumer durables are an important area to investigate this relationship as they represent significant purchases within the household budget. Moreover they represent purchases which are typically made after investigation and the consequences of the decision are manifest over a number of years of the typical life of the product. Consumer durables therefore represent an important area of study. But consumer durables are diverse in nature; thus generalisations can be made across the range, but the investigation needs to be based upon the specific. This study therefore is based upon refrigerators. This particular durable has been chosen for several reasons. Firstly it is a product which all individual consumers make use of, as well as many commercial organisations. Secondly it is not a high technology product and not subject to rapid technological changes in the same manner as televisions or computers. Thirdly the market is mature as almost all consumers are already in possession of a refrigerator. Purchases therefore are almost entirely replacements and are based upon need rather than the dictates of fashion. In other words the product tends to get replaced when it gets old and inefficient, rather than because of change in fashion or a desire for something new. Thus the product has a long life cycle. The life cycle is also an important determinant of choosing refrigerators; the long life cycle means that running costs are a significant determinant of choice and not just the initial purchasing cost. Refrigerators therefore represent an exemplar which is ideal to study the phenomenon under investigation, which is why they are used in this study.

Owing to developments in household industries in recent decades, an average house has approximately 10 electrical appliances, with refrigerating appliances considered the second most important, behind illuminating devices. This appliance plays a major part in the welfare and health of a family. Factors such as the population growth, buying power of the families, relative price reduction and by-installment purchases are expected to increase the market of this appliance. The conventional and relatively straightforward manufacturing process of household refrigerating appliances together with a reliable demand market has led to the emergence of so many manufactures around the world.

The energy consumption behavior of a household refrigerating appliance depends on several factors such as the climatic condition of the area in which the appliance is used or the ambient temperature, the type of the appliance - namely freezer, refrigerator, refrigerator-freezer, Frost-free or not - the frequency of opening and closing the door, the volumes of different compartment, etc. Different climate classes contain different atmospheric conditions and the manufacturer accomplishes design and manufacturing according to the specific conditions of each. Therefore, it is necessary to apply the appropriate material and equipment, to allow for proper performance based on the climatic class concerned. Also it is vitally important that the customer would knowledgably purchase a refrigerating appliance suitable for his/her own area of living. Unfortunately so far this important factor has not yet received enough attention and customers usually purchase an appliance without taking climatic classes into consideration. They may buy an appliance not suitable for their place of residence. This way the appliance would soon lose its efficient performance and consume considerably more energy. As an instance, an appliance designed according to climatic class N, would have an approximate compressor run 20% more when used in tropical areas.

A refrigerator is basically a heat exchanger, cooling the air within it at the expense of the ambient air temperature. The objective for sustainability is to make this heat exchange as efficient as possible by making the refrigerator energy efficient. Over time this is happening as the figure below indicates. This supports findings by Parker and Stedman (1992).

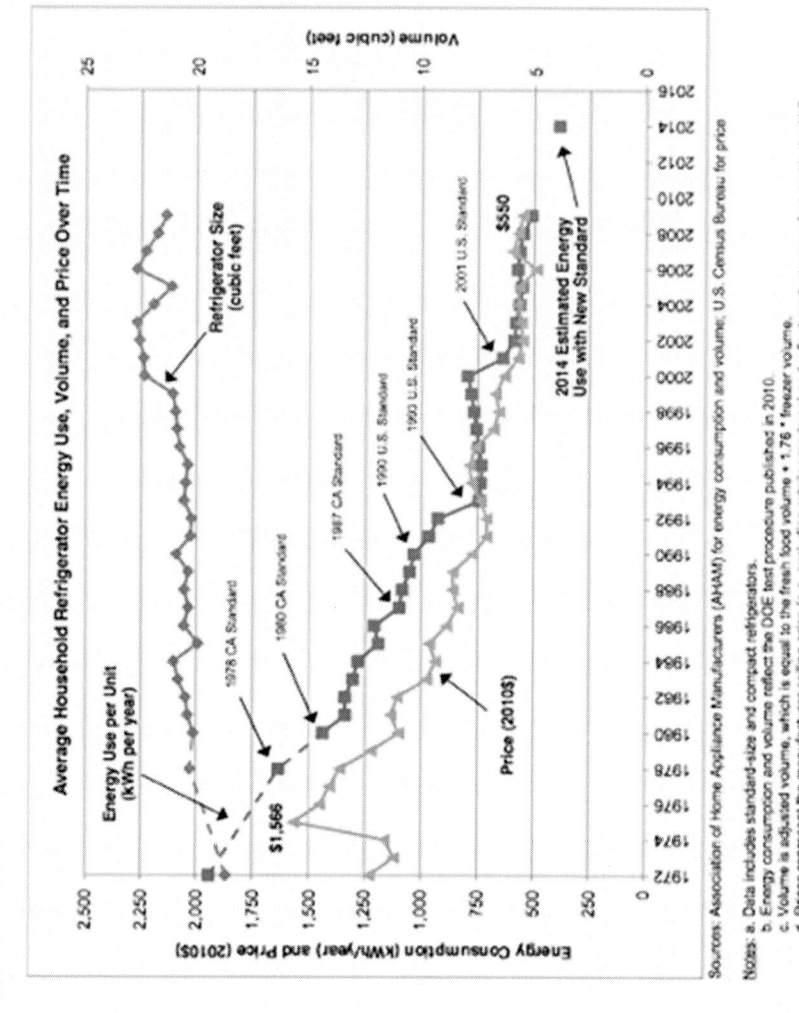

Figure 8.2: Increasing refrigerator efficiency and reducing cost

It was calculated that the fit of a multiple regression model to daily use data from a refrigerator is affected by door opening and explained by the following model:

kWh = -5.05 + 0.084 (Kitchen Temp.) + 0.0092 (Door Openings)   (1)

Where:

kWh = daily refrigerator kWh
Kitchen Temp= °F
Door Openings= number of refrigerator door openings per day
R-squared = 0.85

Applying industrial engineering techniques to understand the issues

In this chapter we are primarily concerned with the effects of energy labelling on refrigerator purchasing. The techniques of IE can be helpful to our understanding and will help to show that better energy labelling will lead to different decision making so we now explore how this can be so. First we start by considering the use of Bayes' Theorem. In the eighteenth century the Reverend Thomas Bayes (1702-1761) became interested in mathematical applications of probability theory, particularly in the way in which probabilities changed depending upon the acquisition of additional information. He developed what became known as the Bayes theorem of conditional probability which states that:

Probabilities can change when additional information is acquired from subsequent events. Probability is therefore of consequential value in decision making.

Bayes theorem of conditional probability can be expressed algebraically as:

$$Pr(A \mid B) = \frac{Pr(AB)}{Pr(B)}$$

(2)

In the case of refrigerators we can consider that 80% of people would like to buy an energy efficient refrigerator because it has lower operating costs. But half of these people will only do so if they understand the information being provided on the label. As such, the Bayes theorem can be used to show that the probability of buying an energy-efficient appliance will change if additional information is provided through labelling. This can then be compared with the cost of providing this information. This additional information will facilitate decision making for the manufacturer.

Bayes' Theorem can therefore be seen to be of value in management decision making (Crowther 1996) through its use in quantification of the value of additional information and a consideration of how this additional information changes the decision which might be made by managers. Equally the use of this theorem focuses attention upon the salient features of decision making through its quantification of the risks associated with any course of action in comparison with the gains which might ensue, thereby making a comparative analysis of the effects of alternative courses of action more rigorous through quantification. Use of the theorem can also actually help identify the choices which are available through this rigorous quantification. It is therefore a valuable part of IE.

There are, however, problems with the use of this technique in practice, which revolve around the ability to quantify the effects of alternative courses of action and to assign probabilities to their likelihood of occurrence. The value of the quantification is obviously only as good as the value of the evaluation of the costs of the alternatives and the probabilities assigned to them. If these are not particularly accurate then the analysis based upon them will not be accurate and this quantification will not form a satisfactory basis for decision making. Currently research is being undertaken to arrive at a more accurate assessment of the relevant probabilities. One of the problems with this kind of analysis is that, unless these decisions are made on a regular basis and some experience is therefore built up, the evaluations are necessarily subjective and the decisions made based upon them therefore questionable. The main use of this technique therefore is in introducing a certain degree of rigour into the decision making process through a forced identification of choices available and consequences of making each individual choice. This in itself is likely to improve the quality of managerial decision making without an accurate quantification. One further problem with Bayes' Theorem is that it assumes that the decision in question can be made in isolation and will not affect, nor be affected by, any other decision which might be made within the organisation. In practice this is rarely the case and any individual decision is inter-related with other decisions.

Risk analysis

Obviously there is an element of risk attached to any operational decision, and this risk arises because we are attempting to predict outcomes in the future of decisions made now (Crowther 2004). Various techniques exist which can help a manager to understand the nature of risk associated with any decision and to quantify the effects of that risk. One such technique is Risk Analysis which is based on clearly distinguishing risk from uncertainty and then treating risk probabilistically in order to make the best decisions. In all cases of strategy development the selection of an appropriate strategy depends upon a realistic assessment of the risk and a quantification of possible effects through analysis. Therefore, it is to risk analysis that we now turn.

When a range of possible outcomes for an event exist then obviously the sum of the probabilities for all of the possible outcomes must equal 1 – as one of the outcomes must occur. The assignment of probabilities to each of the outcomes however enables us to construct a probability distribution showing the range of possible outcomes and their respective probabilities. Such a distribution may well be important to the analysis because merely selecting the most likely outcome may well not reflect the level of risk involved.

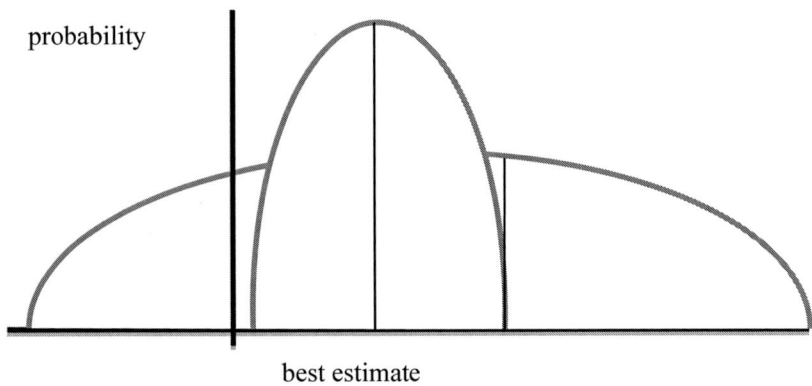

Figure 8.3: Differing probability profiles

For example in the two projects shown below the best estimate of profitability for each of the projects is identical but it can be seen from the probability distributions (figure 8.3) that the risk associated with them is quite different, with one of the projects having a risk of incurring a loss (project B). Without the probability distributions therefore a firm would be indifferent as to which project was chosen but with an understanding of the distribution of risk then it can be seen that project A is the preferable project, providing always that the expected returns for the two projects are similar. Risk analysis can be used to quantify the expected values of the return from each project but assessing the relative relationship between risk and rewards inevitably relies upon managerial judgement and a person's attitude to risk.

Risk analysis as a technique is based upon probability theory (Crowther 2004) and upon the ability to construct probability distributions. It is a technique which is designed to enable individual risks associated with a project to be combined and summed to find the overall risk for the project. It is based upon assigning a probability distribution for each risk factor, rather than merely assigning a best estimate. These probability distributions are then combined using Monte Carlo Simulation techniques to arrive at an overall assessment of risk (Crowther 1996).

This kind of analysis can lead to a very different assessment of risk for a particular decision than would be our assessment if we based our quantification solely upon mean values from our understanding of the probability of particular outcomes. In complex problems with a range of possible outcomes and a variety of factors to be included, this technique therefore can help in our understanding of the risks involved and hence can affect our decision making in such cases. It is therefore an important tool for IE which can be used in the analysis of the problem concerning energy-labelling discussed in this chapter. For example current understandings concerning energy efficiency (see diagrams below) and future demand enables probability distributions to be calculated concerning the effects of producing increasingly energy efficient refrigerators, the effects of improving labeling and the costs of doing so (and hence selling price). Risk analysis techniques enable these to be quantified to make the best decisions regarding future production.

Games theory

Although risk analysis can be a useful tool, when it comes to making strategic decisions the most useful tool is Games Theory. This is particularly helpful when deciding about refrigerator labelling because just as in making many engineering and management decision it is important to recognise that the decision is not made in isolation and that the effects of the decision cannot be realistically quantified as if that decision is made in isolation. This is particularly true when the external environment is affected by the decision, such as when a firm is considering the launch of a new product, a change to its prices, or the conduct of an advertising campaign. In such circumstances it is not sufficient to consider how the decision might affect the firm itself or how it might be received by its customers. It is also necessary to recognise that the firm's competitors will

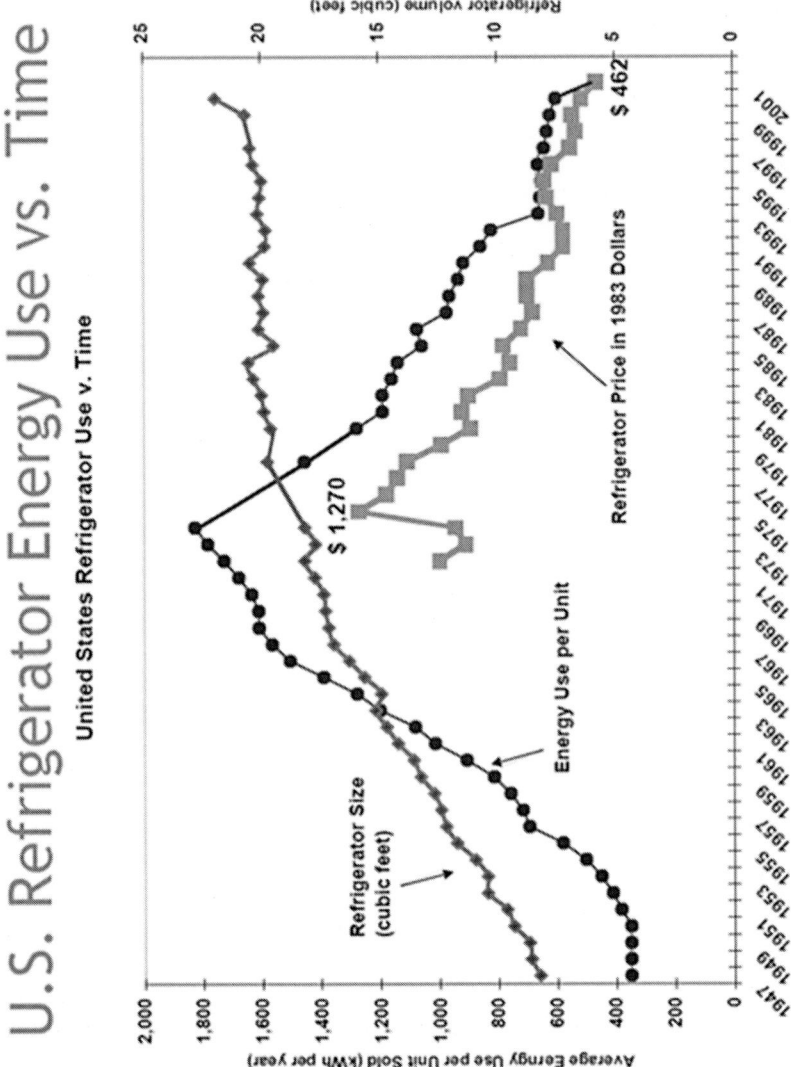

Figure 8.4: Refrigerator energy use over time

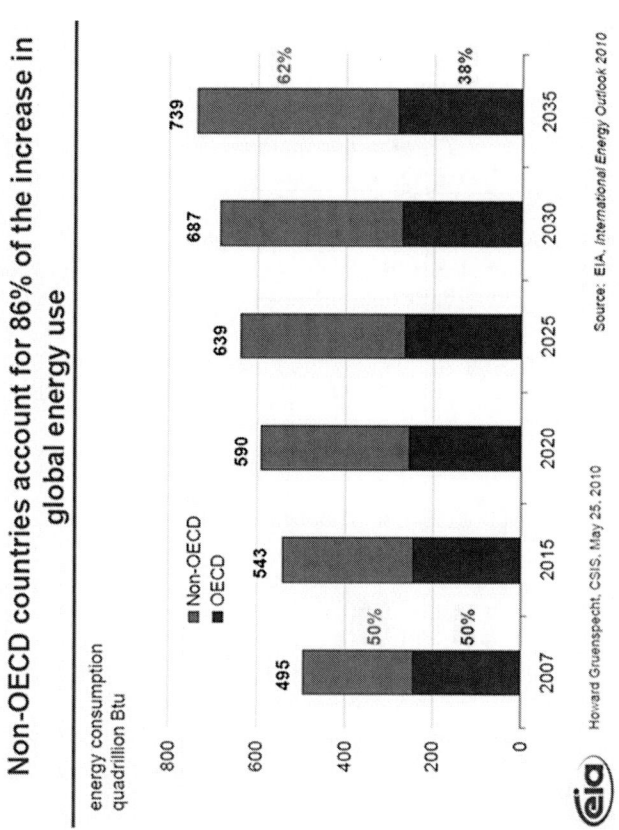

Figure 8.5: Projected increased demand for energy

be affected by the decision and may very well decide to respond to the actions of the firm. In such a situation the firm and its decision makers can be regarded as either in competition with another firm and its decision makers or in conflict, and the generic term to describe this kind of situation is that of a game and Games Theory can help to model this kind of situation (Crowther, 2004) and therefore improve the decisions which are made.

In games the participants are competitors and the success of one is usually at the expense of the other, such as when one firm gains market share through the use of an advertising campaign at the expense of the other firms in the industry – or through its labelling strategy. For the purposes of Games Theory in such a situation the number of players can very often be simplified to two players – the firm and the competition, with all competitors being regarded as a single player. It is possible to model the actions and reactions of all competitors separately through Games Theory but this makes the mathematics very complicated, often without significantly changing the analysis. Games Theory provides a method of formulating a business situation in terms of strategies – the strategy of the decision maker and the strategy of his / her opponent – and in term of outcomes. Each player in the game selects and executes those strategies which (s)he believes will result in 'winning the game', that is will result in the most favourable outcome to the problem situation. In determining this strategy for winning each player makes use of both deductive and inductive logic and attempts quantification of the outcomes.

Conclusions

The main purpose of this chapter has been to consider the issues concerned with sustainability and energy consumption and then show how it is possible to use industrial engineering tools like risk analysis to assess how sustainable our current energy consumption is and what can be changed through the use of these techniques. For this purpose refrigerators are taken as the sample for analysis. This is due to general usage of refrigerators by all people everywhere and due to their major part in worldwide energy consumption. Energy labels are nowadays a common feature of refrigerators put into the market for sale, although this trend is diverse in different parts of the world. This is part of an ongoing research project and the current stage is concerned with the collection of data which will enable mathematical calculations to be incorporated into the industrial engineering problems which have been identified.

References

Aras G & Crowther D (2008a); Corporate sustainability reporting: a study in disingenuity?; *Journal of Business Ethics*, 87 (sup. 1), 279-288
Aras G & Crowther D (2008b); Governance and sustainability: An investigation into the relationship between corporate governance and corporate sustainability; *Management Decision* Vol. 46 No 3 pp 433-448
Aras G & Crowther D, (2009); The Durable Corporation: strategies for sustainable development; Aldershot; Gower
Coombs HC (1990), *The Return of Scarcity, Strategies for an Economic Future*, Cambridge, Eng. Cambridge University Press.

Crowther D (1996); *Management Accounting for Business*; Cheltenham; Stanley Thornes

—. (2002); *A Social Critique of Corporate Reporting*; Aldershot; Ashgate

—. (2004); *Managing finance – a socially responsible appr*oach; London; Elsevier

Crowther D & Martinez E O, 2004). Corporate Social Responsibility: history and principles; in Social Responsibility World; Penang; Ansted University Press, 2004, pp 102-107

Crowther D & Seifi S (2010); *Corporate Governance and Risk Management*; Copenhagen; Ventus

Daly, H. (1992), "From empty-world to full-world economics: recognizing an historical turning point in economic development", in R. Goodland, H. Daly, S.El-Serafy, B. von Drost Eds. *Environmentally Sustainable Economic Development: Building on Brundtland*, Malta: Center for Development Studies, pp. 29-41

Ekins, P. (1992), *A New World Order, Grassroots Movements for Global Change*, London, Eng.: Routledge.

Goodland R, Daly H, El-Serafy S & von Drost B. (eds.) (1992), *Environmentally Sustainable Economic Development: Building on Brundtland*, Malta: Center for Development Studies.

Hawley, A.H. (1986), *Human Ecology*, Chicago, IL: The University of Chicago Press.

Korten, D.C. (1995), "The ecological revolution", in *When Corporations Rule the World*, London, Eng.: Earthscan, pp. 261-76, 1995

Martinez-Alier, J. (1987), "Methodological Individualism and Inter-generational Allocation", in *Ecological Economics, Energy, Environment and Society* (Oxford, Eng: Basil Blackwell.

Parker, D., Stedman, T., "Measured Electricity Savings of Refrigerator Replacement: Case Study and Analysis", ACEEE 1992 Summer Study on Energy Efficiency in Buildings, Proceedings - Commercial Performance: Analysis and Measurement Panel 3, American Council for an Energy-Efficient Economy

Seifi S, Zulkifli N & Crowther D (2010); Promoting sustainable consumption: the case of refrigerators; *Discussion papers in Social Responsibility* No 1001; Social Responsibility Research Network, UK

Seifi S & Crowther D (2010); Supporting sustainable consumption of consumer durables; in G Aras, D Crowther & K Krkac (eds.), *Proceedings of 9th Conference on CSR*; Zagreb; 777-87

Sudarwo, 2008).*Meeting the expectations of developing countries*; *ISO Focus*; The way forward - Developing countries and emerging economies; September 2008

US Department of Energy, US Energy Information Administration, state energy information, detailed and overviews, http://www.eia.doe.gov/state - accessed: 20.02.2011

Walker, M. and Unterhalter, E. (2010), "The Capability Approach: Its Potential for Work in Education", in *Amartya Sen's Capability Approach and Social Justice in Education*, eds. M. Walker & E. Unterhalter, London, UK: Palgrave Macmillan.

WCED (World Commission on Environment and Development) (1987); *Our Common Future* (The Brundtland Report); Oxford University Press; Oxford.

World Energy and Economic Outlook (2008), International Energy Outlook 2008, Report #:DOE/EIA-0484: June 2008) http://www.xof1.com/energyConsumption.php

CHAPTER NINE

GLOBAL SOURCING:
A SOURCE OF CONFLICT BETWEEN GLOBAL
AND LOCAL GOVERNANCE.
SAUDI ARABIA AS AN EXAMPLE

MAZEN F. RASHEED
AND MICHAEL VON GAGERN

Introduction

The organizers of the 2nd Organisational Governance Conference suggested that the agents of changes of mentality should be examined in greater detail. If, for example, it is true that the consciousness about environmental and social issues is increasing globally, will this increase be strong enough to change people's behaviours? How can this behaviour be governed globally as well as locally?

Given that, by the year 2030, the likelihood of Saudi Arabia needing all the oil they produce for internal use is very high, how can they ensure sure that they will continue to have something to sell in the global market? Will it be solar technology? Infrastructure management? E-governance? E-learning and education? Date products, perfume, gold and zinc? Tourism? Will all these alternative sources of income be enough to safeguard a decent standard of living? Is self-reliance an alternative path towards sustainable development?

This scenario is particularly interesting as, unlike many other Arab states, Saudi Arabia seems to still have the time and resources to contemplate and experiment with alternative developmental strategies. Furthermore, the discussion is particularly interesting in the context of conflicting interests between global governance and local government issues.

This chapter will thus:

- Look at the increasing importance of global sourcing and its impact on Local Economies
- Conclude that it is becoming more difficult for economies, which are not factor-competitive to sell anything in this market: if you have nothing to sell, you cannot buy anything.
- Taking the example of Saudi dependence on petroleum reserves, we will show that it is evident that Saudi Arabia must be prepared and able to develop alternatives to its oil-centred economy. Corporate governance is currently caught in a conflict between global and local government rationale.
- Show that the major players in Saudi Arabia are not sufficiently aware of these problems, and that solutions must therefore prioritise solutions to this awareness–deficit.

Global Sourcing and its Impact on Local Economies

Global Sourcing is the art of scouring the planet for the easiest, fastest, and cheapest access to anything which may add value to the transnational process of organizing, producing, delivering, and maintaining goods or services. The highest added value for companies comes from reducing cost.

The power of cost reduction may be seen, for example, in the case of a company with a return on sales of 5%: a 3% reduction of the material cost is equivalent to a sales increase of 36 %,[1] which, of course, is a lot. Global economic players learn how to manage different markets and purchasing situations by applying different purchasing strategies. Furthermore, with the shift from homeland purchasing to purchasing in industrial countries, and from there to global sourcing in low wage countries, a whole new breed of purchasing managers has taken upon themselves the task of screening the markets, assessing the risks, and reducing the cost before, during, and after the transaction.[2]

As soon as a source country loses its competitive advantage, global economic players move on to another place or environment.

Competitiveness is the name of the game and there is even an annual Global Competitiveness Index edited by the World Economic Forum, where countries are ranked according to their ability to attract investors on

---

[1] The example is taken from a paper on *Corporate Social Responsibility & Purchasing Management,* by Dr Mansour Iskander, Siemens, June 3rd 2012 King Saud University, Speakers Series
[2] ibid.

the basis of their competitive edge. Factor competitiveness is the most widely-known component here, while the two other kinds of competitiveness most commonly mentioned are efficiency and innovation competitiveness. They are characteristic for the more developed industrial countries.[3]

One lesson already learned from this relatively new facet of globalization is very simple: if a country does not move fast from factor competitiveness to efficiency and innovation competitiveness, it will lose the benefits of what it may have gained during the time it was factor-efficient. Local governments must be prepared, because the current economic situation represents a very destructive moment for their development strategies. Countries dependent on monocultures currently face this situation, as do the rich petroleum exporting countries and even China with its cheap labour.

One day these countries will be confronted with the sad matter of fact: if you have nothing to sell, you cannot buy anything (at least not in the global market or to the extent you were used to). This simple fact indicates that there is a latent conflict between global and local interests, and shows that this problem must be governed, both globally and locally. This is the main concern of this chapter.

Factor-Competiveness in Saudi Arabia

Saudi Arabia has an oil-based economy with strong government controls over major economic activities. It possesses about one-fifth of the world's proven petroleum reserves, ranks as the largest exporter of petroleum, and plays a leading role in OPEC. The petroleum sector accounts for roughly 80% of its budget revenues, 45% of its GDP, and 90% of its export earnings. [4] As such, the country's factor dependency is extremely large.

The Saudi Government and all the relevant decision makers are now aware of this fact, and realise that, according to current estimates, the amount of petroleum pumped from Saudi wells will eventually be fully consumed by local consumption. This could be as early as 2030, but the surplus might as well last until 2050.

---

[3] The Global Competitiveness Report 2012–2013 Klaus Schwab, Geneva
Copyright © 2012 by the World Economic Forum
[4] Saudi Arabia Economy 2012
http://www.theodora.com/wfbcurrent/saudi_arabia/saudi_arabia_economy.html
SOURCE: 2012 CIA WORLD FACTBOOK AND OTHER SOURCES

So, what is the government reaction inside the country and what strategies are in place to cope with this challenge?

The challenge is twofold: both global and local. On the global scale, Saudi Arabia has developed instruments to control its factor dependency with contracts and pricing policies (OPEC) and technological innovation, as well as having improved technological infrastructure (industrial cities) to attract foreign investment and know-how. These are very farsighted strategies and aim at a future with less factor dependency.

Internally, the country follows the policy of building a knowledge-based society, which, in the long run, would be able to handle the challenges of innovation competitiveness. The paradox of this very wise move, however, is: the more you prepare for efficiency and innovation competitiveness by introducing technology and industry into the bouquet of your economic strength, the more you are consuming your own factors. This may put an early end to your factor competitiveness. Thus, sooner or later, the time will arrive when you will have little to sell and therefore little money to shop with in the global markets. This would be the end of the technology and other transfers which are used to prepare for higher degrees of competiveness.

But what if development strategy and technological development are geared in a way that the focus switches from consumption to sustainability? Luckily, the country has time to reengineer; much more time than most other countries in similar circumstances.

The question, however, is: how will this be done?

To answer this question, it might be useful to look at the above-mentioned World Economic Forum Competitiveness Report, because it shows where the strengths and the weaknesses of the country lie.

One may or may not agree with the analysis given in the report. The report lays open its methodology and it is definitely interesting to look at the ranking, which is very high for Saudi Arabia, as it occupies rank 18 among 144 countries, who together add up to 98% of the world's gross national product.

The Global Competitiveness Index

	Rank (out of 144)	Score (1-7)
GCI 2012–2013	**18**	**5.2**
GCI 2011–2012 (out of 142)	17	5.2
GCI 2010–2011 (out of 139)	21	4.9
Basic requirements (43.4%)	**13**	**5.7**
Institutions	15	5.3
Infrastructure	26	5.2
Macroeconomic environment	6	6.5
Health and primary education	58	5.8
Efficiency enhancers (47.5%)	**26**	**4.8**
Higher education and training	40	4.8
Goods market efficiency	14	5.1
Labor market efficiency	59	4.5
Financial market development	22	4.9
Technological readiness	35	4.9
Market size	24	4.9
Innovation and sophistication factors (9.2%)	**29**	**4.5**
Business sophistication	25	4.9
Innovation	29	4.0

Stage of development

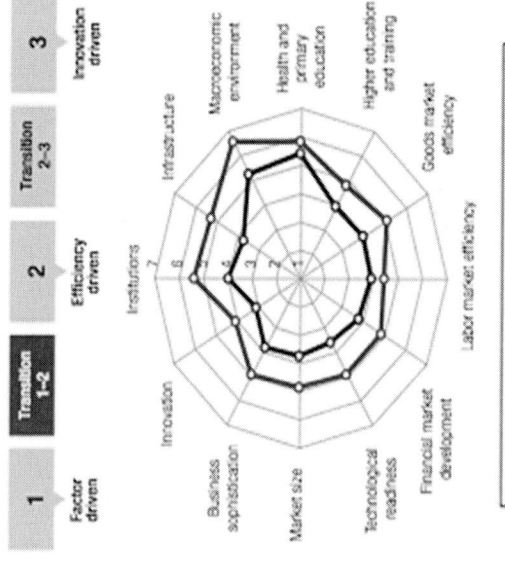

1	Transition 1-2	2	Transition 2-3	3
Factor driven		Efficiency driven		Innovation driven

Saudi Arabia

Economies in transition from 1 to 2

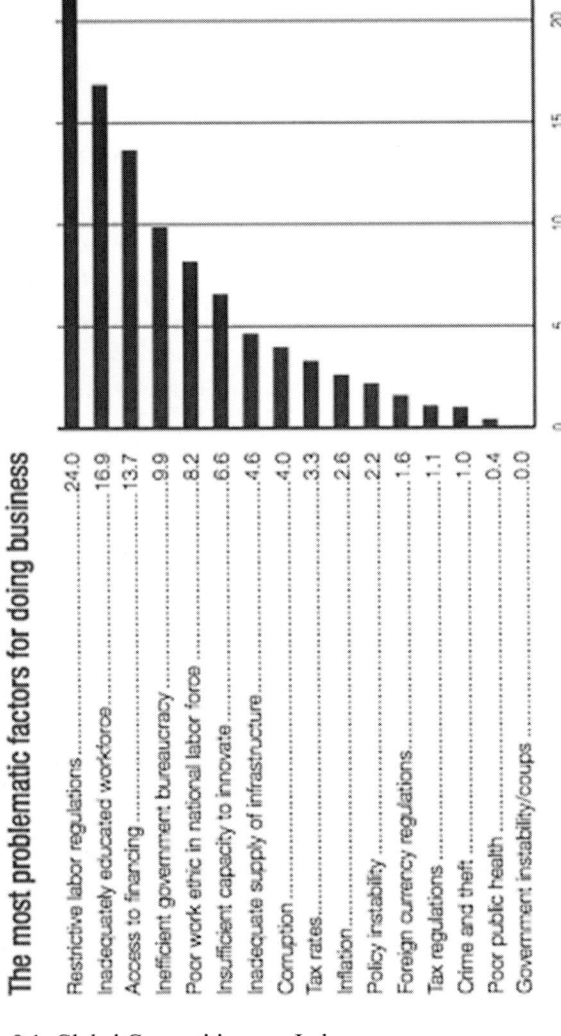

Figure 9.1: Global Competitiveness Index

Interestingly enough, the authors of the report seem to begin doubting, whether their methodology is still sufficient enough to account for the many changes which have occurred during the assessment of what good business may be. They feel, in particular, that the whole complex issue of long-term, or sustainable, business should be given more attention. This is why the new reports added a chapter on sustainability and how measuring and accounting for it would affect the ranking:

> in terms of environmental sustainability, the existing (consumption-driven) economic model coupled with a rising population has brought about increasing pressure on natural resources such as water, energy, and mineral resources, which are becoming scarcer in the face of rising demand. The undesirable environmental consequences of human activity, such as pollution, are leading to a less habitable world. The unpredictable consequences of climate change are also raising the costs of environmental management. Together, these alterations call into question the feasibility of an economic model that does not fully take them into account.[5]

Saudi Arabia is not yet listed in this Index of 70 countries.

The requirement for an awareness of sustainable development

It must be noted that the ranking according to the sustainability index turns out to be not significantly different from the ranking using the old methodology. This can mean that the countries who are doing well are doing well because of, and not in spite of, their sustainability efforts. However, what about the countries on the lower ranks of the scale?

If we assume that caring about sustainability is good for the economy, then not ranking high on this list either means that the country is not aware of the benefits of sustainability and responsible resource management, or that they are being abused by higher ranking countries because they are factor-dependent. In both cases, it is highly likely that the awareness of the high importance of sustainability orientation would be less developed in these countries. It is also implied that the conflict between global and local governance is not thoroughly understood. This is the reason why accountancy for the supply chain has become such an important factor in the CSR debate.

A question, which seems to be worth answering would then be the following:

---

[5] The Global Competitiveness Report 2012–2013 | 49

Is the current level of awareness throughout a specific society high enough to move away from factor dependency and promote the spirit of sustainable competiveness and innovation?

In the last few years we have seen the impressive international SAGIA conferences[7] on sustainable competitiveness, the creation of a Saudi competitive index by the RCI, the efforts of the Saudi Chamber of Commerce, different public and private committees and initiatives for CSR, and, also, the activities of the NCB research chair for CSR. Many public and private institutions have invested a lot of effort in increasing awareness for the sake of improving efficiency, innovation, competitiveness, and responsibility.

At the same time, we encounter a seemingly high degree of ignorance concerning sustainability issues among university students.

In a recent study on students' awareness of their university CSR or sustainability efforts we found two particularly important facts:

1. There are at least as many students who do not know or are uncertain about the CSR/sustainability vision of their university as those who do;
2. Most students do not know of any efforts made by their university concerning the environment.[6]

In this study, it was concluded that there is a grave need for changes in the curricula – and not just in the curricula of the business school. All students should be made aware of the problems and of the technical, social, and economic possibilities of development from factor dependency to sustainable efficiency and innovation competitiveness.

Conclusion

Global sourcing as part of transnational business is a race against time. Saudi Arabia is in a good position because it has still the means to buy time for moving from a factor-dependent to an efficiency-driven and innovation-competent player. But along the way it will again meet with tough competition.

---

[7] See http://www.gcf.org.sa/
[6] The paper is a pilot study and has not yet been published. It shows that even though large efforts have been made by the university to implement CSR-guided measures, they are obviously not communicated to the closest stakeholders, the students.

Yet even without oil, Saudi Arabia is able to mobilize strong resources with a competitive advantage, strengthening the ability to spend less and benefit more. An example of such a resource is the country's solar technology, which has not yet been explored sufficiently. More highly-developed solar technologies could then be exported while also being consumed almost indefinitely and for free in Saudi Arabia. As such, there would be no real conflict between local and global needs. Another example is the huge potential of young people, who, when properly motivated, are willing to learn and able to contribute to national and international ventures. Thus, peak oil and other such negative scenarios are not cogent as long as we look at economic value creation in a sober way. In the current case, the solution is to move from being consumption-driven to a sustainable model of well -being.

PART III:

REGIONAL UNDERSTANDINGS

CHAPTER TEN

THE AUDIT OF THE SUSTAINABLE DEVELOPMENT AND SOCIAL RESPONSIBILITY: A PROPOSAL OF METHODOLOGY. THE CASE OF MOROCCO

EL MANSOURI MOULAY HASSAN

Introduction

The 20th century has undoubtedly been a century of significant and deep-rooted political, economical, technological and social changes. Any maturation of the processes of sustainable development collides with the perspective of the continual changing of the nature and structure of the situation. Indeed, sustainable development is a highly dynamic process, and it would be very risky to claim to be able to illustrate it precisely. It is, nevertheless, possible to find heavy trends which persist, while the factual information quickly becomes obsolete. It is mainly for that reason that this article articulates around the actors, the processes and the poles involved in sustainable development, rather than around the events. Apparently, new facts will arise during the coming years and decades which will confirm or deny several statements proposed by this chapter.

Historical reminder of the concepts and standards of sustainable development

Since 1987 and the publication of the historical report of the Brundtland Committee [1], reflections on sustainable development have progressed considerably. The fundamental principles of the report suggest that our acts have to take into account their effects on the environment, the

---

[1] P.D' Humières and all, Sustainable development: the management of the responsible company, the publishing (editions) of organizations, on 2005, p: 107

economy and the society, and must compromise the well-being of future generations.

Numerous important advances in business have been realized in the past twenty years. Audit firms and big-name companies from most countries throughout the world have begun to integrate sustainable development into their actions and their planning activities. All around the world, dynamic companies are making more sustainable products and processes. Initiatives have also been successfully implemented on the local level to make citizens more aware of the importance of their involvement in the processes of producing less waste, urban renovation and other related projects.

Definition

The expression "sustainable development" began to be widely accepted at the end of the 1980s, having appeared in the document "Our Common Future" (also known as the Brundtland Report[3]). This report is the fruit of the committee gathered by the UNO to propose "a global program for change" concerning the concept and the practices of development. The Brundtland Report shows that a rethinking of our ways of living and governing is urgently required. "To answer in a responsible way the objectives and the aspiration of the humanity", it is necessary to find new methods of approaching old problems, as well as to set up a method of international cooperation and coordination.

The World Committee for the Environment and the Development – to give it its official name - intended to draw the attention of the world to "*the degradation accelerated by the environment and the natural resources, as well as [...] its consequences on the economic and social development*"[4].

By establishing the Committee, the General Assembly of the UNO explicitly emphasized two important ideas:

- The "well-being" of the environment, economies and populations are inextricably connected;
- Sustainable development requires cooperation at the international level.

---

[3] The Brundtland Report, Our Common Future, 1987, Available at www.un-documents.net/wcedocf web site.Htm.
[4] OECD contribution to the United Nations Commission on Sustainable Development: Energy for Sustainable Development 2007

At the heart of sustainable development, we find the necessity of simultaneously taking into account three main factors, namely society, the economy and the environment. Whatever the context is, the basic idea remains the same: the persons, the housing environments and the economic systems are inter-connected. It is possible to ignore this interdependence for a few more years or decades, but history shows that alarming signs or crises always eventually remind us of their existence.

In June 1992, representatives of 179 countries met in Rio de Janeiro to participate in the Conference of the United Nations on development and the environment, commonly called the Earth Summit of Rio. One of the main agreements signed during this meeting was the program entitled Agenda 21. This document of 900 pages describes the initial stages which the world has to undergo in its progress towards sustainable development, both at national and international levels, during the 21st century. The signatories made a commitment to lead the action in four domains, namely:

- The social and economic dimension, particularly the struggle against poverty, and the promotion of sustainable town planning;
- The conservation and management of resources, especially the protection of fishing zones in the oceans and the fight against deforestation;
- The strengthening of the role of collectives, such as women, local governments and NGOs (Non-Governmental Organisations);
- The tools of implementation, such as the use of eco-technology.

Chapter 28 of the document, "Initiatives of local authorities in support of Action", for example, encourages local and regional governments and civil society to participate in the development of a program for action at the community level. Ideally, the coordination of efforts in favour of sustainable development, from the international level down to local municipalities, should support the efficiency of all actions. From Surabaya (Indonesia) to Seattle (the United States), cities all around the world have implemented such plans in order to promote sustainable development at the local level.

Is sustainable development really a guiding principle, as many of its supporters assert? Or is it, rather, a concrete objective or a set of objectives which can be measured, estimated and considered as "achieved"? In the impressive corpus of literature dedicated to the subject, these two points of view, as well as various others, are abundantly discussed[5]. It is not, however, necessary to choose between these options. All the advances of previous generations were the fruit of a permanent process of translating big ideas into concrete practices. This always implies a multitude of experiments, learnings, failures, errors, as well as constant efforts to adapt and refine current methods.

Sustainable development also allows consideration of unifying relations, in order to propose viable solutions. As the Brundtland Report asserts, "sustainable development is not a fixed state of harmony, but rather a process of evolution". It is the tool which obliges us to examine factors which we would rather ignore for the benefit of short-term profits, such as in the case of a polluting industry which is particularly concerned about its profits for the current year, or about a pension plan which does not take into account the increasing number of retired people with regard to the number of contributors.

Brice Lalonde, the former French Secretary of the Environment, proposes the following definition of sustainable development:

> "the idea, for me, is the one of an economy which should allow us to live better while improving our environment and our societies, from now on and in the context of globalization."

In this perspective, sustainable development promotes the possibilities of progress: the economy is a tool which helps us reach global and collective objectives such as improving the quality of life at the world level. The success of sustainable development is dependent on the uniting of the three aforementioned pillars (society, the economy, and the environment) in the same trajectory of progress.

Standards of sustainable development

Respect for ethical rules is a constant concern in all companies. Systems of control and audit have been set up to prevent and fight against bad practices. As underlined so well by A. Chaveau and J.J. Rosé[6], the first reaction of multinational organisations to the implementation of the guiding principles of sustainable development was to deny them or to claim that they were not their responsibility. This is no longer the case

---

[5] OECD, Guiding Principles of the OECD for Multinational Companies, Revision 2000

[6] A Chaveau and J.J.Rosé, The responsible company, the publishing (editions) of organizations, on 2003, p: 225

today, of course. After such initial reactions, companies began to establish internal codes of conduct. The adequacy of these codes depends primarily on the quality of their contents, which are often uncertain. In a 1998 study of 215 codes of conduct, BIT found to be them to be very incomplete and insufficient.

N. Klein adopts a rather critical, but just, view of these codes: "the codes of conduct are of a formidable subtlety. Unlike the laws, they are not applicable. And unlike the labor-union contracts, they were not drafted in association with factory managers to meet the requirements and the needs of the employees."

These ineffective soft laws were eventually replaced by several standards of sustainable development defined by professional organizations, such as:

- **Environmental Eco Audit EMAS[7] management system and audit**: EMAS is a voluntary initiative intended to improve the environmental performance of companies;
- **SD[8]21000 sustainable developments**: Rather than a set of standards, this is a framework of advice and recommendations proposed by AFNOR (French National Organization for Standardization), thus limited to France;
- **The reference table[9] SA8000**: This was realized by Social Accountability International (SAI). The slogan of SAI is "Making Workplace Human Rights a Vital Part of the Business Agenda", and its intention is to assure the promotion of the human rights of workers worldwide. The SA8000 standard concerns the following issues:
  - Child labor and hard labor
  - Hygiene and safety.
  - Freedom of association and right for collective bargaining
  - Ban on discrimination regarding remuneration, training, dismissal and pension
  - Working time
  - Remuneration
  - System of management

---

[7] EMAS: Environmental Management Audit System
[8] SD for Sustainable Development: An Anglo-Saxon term indicating sustainable or steady development
[9] LIMITED COMPANY 8000 for Social Accountability 8000 Standard

The EMAS regulation defines the requirements for setting up an EMS (Management System of the Environment). More complete than ISO 14001, it particularly recommends that the fixed objectives of improvement are verifiable and require environmental communication.

The company has to make an environmental statement at the disposition of interested parties.

Indicators of operation, environmental performance, and management serve as communications tools, and must, as such, be "understandable and without ambiguity". [10]

ISO 14000 environmental management: ISO 14000 was established as a set of standards dedicated to environmental management. It specifies the requirements expected from environmental management systems, and allows the organization concerned to define and to apply its policies and objectives while taking its major legal and normative requirements into account[11]. In its logic, the ISO 14000 is rather similar to the classic ISO 9000 of quality management. In both cases, the idea is to certify correctly the process and not the products of the work. Environmental management systems subject to ISO 14000 are certified by an accredited third party body, independent from the company. Similarly to ISO 9000, ISO 14000 requires a permanent improvement of environmental management from companies having chosen to implement this standard.

The list of the standards presented in this article is not extensive, but it seems convenient here to use only the ones referenced above.[12]

Further to the proliferation of standards, it has been convenient for certain international bodies to develop their own precise frameworks on sustainable development. As such, after 5 years of negotiations and an unprecedented international mobilization (of more than 500 experts from 99 countries and international organizations such as the ILO (International Labour Organization)), the members of ISO approved the framework ISO 26000 at the end of 2010.

ISO 26000 is, undoubtedly, a large innovation in the field of sustainable development. But what exactly is its role? What impact will it have on the working environment of organizations? What operational tools

---

[10] Cf eur-lex.europa.eu.

[11] The standard ISO 14001 does not specify the specific criteria of the evaluation of environmental performance.

[12] Other standards which are described by Ecopass include a guide of the reference tables of sustainable development: which provide tools for a strategy of sustainable development; available on the website http://www.ecopass.fr/developpement-durable-2.html

are required to set it up? To answer these questions, we will investigate the practical methodology of this standard in the next paragraph.

ISO 26000

ISO 26000 is the name of the international standard which designs guidelines for organizational sustainable development and corporate social responsibility. This standard is applicable for organizations of any type, in both the public sector and the private sector, and in both developed countries and developing countries. ISO 26000 contains guidelines and not requirements, and is, thus, not intended for certification, unlike the standards ISO 9001: 2000 and ISO 14001: 2004.

According to AFNOR,

"tomorrow, any organization of any country, whatever its activity and its staff, will have a reference text, recognized at the international level the objective of which will be to guide it in the implementation of best practice regarding corporate social responsibility."

The AFNOR standard, as related by its French representative, establishes the distinction between two notions[13], namely:

- **Sustainable development**: This meets the needs of the present without compromising the capacity of future generations to make choices in their own. It covers three areas: economy, society and environment.
- **Corporate social responsibility**: This is the contribution of organizations to sustainable development. It is the willingness of the organization to assume responsibility for the impacts of its decisions and activities on both the company and the environment, and to report them.

The standards of the management system - ISO 14011, ISO 9012 - are complementary and compatible with the standard ISO 26000. The latter allows the strategic reflection of organizations, and is thus situated more upstream. It can lead, for example, to the adoption of an ISO 9001 approach in order to optimize the relationship with the customer, or of an ISO 14001 approach to organize and support the consideration of the environment in the functioning of the organization. This is also the case for tools such as OHSAS 18013, GRI, and Carbon Assessment® which

---

[13] AFNOR, ISO 26000 in 10 questions, on 2010, P. 5

provide methodological and operational answers or recognition on certain aspects of the implementation of the standard ISO 26000.

The detailed contents of ISO 26000 will evolve over time. However, the current standard covers the following issues:

1 - Field of application
2- Terms and definitions
3- The understanding of corporate social responsibility
4- Principles of corporate social responsibility
5- The identification of corporate social responsibility and the ability have dialogue with stakeholders
6- Guidelines on the central questions of corporate social responsibility
7- Guidelines for the implementation of the practices of corporate social responsibility.

With these guidelines, ISO 26000 offers an environment of work and reflection for the implementation of a strategy of sustainable development and corporate social responsibility for companies. The ISO 26000 approaches seven central questions of corporate social responsibility defined in the standard and represented in the plan below:

Governance and organization: This is the essential element, given that the standard considers governance as the "place" where the company becomes responsible by taking responsible decisions and by allocating the means to reach its objectives.

It is at the level of governance that sustainable development is operated and strategised. As such, without clarity and assertiveness from the management, sustainable development will at best be a set of measures with a marginal impact on the environment and society, and at worst a friendly posture.

Human rights: An organisation must respect the prescriptions of the bill of rights, and must adhere to the following:

- Constant vigilance (particularly against discrimination)
- The prevention of situations presenting a risk for human rights
- Prevention of complicity
- A refusal to violate human rights
- Following civil and political, and business, social and cultural laws
- The fundamental rights of workers.

Relations and working conditions: The auditor will examine if the rules promulgated by labour laws and by the international recommendations of the work office are respected, specifically focusing on:

- Working conditions and social welfare
- Social dialogue
- Health and safety at work
- The development of human resources and vocational training

Environment: It must be ensured that the principles promulgated by the Kyôto protocol, for carbon assessment and for ISO 14011 are respected. Efforts for the following must also be in place:

- Prevention of pollution
- Sustainable use of resources
- Mitigation of climate change and adaptation
- Protection and rehabilitation of the natural environment
- The consumption of fewer resources, protection of biodiversity, and the prevention of climate change
- The best business practices available
- The fight against corruption
- A responsible political commitment
- Loyal competition
- The promotion of corporate social responsibility in the sphere of influence
- Respect for property rights

Questions related to consumers: The following must be in place:

- Best and sustainable practices regarding marketing, information and contracts
- The protection of the health and safety of consumers
- Sustainable consumption
- After-sales service and assistance, and the resolution of consumer disputes
- Protection of data and the privacy of consumers
- Access to essential services

Commitments regarding local populations and their social development: These include:

- Territorial anchoring
- Education and culture
- Job creation and the development of skills
- The development of technologies
- The creation of wealth and income
- Social investment

Towards a proposal for sustainable development auditing: For the past few years, auditing and risk management in particular have assumed greater importance due to the financial scandals that plagued the world at the end of the 20th century.

The auditing of the sustainable development of an organization aims primarily at determining the impact of the decisions and activities of the organisation on both the company and the environment, motivated by a transparent[14]and ethical behavior which:

- Contributes to sustainable development, and the health of individuals and the well-being of the company;
- Takes into account the expectations of stakeholders;
- Respects current laws, and is compatible with the international standards, is integrated in the organization as a whole and implemented in its relations

Furthermore, according to a poll conducted by KPMG[15] (a specialist in audit and counseling) in partnership with The Economist Intelligent Units, CSR strategy is beneficial for the majority of large companies.

The results show that the CSR strategy brings a significant amount of profit to the companies which utilise it, including improvements in relationships with customers (while also appealing to new customers and developing customer loyalty in existing customers for 32% of the respondents). Furthermore, profitability was increased (for 31.5% of the respondents) and new products and services of better quality were developed (for 25% of the respondents).

Vincent Neat, Head of Climate Change and Sustainability at KPMG comments that:

---

[14] Cf standards ISO 26000, as quoted

[15] International KPMG, Corporate Sustainability: Progress adjournment, 2011 available on the website
http://www.kpmg.com/global/en/issuesandinsights/articlespublications/pages/corporate sustainability.aspx

"Whereas most of the companies which we questioned had set up a RSE
strategy with the aim of improving their notoriety and satisfying the new
legislative constraints, these same companies, saw their profitability
increasing, benefited the development of new products and services of
better quality and noticed the improvement of the mood of their
employees."

He adds:

"…it is a positive point to notice that the majority of 400 world companies
which we addressed had a sustainable or already established development
plan or one in the course of implementation."

This poll confirms that what initially urges companies to set up
strategies of sustainable development is generally primarily the desire to
improve their reputation, or the obligation to comply with the social and
environmental standards.

Nature of the Mission of Audit

The auditing of sustainable development and social responsibility
consists of all of the checks that a statutory auditor or audit firm must
realize in order to have a precise idea about the situation of a company.

Ms. G.R. Giordano[16] reflects on the nature of the environmental
check[17] and notices that it has numerous similarities with the financial
audit, justified by the use of the same terminology.

She also specifies that these missions are the privilege of the biggest
audit firms, such as PricewaterhouseCoopers, Ernst and Young, KPMG,
Deloitte, and Mazars. The methodology used by them is considered by the
auditors to be similar to that used in the financial audit, except that the
units of measure and the documentary evidence are specific to the
environmental domain.

Before beginning an audit for a company with an industrial past and
potential problems of pollution, such investigations will help to take into

---

[16] G.R. Giordano, "The quality of the societal information: an experiment relative
to the environmental audit"; doctoral thesis supported at the University of
Montpelier 1; Option: Science of Management; defended on December 3rd, 2007
[17] The objective of this article is not to list an extensive review of the literature
concerning the auditing of sustainable development. For further thoughts on this
subject refer to the doctoral thesis defended by Claire Gilletle on November 23rd,
2010 at the University of Montpelier entitled "The Study of the Determiners of the
Check of the Societal Information in the French Context".

account the environmental liabilities of the site during the calculation of its real value. An environmental evaluation of the plans will provide an understanding of the problems related to the contamination of a site. In such a case, the auditor will help the company determine the responsibility for the operations of purification. An audit of sustainable development will also study the potential legal, social and civil damage which can arise, including the implications of commercial real estate transactions.

Furthermore, the audit firm ensures that the company respects the prescriptions regarding the broadcasting of societal information: every country has its own regulations. Indeed, in numerous countries, companies must legally communicate societal information.

Finally, when the appointed verifier is a statutory auditor, and since the mission has a conventional character, he is free to accept or to refuse this mission. In case he accepts the mission, he must respect the fundamental principles of behavior and the main rules defined in the Code of professional ethics. He has to implement a process of checking in compliance with the abstract frame of the missions of insurance of IAASB, particularly the standard ISAE3000 (Rivière-Giordano, on 2007).[18]

So, the three parts concerned in the checking mission are: the company, the supplier of the insurance benefit, and those parties that have an interest in this check.

As mentioned by Gillet[19], "most of the information required by the national regulations concern environmental information. When the information with social character or when the reporting concerns more widely the extra-financial data, these are never explicit as for their contents. Secondly, in the majority of the presented statutory regimes, companies liable for the obligations of reporting are the ones which are already forced by legislations on the environment. Besides, companies concerned by these obligations are, for the majority of countries, highly-rated companies, with the exception of Norway and of Canada where all the companies are subjected to these obligations".

---

[18] Op cit
[19] C.Gillet, op cit.

Chapter Ten

Table 10.1: The national statutory regimes regarding societal information

Country	Legislation	Impact	Shape
South Africa	Report King II (2002) Code of corporate practices and conduct	All the companies quoted in the stock exchange (JSE securities Exchange)	Publication of an independent report according to the standards of the GRI
Germany	Accounting law bilanzrechtsrefonngesetz (October, 2004)	The companies quoted in the stock exchange	Disclosure obligation of extra-financial data. Companies have to describe their main risks, as well as supply key data of environmental and social performance
Australia	Accounting law Corporation Act (2001)	The companies which have activities liable for the Australian regulations regarding environment	Information detailed on the performance of the company with regard to the regulations on the environment and integrated into the annual report of the board of directors or the management board
Canada	Regulation adopted by the committee of securities: regulation 51-103 and appendix 51-102A2 "Annual Note" Regulation 52-109 Regulation 58-101 (2004-2005)	All the companies liable to Canadian regulations	The annual report has to describe the social or environmental policies which the company implemented and which are fundamental for its activities, as well as the measures taken to operate them (Regulation 51-102 A2 column 5.1)
Denmark	Green Accounting Act (1995)	Companies having an environmental impact are subjected to the procedures of authorization planned by the environmental regulation	An independent report which contains environmental information ("green accounts"), and follows the regime of the annual reports

	Accounting law Danish Financial Statement Act (2001-2003)	Certain average and large companies and all highly-rated companies	Inclusion in the annual report of their impact on the environment and the environmental programs in position
	Accounting law Act amending the Danish Financial Statement Act (report on social responsibility for large business) (December 2008)	The biggest companies	Report in the annual report of their activities RSE, or justification of the absence of such information
USA	Right To Know Act (1996) Toxic Release Inventory (TRI) (1987) SEC (Securities and Exchange)	For the most toxic companies, the activities of which are susceptible to cause damage	Publication of certain information (broadcasts issues of toxic products) for the agency of environmental protection (EPA)
		For all the listed companies in the USA	Publication in the document 10-K of information in conformity with the laws, the legal proceedings and the debts bound to the environment (Regulation S-K Point 101.103 and 303)
	Sarbanes-Oxley Act (SOX) (2002)	For all the listed companies in the USA	Section 401: the reporting has to include information with no financial character to supply to the investors a precise and complete vision in terms of materiality (no reference clarifies in the societal aspects)

Japan	Law N 77 "law for the promotion of the activities of companies and consideration of the impact on the environment of certain specific companies, etc., and for the facilitation of the access to the information relative to the environment and to the other measures" (2004-2005)	Japanese companies considered to be specific according to the ministerial prescription	Publication of a specific environmental report (article 9)
Norway	Accounting law Accounting Act (1998)	All the Norwegian companies which have to hold accounting documents and all the foreign companies carrying out activities in Norway and paying tax there	Companies have to supply environmental information detailed in the financial annual report
Netherlands	Environmental Management (1997)	The establishments which could have negative impacts on the environment defined according to precise criteria according to the sector, the production capacity, etc.	Publication of both sorts of environmental reports: A report for the government and a report for the public
United Kingdom	Operating and Financial Review (OFR) (2004) Abandoned	All the listed companies	Publication of a report OFR (in the form of separate report - an integral part of the audited annual report) containing social information
	Company Law Reform Bill (2006)	All the listed companies	The "examination of companies" of a listed company has to contain information on environmental issues, on employees of the company and on community questions (law less precise than the OFR)

Source: adapted from C. Gillet, op cit Pp. 40-41

Methodology of the audit of sustainable development

Audit firms formulate various types of recommendations being able to interest numerous actors, such as shareholders, banks, customers, NGOs and companies. In particular, they can help companies to better understand concepts and principles that must govern the behavior of companies. The evolutionary frame of sustainable development gives orientations in domains such as:

Central question: Human Rights
Sphere of action 1: duty of vigilance
Sphere of action 2: situations presenting a risk for human rights
Sphere of action 3: prevention of the complicity
Sphere of action 4: remedy infringements of human rights
Sphere of action 5: discrimination and vulnerable groups
Sphere of action 6: civil and political Laws
Sphere of action 7: business, social and cultural Laws
Sphere of action 8: fundamental Principles and right to work
Central question: Relations and Working Conditions
Sphere of action 1: employment and employer / employee relations
Sphere of action 2: working conditions and social welfare
Sphere of action 3: social dialog
Sphere of action 4: health and safety in the work-place
Sphere of action 5: development of the human resources
Central question: Environment
Sphere of action 1: prevention of pollution
Sphere of action 2: sustainable Use of resources
Sphere of action 3: Loyal competition
Sphere of action 4: Promotion of corporate social responsibility in the chain of values

In certain cases, these instruments directly address companies (for example the law NRE or the law Grains in the French case). In other cases, they constitute for the governments an obligation to transpose certain concepts and principles issued from international organizations (for example, the principles of the work of the United Nations Global Compact Guide for companies) which, in turn, modifies the legal obligations of companies. In their overseas activities[21], including in zones with deficit of

---

[21] When the company establishes strengthened accounts, the information to be supplied will be strengthened data (on the company itself as well as on all

governance, companies should respect the law and the concepts and the established international principles.

These principles of sustainable development can help the subcontracting companies operating in zones with deficit of governance to better detect and understand the risks from negligence of social responsibility.

Even reduced to the questions concerning the organization and the environment, such as their consequences on the employment and working conditions, the field of practices covered within the article has proved so wide it seemed necessary for us to examine the field of practices, or to reduce it (we had no right to dismiss any of the good practices), and at least to organize it by determining the priority grounds with regard to the thorough question put to the CSR, which seems to us to be that of the sustainability development audit's report.

Human rights

Today, the majority of the Member states of the UN[22] favor international agreements regarding human rights. They have the entire legal obligation to respect, protect and implement rights and fundamental liberties.

The majority of them signed the Statement adopted during the Conference of Vienna on human rights in 1993, which reaffirmed "that the protection and the promotion of human rights are a priority question for the international community" and "that no argument, even the development, can justify a limitation of the rights and the liberties".

The general principle of nondiscrimination

With the principle of equality, the principle of nondiscrimination constitutes one of the fundamental elements of the international law of human rights, as shown by the DUDH, both Pacts of 1966, the international Agreement on the elimination of all the forms of racial discrimination (CERD), and the Agreement on the elimination of all the forms of discriminations towards women (CEDAW), and Agreement on children's rights.

---

subsidiaries in the sense of the article L. 233-1 or the companies which it controls in the sense of the article L. 233-3 1 of the Law N 2010-788 of July 12th, 2010 published the official journal of July 13th, 2010).

[22] The article 55 of the Charter in its paragraph states that United Nations will favor: "the universal and actual respect for human rights and for fundamental liberties for all, without distinction, for sex, for language or for religion."

The forms of discriminations can be multiple and the problem of the groups and the vulnerable, marginal, disadvantaged individuals or socially excluded is at the heart of the international law of human rights.

The principle of participation in the decisions

The normative frame of human rights internationally recognized includes the right of the persons affected by key decisions to participate in the relevant decision-making process. It states the right to participate in numerous international instruments, in particular the international Pact concerning the business, social and cultural laws and the Statement on the right for the development. A policy or a program which is elaborated without the active participation by the concerned persons has little chance of being effective.

Due diligence is performed with respect to human rights, and particular attention of the auditor will concern the following elements:

- Fire-ups due to racial discrimination;
- The complaints put down by associations or NGO;
  o In the socio-cultural distribution of the company;
  o In the trials instituted to the company;
  o In its values;
  o In the complaints put down in the service of the human resources for racial prejudices;
  o In the board of the promotions and in the balance sheet of the skills;
  o In the paid salary and in the fair processing of the employees.

Relations and conditions of work

According to P. Auer, G. Besse and D. Méda[23], the reasons for which the international standards were organized since the creation of the ILO (International Labor Organization) are always valid: a competition not regulated on the labor market engenders negative effects on the working conditions.

Rules and regulations having a binding effect are necessary to prevent the destructive competition. This is beneficial as the international standards can allow the improvement of the economic performances (by encouraging

---

[23] P Auer, G. Besse and D. Méda, Relocations, standards of the work and employment policy towards a more just globalization? THE DISCOVERY, LA DECOUVERTE Paris, (2005)

the entrepreneurs to innovate, to make productivity gains, to take up little profitable activities).

Among the international standards of work we can quote:

Freedom of association supposes to respect the right of employers [24]and workers to establish, join and manage free, voluntary organizations, i.e. labor unions, to promote and defend their professional interests.

The workers and employers have the right to do this without intervention from the company. The employers cannot interfere with the decision of the workers to join; nor can they try to influence their decision or exercise discriminatory measures against the workers, or their representatives, who decide to join.

The right of the workers to negotiate freely with the employers is an essential element of the freedom of association. The collective bargaining[25] is a voluntary process which allows the employers and the workers to discuss and to negotiate their relations, in particular as regards the working conditions. The participants in the negotiation understand the employers themselves or their organizations, and labor unions or, in their absence, the representatives freely appointed by the workers. The collective bargaining can work effectively only if it takes place freely and honestly, with the cooperation of all the parties.

It supposes :

- To make efforts to reach an agreement;
- To hold constructive and honest negotiations;
- To avoid inexcusable delays;
- To respect the concluded agreements and to apply them honestly; and to give to the parties enough time to discuss collective disputes and to reach a regulation.

Besides the fact of being a right, the freedom of association allows the workers and the employers to group together to better protect not only their economic interests, but also their civil liberties such as the right to life, in safety and in integrity, as well as their personal and collective freedom. This principle, consubstantial with democracy, is essential for the respect for all other principles and fundamental rights for the work-place.

---

[24] International Labour Office, The principles of the work of the World Pact of United Nations. Guide for companies. Geneva, (2010)
[25] Collective bargaining: in the working right it is translated by collective agreement

The collective bargaining is a forum of exchanges which allows the employers and the workers, or their respective organizations, to discuss in a constructive way their relations and conditions of work and employment. It is often more effective and more flexible than the state regulations. It can identify the potential difficulties, and set up mechanisms allowing for them to be adjusted peacefully. Collective bargaining can also identify solutions which take into account priorities and needs of the employers, as well as workers. Harmonious collective bargaining is advantageous both for the management and for the workers, as it favors peace and stability, which benefits the company overall. The collective bargaining can constitute an important mechanism of good governance, in that it allows increasing the degree of commitment of the persons who participate in it, by involving them in the decisions which affect them directly.

In Morocco, the article 96 of the labor code states that the collective bargaining takes place once a year, at the level of the company that is between the employer and the labor unions of the most representative employees, as well as at the level of the sector between the employer or the professional organization of the employers and the most representative labor unions at the national level.

Hard labor[26] is a fundamental violation of human rights, which represents a challenge for most of the countries worldwide. The BIT considers that at least 12.3 million people are victims of hard labor in the world, among which 80% are in the hands of the private agents. Most of the victims receive a low remuneration, sometimes even nothing, and work for long hours in deplorable conditions of safety and health. Hard labor is really a worldwide problem in the developed countries where it affects mainly the victims of milking among the migrant workers. It concerns men and women, but also children, who represent at least 40% of all the victims.

Also, working contains risks. It is evident, because work is a human activity, and because any activity involves factors of uncertainty and unknown combinations. These dangers, which appear in the shape of personal accidents and diseases of varied gravity, are called occupational hazards.

---

[26] The hard or compulsory labor appoints any work or service (department) required (demanded) from whomever, under the threat of a penalty, and where this person did not offer his/her self or his/her own free will. The fact that the concerned worker receives a salary or another shape of remuneration does not mean inevitably that the work does not dress (take on) a forced or compulsory character

According to the gravity of the injury, we distinguish four types of occupational accidents, corresponding each to specific modes of repair.

The first type is occupational accidents without a sick leave, which are generally mild and can be looked after on the spot in the infirmary of the company, and which require only a few hours of rest or care. These accidents are not to be necessarily declared, but must be recorded on special registers of the company doctor. These type include small wounds (cuts, scratches, shocks and mild traumas), of very light poisonings and small projections of aggressive products on the skin causing very superficial burns.

The second type is occupational accidents with sick leave, of a few days to several months. It involves temporary disabilities, depending on the duration of the work leave, until total or partial resumption of the work. These are graver accidents, requiring prolonged and intensive medical or hospitable care as well as extensive days of rest.

A fracture of bones, a sprain or significant burns, but which can be looked after without leaving permanent damage, are considered as temporary disabilities and repaired as such. By virtue of the article 14 of Dahir of June 25th, 1927, any occupational accident must be declared to the local authority within 48 hours from the moment the accident happened.

The third type is occupational accidents that cause permanent incapacity, correspondent in definitive injuries and lasting damage susceptible to reducing the working capacity. According to the gravity of the physical injury, there are several degrees of permanent incapacity, resulting in compensation determined by following a scale defined by statutory texts. A cut finger, a leaky eye, a deformed leg and a partially damaged lung are the types of compensation whose amounts are variable.

The fourth and final type is mortal occupational accidents with immediate or deferred death, further to complications from accidents. In that case it is the legal successors who receive life annuities.

Finally the auditor will pay particular attention to the following elements:

- To respect Guaranteed minimum wage and for the Minimum wage;
- Agricultural Guaranteed (SMAG) to eliminate the risk of hard labor;
- To give to the union representatives the possibility of negotiating collectively with interlocutors who hold a real decision-making power;
- To supply the information necessary for constructive negotiations;
- The existence of the mechanisms of dispute settlements;
- The existence or not of strikes;

- The existence of hard labor by revealing signs such as: food deprivation, the non-payment of salary; exercise against the employees of physical violence or sexual abuse; restrict their movements or imprison them;
- the existence of a committee of safety and hygiene for companies employing at least 50 employees;
- To identify the occupational hazards within the company;
- To honor the application of the legal prescription relative to the health and safety of the workers, in particular the decree n°2-09-197 of March 22nd, 2010; fixing the model of the annual report that has to establish the committee of safety and hygiene;
- To make sure that instruments and safety devices are suitably used and that the company respects the prescription of the safety guides, against risks of fire and panic elaborated by the Management of the Disaster and emergency services;
- The existence of a working doctor, a possibility of psychological consultation and the statements of working actions put down in the local authorities;
- The use of the grade-related method of certain number of ratios such as: the rate of absenteeism, the number of statements of professional diseases, the staff turnover. It is also necessary to record the increase in the demands of consultation "Human resources" or with the hierarchy, as well as that of the number of visits to the infirmary or consultations for occasional medical examinations at the request of the employees. In the same way, a record must be made of an increase in medicinal consumption or an increase of sick leave. In the case of an increase in the rate of occupational accidents, a check for an increase in road accidents (missions, routes) can be useful because these indicators can affect the other indicators so meaningfully, such as the number of meetings of Representative Authorities of the Staff and the number of demands for departure in training.

The environment

According to the standard ISO 31000 version 2009, the risk defines itself as the possibility that an event arises and whose consequences (or effects of the uncertainty) may affect the persons and assets (active persons) of the company, its environment, the objectives of the company or its reputation.

This general definition applies obviously to the environmental risks. The event associated to be at risk in relation to the environment, such as defined within this standard, thus can be of diverse nature, but it contains inevitably sources or environmental consequences.

So, by risks we mean having to do with the environment:

1. The industrial or technological risks generated by the company (internal risks) impacting on the environment: water, air (sight), sites and grounds, noise, etc.
2. The risks of outside attacks (external risks), the environmental dimension of which impacts on the company, such as:
   - The natural risks: flood, movement of ground, storm, lightning, drought
   - The outer accidents at the origin of environmental damage: damange to dikes, accidents caused by a nearby dangerous activity …

The consequences for the company of the risks connected to the environment can indeed be of several orders:

- Affected the environment: water, air, grounds, landscape, natural resources, etc.
- Reached the human integrity: health and safety of the employees, the users of products and departments, etc.
- Financial Losses: loss of income, costs of the damage, the insurances, etc.
- Possible legal penalties: penal, civil and administrative,
- Degradation of the image of the company: risk of reputation, etc.

Except the quoted risks or except those located during the operation of audit or attuned to the stakeholders (NGO or employees), new risks can appear:

- The "environmental liabilities" of a site, which shows itself often only late and sometimes when the person in charge of the situation is no longer capable of assuming it and of repairing the consequences,
- The risks of natural disaster,
- The risks of development related to new activities or to new products,
- The statutory risks, in particular those led by the new European directive on the Environmental responsibility, or still by the law Sarbanes-Oxley concerning companies listed in the United States,
- The new economic risks led by environmental problems (example of the market of the quotas of emission of CO_2),

- The risks of collective actions on behalf of consumers or other stakeholders,

The operation of audit takes place by an interview which has to allow for classifying the risks according to their existence, the nature of their environmental impact, and their temporal origin:

Existence of environmental risk: Risk exists when it is spotted in the considered perimeter (such as installations, products, and activities), that is the probability of appearance of the generative fact is recognized as not null. The risk is potential when it is not spotted in the considered perimeter but when it was it already in installation or in similar conditions.

Nature of the environmental impact of the risk: The environmental impact is recognized in case of realization of the generative fact (we can speak about turned out risk). The environmental impact is supposed but not demonstrated scientifically in case of realization of the generative fact (we can speak about plausible risk).

Origin of the environmental risk:

- The risk can result from the past activity of the company,
- Or of a present activity,
- Or of a future activity,

So, points to be evoked would be in particular the following:

Setting-up of production sites

- What natural environment (groundwater, river? Nature of the ground? Rosette of winds?),
- What industrial environment (the other companies nearby? Among which are some at risk?)
- What human environment (houses, schools, hospitals nearby?),

These questions apply to the transportation of goods and products related to the activity of the company.

In addition, these factors also apply to the services of the company, and also the products of the company, i.e. bad storage use or product recycling by the user or the consumer can have environmental impacts.

Statutory risks (current non-compliance, or risk of hardening of the legislation)

Sectorial Benchmark regarding risks:
- Environmental risks of the sector,
- Positioning of the company in its sector (best in class or worst in class regarding risks?).

Environmental image of the company:
- Reputation, embellish with images (institutional image and image of the products),
- Reliable level with the stakeholders,
- Crises and dispute (past, current or plausible),
- Press articles,
- Certifications,
- Classification in the indications of financial extra notation (ASPII, F4Good, etc.),
- Environmental prizes, quotations,
- Signatures of charters, international treaties, etc. (Global Compact, OECD,
- WBCSD, etc.).

Sectorial Benchmark regarding image:
- Environmental image of the sector,
- Positioning of the company in its sector (best in class or worst in class regarding image?).

The same questions on the main suppliers of the company:
- The suppliers can cause environmental risks for the company because of products or services which they supply ;
- The suppliers can also create risks of reputation: in an environmental crisis at the supplier, the contractor could be blamed for having those practices, or for not having pressed enough so that his supplier stops or improves those practices, even not listing them.

The same questions on the main customers of the company:
- The reputation of a company can be affected if it works for a customer whose environmental practices are disputed.

The management of environmental risks can be estimated under four aspects: policy, organization, men (people) and means.

Policy:
- Contained by the environmental policy: axes, ambitions, commitments, principles, level of priority, considered perimeters,
- Coherence with the other corporate policies,
- Level of distribution and in-house appropriation,
- Charter interns (or charter external but spread and applied in house) formalizing the policy, the commitments of the management, etc.
- Attitude with regard to the possible evolutions of the legislation: waiting-game or anticipation?

Organization:
- Organization of the function environment: links with the management, with the production sites, etc.,
- Existence of a Management committee of the risks: and in that case, composition and functioning of this Committee as regards to the aspects of environmental risks,
- Organization of the function Risk Manager: links with the function environment, with the legal function, etc.,
- Organization of the regulatory monitoring,
- Organization of the technology watch (Best Available Technologies, etc.), relations with the academic community concerned by the environmental problems.

Human factor:
- Skills of the persons in charge of the environment,
- Environmental skills of Risk Manager and the Management committee of the risks,
- Raising awareness and environmental training of the staff, in particular
- Operational managers in the various functions,
- Environmental objectives given to these managers and corresponding penalties

Tools and means :
- Tools of mapping / of management of environmental risks,
- Technical means of detection and prevention of set up risks,

- Management systems of the Environment (EMS) or the internal procedures, the reporting: nature of the environmental indicators follow-ups, certification, standards,
- Internal or external environmental audits, and processing of audit reports, policy of green purchases,
- Audits and supports of the suppliers on environmental criteria, density and efficiency of the environmental regulations concerning the activities of the company (and thus on which it can or cannot rely on centering its environmental management),
- Rising and structuring of the environmental expense of the company (including reserves for responsibilities),
- Experience feedback on the incidents, the accidents, or the crises environmental,
- Analyses of life cycle of products / steps of eco-design,
- Membership in a network of companies

The loyalty of the practices

Fraud remains one of the main problems with which companies are confronted in the world, which are their countries of presence, their branch of industry or their size. A vast study led in 2007 with 5428 companies of 40 countries[27] revealed that more than 43% of them had been victims of one or several considerable economic offences during the previous two years. In spite of the attention of the authorities of regulations and the investments of companies in the controls, the real level of the economic offences and the financial or other damage which ensue from it did not decrease in a significant way.

Economic fraud destroys the shareholder value, threatens the development of the company, compromises the possibilities of employment and harms good economic governance.

Companies should consequently intend to set up internal tools effectively and be prepared to fight economic fraud and fight against corruption. Studies show that the companies which use effective guiding principles and programs of voluntary membership are much less vulnerable in the economic offences.

So according to the anti-corruption Committee of the international chamber of commerce, the fraud can be detected by means of internal or

---

[27] PricewaterhouseCoopers, Services (Departments) of inquiries and juricomptabilité, Economic crime (murder): celebrity, culture and controls, biennial world survey (investigation) " Global Economic Crime Survey", on 2007, p. 22.

external audits, of the management of the risk or the safety of the company, but also, and to a large extent, by devices of ethical alert.

The concerning legal requirements internal or external, ethical warning devices, are indicated below, because they give useful indications for the organization of the descriptions within companies:

- The Inter-American Agreement against the corruption of March 29th, 1996 (article III,8) mentions that the parties intend to adopt " systems for protecting state employees and persons who denounce honestly the acts of corruption, including the protection of their identity ";
- The Agreement of United Nations against the corruption of December 9th, 2003 (article 33) mentions that every Part state intends to incorporate into its internal legal system " measures suited to assure the protection against any inequitable processing of every person which indicates to the competent, honest authorities and on the basis of reasonable suspicions, any facts concerning breaches established according to the agreement ";
- The penal Agreement on the corruption of the Council of Europe of January 27th, 1999 (article 22) states that every Party adopts " measures suited to assure protection against any inequitable treatment of every person which indicates to the competent, honest authorities and on the basis of reasonable suspicions, any facts concerning breaches established according to the agreement ";
- The civil Agreement on the corruption of the Council of Europe of November 4th, 1999 (article 9) states that every Party plans " in its internal law an adequate protection against any inequitable penalty towards the employees who, honestly and on the basis of reasonable suspicions, denounce facts of corruption to the persons or responsible authorities";
- The Agreement of the African Union on the prevention and the fight against corruption of July 11th, 2003 (article 5) states that States parties adopt " measures to make sure that the citizens indicate the cases of corruption, without being possibly afraid of reprisals ";
- In the United Kingdom: Public Interest Disclosure Act 1998 (PIDA) grant a specific protection to the persons who reveal certain honest facts and in the public interest, and allows them to lodge a complaint in case of ragging;
- In the United States: the law Sarbanes-Oxley of 2002 (article 806) grants the employees of listed companies in the stock exchange to a specific protection against reprisals in business fraud;

- The Listing Manual New York stock exchange (NYSE) (article 303A.10) arranges that listed companies have to adopt a code of ethics for the administrators, the executives and the employees. In the comment, it is underlined that any code of ethics has to contain standards and procedures of stake in conformity intended to facilitate its effective application and, among others, ethical warning procedures and a protection for the informers;
- In France: the law N 2007-1598 of November 13th, 2007 (article 9) modifies the labor code and forbids any discriminatory measure to a person having told or testified, honest, either to his/her employer, or to the judicial or administrative authorities, of facts of corruption. Any discriminatory measure is invalid;

By way of conclusion, sustainable development is henceforth a part of the communication of large companies. It is what all the interested parties wait for (for "stakeholders": used, customers, local residents, labor unions (syndicates), authorities, NGO, shareholders, etc.).

We can wonder however legally if this communication is not an effect of facade "a window dressing room". How many concrete and effective actions can these companies boast? When they exist, are these actions integrated into the strategy of the company or are they only intended to be isolated initiatives to feed the annual report? It is this which we will try to develop in our next research.

References

AFNOR (French National Organization For Standardization), ISO 26000 in 10 questions, (2010), P. 5

Auer, P., G. Besse and D. Méda, "Relocations, standards of the work and employment policy towards a more just globalization? "THE DISCOVERY, (Paris, 2005)

Chaveau, A. and J.J. Rosé, "The responsible company, the publishing of organizations", (2003) P. 225

D'Humières. P. and all, Sustainable development: the management of the responsible company, the publishing of organizations, (2005) P.: 107

Ecopass: guide of reference tables of sustainable development: which tools for a strategy of sustainable development available on the web site http: // www.ecopass.fr/developpement-durable-2.html

Gillet, C. "The study of the determiners of the check of the societal information in the French context"; Doctoral thesis in science of management supported on November 23rd, 2010 at the University of Montpelier.

Giordano, G.R. "The quality of the societal information: an experiment relative to the environmental audit"; Doctoral thesis supported at the University of Montpelier 1 option: science of management, supported publicly on December 3rd, 2007

International Labour Office, "The principles of the work of the World Pact of United Nations. Guide for companies", (Geneva, 2010).

OECD, "Guiding Principles of the OECD for the Multinational Companies", Revision 2000

OECD Contribution to the United Nations Commission on Sustainable Development: Energy for Sustainable Development 2007

PricewaterhouseCoopers, "Departments of inquiries and law and accounting, Economic crime: celebrity, culture and controls, biennial world investigation «Global Economic Crime Survey", (2007) P. 22.

Report Brundtland, Our Common Future, 1987, available on the web site www.un-documents.net / wcedocf.htm.

CHAPTER ELEVEN

ACCOUNTABILITY IN GOVERNANCE: THE CASE OF JUDGEMENT / SETTLEMENT DEBT PAYMENTS IN GHANA

RUBY MELODY AGBOLA AND EVANS SOKRO

Introduction / Background

Corruption and fraud in the procurement of goods and services for the public is a major problem that plagues most governments across the world, especially in the developing countries of Africa, and Ghana is no exception. The Government of Ghana under the Mills administration is reported to have paid out a total of GH¢624 million as judgement and settlement debts in its first three years in office (http://edition. myjoyonline.com/pages/news). The majority of these were the payment of debts resulting from a breach of contract in the procurement of certain goods and services for the Ghanaian public. Institutions and individuals who benefited from such payments include Construction Pioneers (€94 million), Waterville Holdings (€25 million), and the businessman Alfred Agbesi Woyome (GH¢51.2 million). Other judgement debt claims yet to be settled include Isofoton and Africa Automobile's claims of USD$1.3million and USD$1.5 billion respectively.

However, investigations into the payments by the Economic and Organised Crime Office (EOCO) revealed that most of the payments made were either fraudulently obtained or resulted from previous governments' disregard for contractual agreements. The Auditor-General's 2010 Report on Public Accounts submitted to Parliament also indicated that GH¢276 million of the total judgment debt paid by the government to various claimants, representing 11% of total government administrative expenditure, could have been avoided if public officials had taken precautionary measures in performing their official duties. Procurement contracts are awarded and cancelled by successive governments in a point scoring match. Contracts are sometimes abrogated through the arbitrary and, in some instances, capricious use of power. In the end, huge sums of money that could have been expended on essential social services are lost senselessly to individuals and firms whose services the state did not enjoy.

Study Objectives

1. To investigate the extent to which the public institutions of accountability and mechanisms of control operate effectively to ensure that those who exercise power account for their stewardship in the use of public funds.
2. To assess the public's perception of the judgement debt payments.
3. To investigate the implications of the judgement debt cases for institutional development in the country.

Literature Review

Judgement/Settlement Debt

Judgment debt is the amount of money awarded by a court to the winner of a court case and payable by the losing party. It is "a legal obligation to pay a debt or damages evidenced by a judgement entered in a court of record and enforceable by execution or other judicial process" (http://www.merriam-webster.com/dictionary). Judgement debt may be obtained by full litigation or by default when the defendant fails to file a defence, leading to a judgement given in favour of the claimant unopposed. Thus, judgement debts are debts that have been reviewed by a judge in a court of law, and found to be valid. Judgement debt must be distinguished from settlement debt, or debt arbitration, which is an approach to debt reduction in which the debtor and creditor agree on a reduced balance, a sum lesser than the original amount that will be regarded as payment in full.

Debt settlement is sometimes preferred to full law suits because a considerable percentage of the outstanding balance can be reduced or forgiven through the settlement negotiations, and the arbitration process avoids lengthy, acrimonious legal wrangling. However, debt settlement robs the debt resolution process of transparency, full litigation and the thorough interrogation of issues, evidence and witnesses leading to an authoritative verdict by a court of competent jurisdiction. Hence, the debt settlement process is open to the fraudulent manipulation of state officials charged with negotiating such settlements on behalf of the state.

In the case of the recent breach of contract debt payments in Ghana, it is important to note that most of the payments were settlements rather than judgement debt payments.

Public procurement

Public procurement refers to the acquisition of goods, services and works by a procuring entity using public funds (World Bank, 1995a). According to Roodhooft and Abbeele (2006), public bodies have always been big purchasers, dealing with huge budgets. Public procurement represents 18.42% of the world GDP (Mahmood, 2010), and in developing countries, it is increasingly recognised as essential in service delivery (Basheka and Bisangabasaija, 2010), and accounts for a high proportion of total expenditure (Tukamuhabwa, 2012). In Ghana, it "accounted for more than 70% of government expenditure after personnel emoluments" (Chairman of the PPGB, 19/09/2012). Due to the huge amount of money involved in government procurement and the fact that such money comes from the public, there is a need for accountability and transparency (Hui et al; 2011).

Consequently, various countries—both developed and lesser-developed countries—have instituted procurement reforms involving laws and regulations. However, the major obstacle has been inadequate regulatory compliance (Tukamuhabwa 2012). De Boer and Telgen (1998) confirm that non-compliance problems affect not only third-world countries, but also countries in the developed world. For example, in the US, for the fiscal year ending September 30, 2006, the government recovered a record total of more than $3.1 billion in settlements and judgments from cases involving claims of fraud (Lander et al., 2010). Odhiambo-Mbai (2003) also observes that the level of accountability in the management of public affairs in Kenya has consistently declined since independence. A report by the OECD notes that, although public procurement has been employed as a vital instrument for achieving economic, social and other objectives, it is regrettably an area vulnerable to mismanagement and corruption (OECD, 2007). Procurement fraud squanders limited funds, threatens safety and national defence, cheats taxpayers, and harms government efforts to obtain required goods and services.

Although fraud in public procurement has long been established as a major problem in Ghanaian public management and despite the recent public and national uproar over huge payments of judgement/settlement debts in connection with procurement and financial engineering, very few, if any, scholarly studies exist which systematically examine public accountability relating to the various judgement debt payments by the government, the mechanisms of control, and the extent to which these mechanisms are effectively implemented and enforced to hold officials entrusted with the disbursement of public funds accountable for their stewardship.

Public Accountability

The Encyclopaedia of Democracy defines public accountability as "the ability to determine who in government is responsible for a decision or action and the ability to ensure that public officials are answerable for their actions". According to Bonsu (1998), accountability is not just the responsible exercise of authority, but is also concerned with ensuring that those who exercise power account for their stewardship to the ultimate source of power – the people. Due to the enormous authority given to public officials, including in particular the exercise of discretionary powers, it has become necessary to hold public officers accountable for their actions as a way of preventing the misuse and abuse of power/authority/position. Whenever an action is taken in the name of the state, the state becomes responsible for that action. Furthermore, because of the massive injection of public and donor funds and loans, it is important to hold public actors accountable for the manner in which public funds are disbursed.

Furthermore, evaluating the ongoing effectiveness of public officials or public bodies ensures that they perform to their full potential, provides value for money in the provision of public services (Bovens ,2006), instils confidence in the government, and ensures responsiveness to the community they are meant to be serving. Basically, public accountability is the cornerstone of modern democracy, and is central to good governance. According to Adefila & Adeoti (2001), it is the parameter for judging the public expectation of fairness, responsiveness and exemplary leadership

According to a World Bank document, the concept of accountability involves two distinct stages: *answerability* and *enforcement*. Answerability refers to the obligation of the government, its agencies and public officials to provide information about their decisions and actions, and to justify them to the public and those institutions of accountability tasked with providing oversight. Enforcement suggests that the public or the institution responsible for accountability can sanction the offending party or remedy the contravening behaviour, (http://siteresources.worldbank.org/public sectorandgovernance/Resources).

Types of Accountability

The concept of accountability can be classified according to the type of accountability exercised and/or the person, group or institution the public official answers to, and can be conceptualized by reference to opposing forms of accountability. Public accountability is therefore classified into horizontal versus vertical accountability, political versus legal accountability, and social versus diagonal accountability.

Horizontal versus Vertical Accountability

Horizontal accountability is the capacity of state institutions to check abuses by other public agencies and branches of government, or the requirement for agencies to report sideways. Its institutions include the judiciary, independent constitutional commissions, the public accounts committee and agencies of restraints on executive and official power. Alternatively, vertical accountability is the means through which citizens, mass media and civil society seek to enforce standards of good performance on officials. According to Professor Gimah Boadi (2005), vertical accountability refers to the accountability that political leaders owe their followers, and to that owed by public officials to tax payers. It is usually secured through a system of campaigns and elections resulting in officials holding office at the pleasure of voters.

Bovens (2006) notes that vertical accountability can also refer to the principal-agent relationship, whereby the principal delegates to the agent and the agent is accountable to their direct superiors in the chain-of-command. For instance, the public official answers to the department/agency minister, the department answers to the minister, the minister answers to parliament, and parliament answers to citizens. Parliament is thus a key actor in terms of holding government officials to account. Parliament, as principal, requires the government and its officials, as agents, to implement the laws, policies and programs it has approved – and holds the government and officials to account for their performance in this regard. Parliament is also an agent, in that the electorate (the principal) elects legislators to enact laws and oversee government actions on their behalf. The electorates then hold legislators to account at election time.

Political versus Legal Accountability

Parliament and the judiciary act as horizontal constitutional checks on the power of the executive. While parliament holds the executive politically accountable, the judiciary holds the executive legally accountable. Together, they provide ongoing oversight in order to keep the government accountable throughout its term in office. Political accountability usually manifests itself in the concept of individual ministerial responsibility in the sense that parliament can call on ministers during question time or through the public accounts committee to answer questions regarding their stewardship. The judiciary holds the executive and other public officers accountable by determining the constitutionality of their actions, and imposes judgement and punishment on those found guilty of contravening the law.

Social versus Diagonal Accountability

The concept of social accountability relies on civic engagement, a situation whereby ordinary citizens, the press and/or civil society organizations participate directly or indirectly in exacting accountability. Mechanisms of social accountability are often "*demand-driven*" and operate from the bottom-up (Goetz & Gaventa, 2001). Where press freedom exists, the press is usually very vocal on matters of accountability, and regularly informs the public of actions bordering on impropriety by public officers. The role of the members of parliament is paramount in providing weight to such grassroots accountability mechanisms. For example, a Member of Parliament can represent the concerns of his/her constituents by questioning a Minister during question time in parliament.

According to the World Bank Institute (2005), social accountability involves mechanisms of diagonal accountability which seek to engage citizens directly in the workings of horizontal accountability institutions in an effort to augment the limited effectiveness of civil society's watch dog function by breaking the state's monopoly over the responsibility for official executive oversight. Mechanisms of diagonal accountability include community advocates' participation in institutions of horizontal accountability, such as independent constitutional commissions and various commissions of enquiry that may be set up to investigate the wrongdoings of public officials; community advocates' ability to access classified information about government agencies; the authority to compel a government agency to answer questions; and the acquisition of the authority of the horizontal accountability institution to enforce the findings or influence elected officials.

Ultimately, parliaments are key actors in what has been termed the 'chain of accountability'. They are, along with the judiciary, the key institution of horizontal accountability, not only in their own right, but also as the institution to which many autonomous accountability institutions report. They are the vehicle through which political accountability is exercised. Along with civil society organizations and the mass media, they are also important institutions in vertical accountability (http://site resources.worldbank.org/publicsectorandgovernance/Resources)

Mechanisms of Accountability in Ghana

In Ghana, a number of control mechanisms are put in place to ensure public accountability in the use of public funds, including the following:

- The Economic and Organised Crime Office (EOCO)
- Parliamentary control
- Professional codes of ethics
- Financial administration laws & regulations
- The Auditor Generals Department
- The courts
- The media
- National elections

The Economic and Organised Crime Office (EOCO)

The Economic and Organized Crime Office (EOCO), was set up by Act 804 of 2010 in line with Article 190 (1(d)) of the 1992 constitution as one of the Public Services of Ghana to supplement and augment the government's efforts in the fight against corruption in the State. The Office was established as a specialized agency of the government to monitor, investigate and, on the authority of the Attorney-General, prosecute any offence involving serious financial and economic loss to the state. The Act replaces the former Serious Fraud Office Act, 1993 (Act 466). EOCO is mandated by Section 3(1) (a), (b), (c), (d) and (2) S.12, and S.13 to investigate any suspected offence provided for by law which appears to the Executive Director on reasonable grounds to involve serious financial or economic loss to the state or to any state organisation or other institution in which the state has a financial interest; to detect crimes likely to cause financial and economic loss to the state; and to take reasonable measures to prevent the commission of crimes which may cause financial or economic loss to the state. Can EOCO be relied upon to effectively investigate government and public officials who commit financial crimes against the state impartially, without fear or favour?

Parliamentary Control

As John Stuart Mills notes, parliaments function to watch and control the government, throw the light of publicity on its acts, compel a full exposition and justification of acts which anyone considers questionable, and to censure them if found condemnable. In Ghana, the legislature has the authority of oversight over the operations of the government and the ability to criticize said operations. This is to ensure that public office holders conduct the affairs of the country in a responsible manner. Parliament uses the Public Accounts Committee, the Estimate Committee, Departmental Standing Committees, and Question Time as means of controlling the acts of public officials. Other methods available for parliament to control the executive branch of government include: impeachment, approval of policies and agreements initiated by the executive, and the motion of censure. Does the Ghanaian parliament exercise effective oversight over the government and other public officials?

Professional Codes of Ethics

Organizations and professions also try to ensure proper conduct of office by instituting codes of ethics and conduct to regulate the excesses of public officers which otherwise could lead to the exercise of uncontrolled power, fraud, nepotism, negligence and inefficiency. The major question in the case of Ghana is: did the public officials involved in the judgement debt payment scandals do due diligence, conduct themselves with professionalism and diligently follow the codes of ethics of their respective professions?

Financial Administration Laws and Regulations

To ensure financial propriety and accountability for their actions, public officers/heads of department, and spending officers are regulated by a set of financial procedures, rules and regulations including the Financial Administration Regulations (FAR) NRCD 123 1979, the Financial Administration Act 2003, Act 654, and the Public Procurement Act 2003, Act 663, which indicate the manner in which the security and custody of assets, as well as expenditure, are disbursed. The Financial Administration Act 2003, Act 654, was established "to regulate the financial management of the public sector; prescribe the responsibilities of persons entrusted with financial management in the government; ensure the effective and efficient management of state revenue, expenditure, assets, liabilities, resources of the government, the Consolidated Fund and other public funds and to provide for matters related to these". Article 17 (1) of the Act states that "a contract that provides for the payment of any money by the government shall not be considered valid without the prior approval of the Minister". The question is, did the Minister of Finance approve the payments made to Woyome, and on what basis was the approval made?

The Public Procurement Act 2003, Act 663, specifies public procurement methods, tendering procedures, the conduct of procurement proceedings and the award of procurement contracts, in addition to establishing the Public Procurement Board charged with the duty to "harmonise the processes of public procurement, secure a judicious, economic and efficient use of state resources and ensure that public procurement is carried out in a fair, transparent and non-discriminatory manner".

Furthermore, Article 62 (1) of the Financial Administration Act 2003, Act 654, states that any public official who conspires with another person to defraud the Government, or provides an opportunity for another person to defraud the Government, deliberately permits the contravention of the law by another person, wilfully makes or signs a false entry in a book or wilfully makes or signs a false certificate, commits an offence, and is liable on summary conviction to a fine not exceeding 5000 penalty units or to imprisonment for a term not exceeding 10 years, or to both.

Unfortunately, the Act is silent over the abrogation of public procurement contracts and compensation for the termination of such contracts, thereby creating room for the fraudulent manipulation of both government and private officials involved in the procurement of goods and services for the public. Are our public procurement laws adequate to protect public coffers against fraud and corruption? Did government officials involved in the procurement process follow all the stipulations of the Public Procurement Act?

The Judiciary and the Courts

The Judiciary, or the law courts, is the branch of government responsible for the settlement of disputes, the enforcement of civil and criminal cases, and the interpretation and protection of the laws of the country. The judiciary exercises legal and horizontal accountability over executives to ensure that government and public officials who break the law are duly punished. The law courts have been deeply involved with the judgement debt cases since their onset; however, questions have been raised about the capacity and ability of the Attorney General's Department to successfully prosecute those accused of illicit involvement in the judgement debt payment issues. Is the government committed to bringing those who default the state to justice?

The Auditor Generals Department

The office of the Auditor-General is extra-ministerial and is given power by Article 187 (2) of the 1992 Constitution to audit all the public accounts of Ghana, including the courts, central and local government bodies, all bodies enacted by an Act of Parliament, and all institutions in which the government has shares or a stake. The payment of all judgement debts by the government has been captured in the Auditor-General's 2010 Report on Public Accounts submitted to Parliament by the Auditor-General. The Auditor-General's Report also indicated that GH¢276 million of the total judgment debt paid could have been avoided if public officials had taken precautionary measures in performing their official duties. Could those public officials responsible for such needless payments be apprehended and prosecuted for their negligence, fraud or corruption?

Media Publicity

The media and civil society groups hold governments socially accountable and play a critical role in public and corporate accountability. Through the media, the general public and the corporate community are made aware of regulatory outcomes (Zubcic and Sims, 2011). Hui et al. (2011) stated that, in Malaysia, the wide publication of tenders in the media such as newspapers and websites could help reduce corruption by increasing transparency and participation, thereby enhancing public procurement compliance. According to Borden (2007), media exposure reduces the incidence of wrongdoing through press coverage that highlights instances of wrongdoing. In an environment of heightened and effective press coverage of misconduct, others contemplating misconduct may be discouraged. Related to this, UNDP (2010) indicated that many procurement scandals have been uncovered by the media, and highlighted that a free and independent press is a powerful tool in the promotion of transparency and accountability.

Ghana currently enjoys a wide degree of press freedom. In 2008, there were over 136 newspapers, 11 TV stations, over 21 radio stations and increasing internet access (http://www.pressreference.com/Fa-Gu/Ghana. html). Does the Ghanaian media report issues fairly and impartially to constitute an effective source of social accountability?

National Elections

The idea that voters use elections to hold governments to account lies at the heart of democratic theory. If governments fail to provide policy outcomes preferred by the majority of the citizenry, they are likely to lose office. In turn, a solid government record that is largely in tune with public demands may secure re-election. Put in the words of Vladimir O. Key (1966, 568), elections allow citizens to act as the "rational god of vengeance and reward". In order for citizens to judge if an incumbent deserves to be re-elected on the basis of past performance, voters need to be aware of government actions and the outcomes of these activities (Vries & Giger, 2012). However, studies show that the extent to which electorates are able to cast their votes based on a logical assessment of incumbents' performance depends upon the individual's political sophistication and the availability of information to the individual electorate (Gomez & Wilson, 2006; Duch, 2001). But are Ghanaian electorates politically sophisticated or well-informed enough to make voting decisions based on a critical analysis of the issues?

Research Methods

Question	Yes	No	Neutral/Don't Know
1. Do you think the EOCO reports are credible in their exposition of fraud in the judgement/settlement debt payments?	80.9%	19.1%	0%
2. Do you think parliament exercises effective control and oversight over the government?	35%	61.3%	3.7%
3. Are Ghana's procurement laws adequate to protect public coffers against fraud and corruption?	53%	25%	22%
4. Do you trust the Attorney General's Department and the Minister of Justice to effectively prosecute government officials and all those implicated in the judgement debt fraud?	31%	56%	13%
5. In your opinion, does the media report on issues in an unbiased and non-partisan manner?	55%	45%	0%
6. Will the judgement/settlement debt cases be the main considerations for your voting decisions in the December elections?	28%	11%	61%

Figure 11.1: Research questions

The research procedure applied was mainly the careful analysis of source materials including newspaper articles, parliamentary proceedings, government documents and public reports, as well as radio and television reports. A 6-item survey questionnaire was also administered to the general public at various parts of Accra (including shopping malls, markets, university campuses and lorry stations) to ascertain the public's opinion on the judgement/settlement debt payment issues. In all, a total of 1568 people were polled. The results were analysed using frequencies and percentages.

Research Findings

The Effectiveness of the Mechanisms of Accountability in the Judgement Debt Payment Cases:

At the outbreak of news about the judgement debt payment fraud, the EOCO was charged by the late President John Evans Atta Mills to investigate the payments. The office indicted a number of people, including present and past government officials, namely:

- Businessman Alfred Agbesi Woyome for making false claims to obtain 51.2 million for the abrogation of a contract that never existed. "Mr. Woyome manipulated documents and information, and riding on the negligence and/or complicity of public officials, managed to receive money which he was clearly not entitled to". (EOCO Reports, 2012).
- Former Chief State Attorney Nerquaye-Tetteh, who refused to contest Woyome's fraudulent claims, leading to a default judgement in favour of Woyome.
- Mrs Gifty Nerquaye-Tetteh, the wife of the above, into whose account Woyome paid ₵ 400,000.00.
- Paul Asimenu, the Director of Legal Services at the Ministry of Finance and Economic Planning, was accused of providing information that aided Woyome in obtaining the fraudulent payments.
- Former Deputy Minister for Education and Sports under the Kufuor administration, Mr. Osei Bonsu Amoah, was accused of not following the laid-down procedures stipulated in the procurement law guidelines when awarding the contract to Waterville Holdings. His political campaign was financed by Woyome.
- Mr. Osarfo Maafo, the Minister for Education and Sports under the Kufour administration, was accused of the illicit abrogation of the contract with Waterville leading to a €25million settlement debt payment.

- Mrs Betty Mould Iddrisu, the former Attorney General, was accused of failing to go to court, preferring to settle the breach of contract claims, some of which turned out to be fraudulent, out of court without due diligence and even disregarding the late president Mills' instruction to go to court.
- Mrs Betty Mould Iddrisu, was also accused of paying an out-of-court settlement of €94million to Construction Pioneers (CP) without due diligence.
- The Minister of Finance and Economic Planning, Dr Kwabena Duffour, for paying out the judgement/settlement debts out of government coffers without due diligence as required by the Financial Administrative Regulations.

The EOCO reports also stated that the late President Mills tried unsuccessfully to stop the Woyome payments, raising questions as to the extent to which the President was in control of the affairs of the government. The former President was reported to have instructed the Attorney General Betty Mould Iddrisu to contest the default judgement obtained by Woyome and to withhold subsequent payment of the remaining amount after the initial payment of over Gh¢17 million in February 2010. Mrs Betty Mould Iddrisu however, disregarded the President's orders and went ahead to negotiate an out-of-court payment plan for an additional Gh¢34 million paid in three instalments. This, according to critics, is "evidence of leadership paralysis, if not deliberate connivance" (http://www.ghanaweb.com/Ghana). The sudden and untimely death of President Mills on the 24th of July 2012 gives further credence to the suggestion that, due to ill health, the former President was unable to exercise full control over his cabinet and staff, leading to rampant corruption and disregard for the principles of probity and accountability by government officials.

The authority of EOCO to investigate the judgement debt payment cases was, however, challenged by the main opposition party, the New Patriotic Party (NPP), on the grounds that EOCO was not an independent institution, and therefore might not conduct a fair and impartial investigation since members of the ruling New Democratic Congress (NDC), officials of the Attorney General's Department, and other government officials were implicated in the cases. Section 4 of Act 466 places the EOCO under the Attorney General. The Director and two Deputies of the office are appointed by the President, and the Minister of Justice and the Attorney General are responsible for the EOCO. However, the then Attorney General was herself implicated in the case. Former president John Agyekum Kufour consequently advised his party members not to cooperate with the EOCO investigations.

However, despite initial objections, our survey shows that 80.9% of those questioned agree that the EOCO reports were credible. Thus, the EOCO reports have come to be accepted by the majority of Ghanaians as a true and authoritative exposition of fraud and corruption within the present government and, to some extent, within the previous government's financial administration of the country.

Effectiveness of Parliamentary Oversight

Parliament has, in the course of these scandals, subjected the majority of those implicated in the case to severe scrutiny by the Public Accounts Committee. The former Attorney General and Minister of Justice Betty Mould Iddrisu was subjected to questioning by the Public Accounts Committee (PAC) for her role in the payment of the GH¢51.2 million to Woyome and the €94 million to CP. The PAC of Parliament also established that Construction Pioneers Ltd. (CP) owed the government 284 million deutsche marks and GH¢5.2 million in tax liabilities at the time that the government entered into an agreement to pay the company €94 million as settlement debts. Irrespective of this, CP was able to claim the €94 million without paying what it owed the government in tax liabilities to the state. Why did the former minister decide to settle the case with CP without taking care to ensure that investigations were conducted into all of CP's dealings with the government before the payment was made? Appearing before the PAC on the 12th of July, the former Minister of Justice informed parliament that she acted professionally and in the interest of Ghana in reducing the €162 million claimed by CP to €94 million through the settlement negotiations.

Some members of the public had called for the impeachment of the late President Mills for "overseeing" the fraudulent payment of the colossal judgement debts, but this was probably farfetched as there has been no proven link between the late President and the "gargantuan fraud". Should parliament have moved a motion to censure ministers involved in the case? The majority of Ghanaians think the Minister of Justice, Betty Mould Iddrisu, should have been censured and prosecuted for her role in the case. Consequently, Mrs Mould Iddrisu has resigned from her post following the EOCO investigation.

Although parliament had been instrumental in ensuring that public officials involved in the judgement/settlement debt cases offered explanations and justification for their conduct, as well as in apportioning blame to those found wanting, it did not call for the arrest and prosecution of suspects. Could parliament do more to ensure that the future occurrence of such cases is prevented? Does the Ghanaian parliament as an institution exercise real and effective oversight over the executive to control the excesses of the government and its officials? Our research reveals that only 35% of those polled believe that parliament exercises adequate oversight over the executive. The majority of those polled are of the view that parliament is too polarised to exercise any real and objective control over the government.

The manner in which the Parliament of Ghana has carried out its oversight role has come under sharp criticism from the Chairman of the Public Accounts Committee, Mr Albert Kan Dapaah, who regretted how the government majority, over time, had endorsed in an omnibus manner whatever was presented by the executive. Speaking on the topic 'Parliament's Role in Ensuring Transparency in the Oil & Gas Sector', the PAC chairman stated that:

> "While we hail the victory of democracy in our country, parliament, which is the central institution of democracy and the key institution in oversight, suffers from a crisis of credibility,"[1]

Ghanaian MPs are noted for voting on party lines and supporting their party's position on all issues without any real justification, even when common sense points to the contrary. This is because criticizing one's own party's position on any issue is seen as disloyalty and treachery. As such, leaving the task of holding the executive accountable for the way state resources are managed in the hands of parliament will only serve to entrench the chronic state of corruption and mismanagement of public funds. Until MPs are ready to defend the constitution of the country and the will of its people in the discharge of their mandate against parochial party, and personal, interests, the ability of parliament to exercise significant oversight over the current government will continue to be severely limited.

The Adequacy of the Public Procurement Laws

Were the public procurement laws effectively implemented and enforced in the procurement processes that resulted in the disputed judgement/settlement debts for the country? The former Deputy Minister

---

[1] http://iamaghanaian.com/index.php?do=/news/ghana-parliament-suffers-credibili ty-crisis

for Education and Sports under the Kufuor Administration, Mr Osei Bonsu Amoah, who was instrumental in the awarding of the contracts to Waterville Holdings for the rehabilitation of the Accra, Kumasi and Elwak sports stadia, was said to have instructed the contractors to start work on the projects immediately after the signing of the memorandum of understanding (MOU) while awaiting the official signing of the substantive contractual agreement; an action which constituted a clear breach of procurement regulation. The question therefore is: was due process followed in the awarding of the contract?

A major flaw in the Public Procurement Act 2003, Act 663, is its silence over the abrogation of contracts and compensation for the termination of such contracts. Consequently, most of the breach of contract claims and subsequent judgement/settlement debts were the result of the illicit abrogation of contracts entered into with the government. The Managing Director of Waterville Holdings (BVI), Mr Andreas Orlandi, argued that Waterville, through an open, fair and international bidding process and in compliance with the Ghana Public Procurement Law, won a contract to construct two new stadia and rehabilitate two others. However, in spite of Waterville being granted approval for the work on the stadia, the government decided to re-award two of the stadia already awarded to Waterville to the Shanghai Construction Group. "The procurement process for the two stadia awarded to Shanghai was not in compliance of the Public Procurement Law" (http://edition.myjoyonline.com/pages/news). This situation is indicative of gross disregard for public procurement laws and a breach of contract causing financial loss to the state.

The then Vice President under the Mills Administration, Mr John Dramani Mahama, now the President of Ghana, having taken over the presidency after the sudden demise of President Mills, stated in an interview with Shaka Ssali of Straight Talk Africa on VOA Africa that most of the judgement debts the NDC government is saddled with were caused by the previous NPP government, which, after coming to power in 2001, abrogated several contracts with many foreign, international and local companies, leading to the crystallisation of many of these debts when the NDC returned to power in 2009.

Most notable among these abrogated contracts are the procurement contracts with: Waterville Holdings for the rehabilitation of stadia which resulted in the payment of €25 million to Waterville and the controversial Gh¢51.2 million to Woyome; Isofoton, a Spanish company contracted to execute the rural solar electrification project for Ghana under the Spanish protocol agreement with the Government of Ghana, leading to a claim of $1.5 million for breach of contract; and African Automobile, contracted by the former NDC government in 1999 to import 86 cross country vehicles which were delivered in 2001 for distribution to local assemblies but have been left to rot in a bonded warehouse because the NPP government which took over office refused to pay for or use the vehicles, claiming a lack of contract, a lack of appropriate documentation, and the vehicles' failure to meet the required specifications. African Automobile is now claiming $1.5 billion from the NDC with whom the initial contract was entered.

The major question here, therefore, is: are our public procurement laws robust enough to insulate the state against fraudulent manipulations by public and private officials involved in the procurement process? The opinion of our respondents on the issue was sharply divided. While 53% believe the laws are adequate, 25% answered 'No' and 22% 'Don't know'. It's important to note that the procurement laws themselves are not the problem, rather it is their implementation and enforcement that are problematic. However, it may also be important to rewrite the current procurement laws to include clear conditions under which contracts with the state could be legitimately abrogated.

While it is legally and morally imperative that a successor government has the authority to review all contracts and liabilities it inherited from a previous government, it is crucial that constitutional or legislative measures are put in place to ensure that legally binding contractual agreements of the state are honoured regardless of which particular government entered into the initial agreement. Hence, any decision to abrogate a contract, particularly those with foreign companies which normally have huge financial implications for the state, must obtain parliamentary approval or be disclosed publicly together with the reasons for abrogation, which should include the cost-benefit analysis.

Capacity of Judicial Oversight

The capacity of the law courts, particularly that of the Attorney General's Department, to effectively prosecute and punish those who have been involved in the fraudulent payment of the gargantuan judgement/settlement debt payments has been called into question. To date, only the businessman Alfred Agbesi Woyome, who is accused of making fraudulent claims to obtain ¢51.2million in default judgement, is currently facing prosecution at the high court. All the current and former government officials and others implicated in the cases have been let off the hook, raising questions about the government's commitment to prosecute these corruption cases and the ability of Ghanaian courts to exercise effective oversight over the government.

Results from our polls show that only 31% of the Ghanaian public trust the AG Department to effectively prosecute government officials accused of illicit involvement in the judgement/settlement debt fraud. No-one, for example, understands why the state, in a dramatic twist, entered a *nolle prosequi* on Tuesday 5th June, on the basis of which the court dropped all charges against the three others being prosecuted for their role in the Woyome case. Why were the charges dropped entirely?

Why did the then Attorney General refuse to contest Mr. Woyome's fraudulent claim against the state leading to the award of the Gh¢51.2 million judgement debt? Why didn't the Attorney General contact the former government officials regarding the award of the stadia procurement contracts in order to ascertain the facts and establish the legitimacy of the claim?

An even more pressing question on the minds of most Ghanaians is why did the state decide to settle the breach of contract cases out of court, rather than vigorously pursue them in court, especially when the legitimacy and legality of some of the supposed procurement contracts were clearly in doubt? It is important to note that most of the prominent so-called judgement debt cases were actually out-of-court settlements negotiated by the former Attorney General Betty Mould Iddrisu. According to Martin Amidu, a former Attorney General who was dismissed by the Mills administration for 'misconduct' in the wake of the Woyome scandal; "As long as the state has a good case, we should not abandon the courts and rush for out-of-court settlement, just to build evidence against others" (http://www.graphic.com.gh/features/page.php? news). The Auditor-General's 2010 report also stated that those who undertook the negotiations and authorised the payments could not always explain and justify the need for such payments.

As the former Vice President and current President John Dramani Mahama explained:

> "Previously we had no rules by which the Attorney General operated; he used his discretion to decide which case to pursue in court and which to settle. But the lesson we have learnt is that you need not leave this discretion to one person"
> (http://www.youtube.com/watch?v=wSomcwdZhWI)

The Cabinet has therefore decided to fix a ceiling of GH¢10 million on judgement/settlement debt paid by the Attorney General. Any amount exceeding this must be referred to the Cabinet for consideration. Although this new ceiling has the potential of reducing the level of losses, one wonders whether the policy is far-reaching enough to curb the future abuse of such discretionary powers.

A more worrying phenomenon has been the ability of the law courts, especially that of the AG Department, to successfully prosecute people who defraud or commit crimes against the state. The state of Ghana under the Mills administration has lost all 13 high profile cases in succession, raising questions about the ability, expertise and motivation of government lawyers charged with the duty of defending the state to deliver on their mandate. Reasons given for the state's frequent loss of cases include:

- undue politicisation of cases;
- the haste of the AG Department to rush cases to court without careful investigation;
- the inexperience or incompetence of lawyers in the AG's office leading to the filing of wrong law suits;
- inadequate personnel at the AG's office to represent the government in certain cases, leading to accused persons being discharged for want of prosecution;
- inadequate budgetary allocation of funds for the training of staff, and provision of necessary materials for effective and efficient professional services to the state;
- corruption in the AG Department, resulting in the lack of interest in ensuring that those who defraud the state are duly prosecuted and punished.

The sacked Attorney General Martin Amidu claimed, among other things, that a government minister was trying to frustrate his attempts to prosecute Woyome who had perpetrated "gargantuan crimes" against the people of Ghana. Mr. Amidu will be remembered for being the one who introduced the word 'gargantuan' into the vocabulary of the ordinary Ghanaian.

Furthermore, the delay in prosecuting Woyome, for example, is partly attributed to the difficulty in recovering documents relating to the awarding and subsequent abrogation of the CAN 2008 stadia procurement contracts. The prosecution has accused former government officials of destroying and/or hiding important documents crucial to the successful prosecution of the case. It is no secret that in Ghana and most developing countries of Africa, public officers normally leave office with the office – taking with them important documents to cover their tracks or simply to frustrate their successors and render them ineffective.

Given the current calibre of lawyers at the AG's office, the institutional weaknesses of the department and the challenges of resource and material constraints, the prospects of the state successfully prosecuting and winning cases against those accused of defrauding or causing financial loss to the state in the judgement/settlement debt saga are very slim.

The Media & Civil Society Groups

The media has been vociferous in exposing corruption, fraudulent dealings and other forms of wrongdoing by government and public officials, as well as corporate and private officials. The Woyome case was first broken by Adom FM back in December 2011, and was fiercely pursued and anatomically digested on a daily basis by most media houses throughout the country. The media's daily exposition on the case has kept the public informed about the judgement debt saga. The use of TV and radio call-ins and social network sites like Facebook and Twitter also enables the public to express their opinions and condemnation for what they see as corruption and abuse of office by the government.

Given the high level of press freedom in the country, one would expect that the media's exposition of issues would objectively inform the public about issues of national importance, thereby giving the public the opportunity to make an informed decision about government activities and the behaviour of public actors. Unfortunately, our polls show that only 55% of the public think the media reports on issues in an unbiased, non-partisan manner.

The Ghanaian media is polarised and is often seen as an instrument of political propaganda for the two main political parties – NDC and NPP, rather than as a reliable source of public information. As such, any revelations of wrongdoings can simply be dismissed by either side of the political divide as mere propaganda aimed at discrediting the opponent, a situation which has limited the effectiveness of the media as a forceful tool of public accountability.

The implication here is that, for effective social accountability, the media cannot be totally relied upon. The onus, therefore, lies with civil society organisations like ISODEC, AFAG and IMANI Ghana to exercise diagonal accountability by intensifying their campaigns against fraud and corruption in public actors. Civil society groups must insist on membership in various commissions of enquiry so as to influence other institutions of horizontal accountability in issues of public interest.

National Elections

No other scandal has consumed the Ghanaian electorate in recent years as much as the judgement debt scandals, particularly the 'gargantuan' payment made to Woyome and the involvement of several government and public officials. The potential of the scandals to influence the voting behaviour of Ghanaians in the forthcoming elections cannot be overemphasised. While the Mills/Mahama government is focused on propagating their "unprecedented achievements" over the last   3–4 years, the opposition parties, especially the NPP, are bent on making the judgement debt scandals a major part of their electioneering campaign and hammering the level of corruption in the government in order to turn the electorates against a government which came to power on the back of promises to fight corruption and restore probity, accountability and good governance. However, the demise of President Mills and the nationwide testimony of his honesty, dedication to country and his 'Better Ghana Agenda', and most importantly, his pursuit of peace, which earned him the title "Asomdweehene", will no doubt affect voters' opinion of the government.

Our investigations reveal that only 28% of the public categorically declare that the judgement debt cases will be the main consideration for their voting decisions during the forthcoming December elections. The majority (61%) is neutral and the remaining 11% answered 'No'. Consequently, the extent to which the scandals will play a decisive role in the outcome of the forthcoming elections depends partly upon how the events, especially the court cases, unfold, and partly upon the economic conditions of the country.

Most people vote based on their personal economic situation – whether they are able to afford daily meals for themselves and their families, pay their children's school fees and meet the basic necessities of life – as well as the general macro-economic conditions of the country as a whole. A significant number of people also vote along tribal lines and dogmatic allegiance to certain political parties.

Although the government has managed to keep inflation in single digits over a sustained period, there is a general feeling of a worsening economic condition throughout the country, partly due to the continuing depreciation of the national currency. The question as to whether the judgement debt scandals will have a significant impact on the December elections is anyone's guess. To prevent a negative impact, the government must take measures to ensure that all those who connived to defraud the state in the judgement debt payments are duly punished. More importantly, the government must take rapid measures to ensure the economic wellbeing of the people in order to guarantee their support and votes in the elections.

Conclusions and Implications of the Judgement Debt Cases for Institutional Development

This study revealed the weaknesses in the country's procurement laws, its institutions of parliament, the law courts and the Attorney General's office, as well as the general application of the various mechanisms of control. The recent revelations of the fraudulent payments of judgement debts by the government are another clear example of the corruption that has bedevilled state institutions for many years now. There is a need for a rethinking and strengthening of our institutions of accountability to ensure that people in authority properly account for their stewardship and are duly punished when they contravene the law. The following ten key factors should be considered in any future institutional development effort regarding governance and accountability in Ghana.

1. There is a need to separate EOCO from the Attorney General's Department, and establish it as an independent state institution with representation from relevant stakeholder groups, especially civil society groups, to ensure the effective investigation of government officials involved in fraud and corruption.
2. The Attorney General's Department must be separated from the Ministry of Justice. The former should be the state's advocate and independent of the latter which is a government ministry to ensure the effective and impartial prosecution of government and public officials who contravene the law.
3. The public procurement laws need to be amended to include stipulations for contract abrogation
4. Constitutional guidance and constraints on the abrogation of government contracts by successive governments must be provided.
5. The powers of the Attorney General in making debt settlement decisions must be carefully regulated.
6. Implementing bodies or agencies involved in the procurement process must ensure the strict observance and enforcement of public procurement laws
7. The media should be depoliticised to ensure objective and impartial reportage of issues of public interest
8. Civil society groups must be supported and given prominence on public commissions of accountability

9. Electorates must be well-informed and educated on the importance of voting based on issues and performance rather than tribe affiliation and blind allegiance.
10. The law courts must be provided with the necessary human and material resources and strengthened to ensure the successful prosecution and punishment of people who commit fraud, corruption and other crimes against the state.

References

Adefila, J.J. & Adeoti, J.O. (2001). The Essence of Accountability in Fraud Prevention and Control: Borno State Ministry of Finance's Perception. Available at: www.unilorin.edu.ng/**adeoti**jo/. *Accessed on 28/05/2012.*

Basheka, B. C. & Bisangabasaija, E. (2010). Determinants of unethical public procurement in local government systems of Uganda: a case study. *Int. J. Procurement Management,* 3(1).

Borden, M. J. (2007). The role of financial journalists. *Fordham Journal of Corporate & Financial Law,* 12, 323-36.

Daabu, M.A (2012). MP's have Failed to Defend accountability. Available at: http://politics.myjoyonline.com/pages/news/201208/92000.php. Accessed: 13/08/2012.

De-Boer, L. & Telgen, J. (1998). Purchasing practice in Dutch municipalities. *International Journal of Purchasing and Materials Management,* 34(2), 31-36.

De Vries, C. & Giger, N. (2012). Holding Governments Accountable: Individual Heterogeneity in Performance Voting. Available at: www.catherinedevries.eu/HoldingGovernmentsAccountable.pdf *Accessed: 27/05/2012.*

Donkor, S. (2012). The Woyome Judgement Debt Saga. Available at: (http://www.ghanaweb.com/GhanaHomePage/features/artikel). Accessed: 20/05/2012.

Duch, Raymond M. (2001). "A Developmental Model of Heterogeneous Economic Voting in New Democracies." *American Political Science Review* 95:895–910.

ETV, Ghana (2012). GHC51 Million Judgment Debt; Alfred Woyome Finally Opens Up. Available at: http://www.etvghana.com/index.php/politics-news Accessed: 15/05/2012.

Goetz, A.M. & J. Gaventa. (2001). *Bringing Citizen Voice and Client Focus into Service Delivery.* Brighton, Sussex: IDS Working Paper No.138. Available at:

www.pnet.ids.ac.uk/guides/citizenship/action.htm. Accessed: 20/05/2012.

Gomez, Brad T. and J. Matthew Wilson. (2006). "Cognitive Heterogeneity and Economic Voting: A Comparative Analysis of Four Democratic Electorates." *American Journal of Political Science* 50:127–145.

Gyasiwaa, A. (2012). IMANI Backs Calls For Public Enquiry into Gh¢58m Judgment Debt. Available at: www.Ghana/Myjoyonline.com. Accessed 12/05/2012.

Hui, W. S., Othman, R. O., Normah, O., Rahman, R. A. & Haron, N. H. (2011). Procurement issues in Malaysia. *International Journal of Public Sector Management,* 24(6), 567-593.

Key, Vladimir O. (1966). *The Responsible Electorate. Rationality in Presidential Voting, 1936-1960.* New York: The Belknap Press of Harvard University Press.

Mahmood, S. A. I. (2010). Public procurement and corruption in Bangladesh. Confronting the challenges and opportunities. *Journal of public administration and policy research,* 2(6).

Odhiambo-Mbai, C. (2003). Public Service Accountability and Governance in Kenya since Independence. *African Association of Political Science Vol. 8 no. 1 ISSN:1027-0353*

OECD. (2007). Integrity in Public Procurement Good Practice from A to Z, OECD Publishing, Paris, France.

Prof. Gimah-Boadi, (2012). Ghanaians can consolidate democracy through civic education. Available at: http://www.hracghana.org/newsdetails.php?news. Accessed: 15/05/2012.

Roodhooft, F. & Abbeele, A. V. D. (2006). Public procurement of consulting services Evidence and comparison with private companies. *International Journal of Public Sector Management,* 19(5), 490-512.

The Enquirer Newspaper. January – April 2012.

The Daily Graphic. February – July 2012.

The Ghanaian Times. February – July 2012

The Ghanaian Voice. February – July 2012

The Independent. January – May 2012.

The EOCO Report (February, 2012) Available at: http://citifmonline.com/index.php. Accessed: 15/05/2012.

The Financial Administration Act, 2003, Act 654. Available at: www.bog.gov.gh/ *Accessed: 25/05/2012.*

The Public Procurement Act, 2003, Act 663. Available at: www.bog.gov.gh/ *Accessed: 25/05/2012.*

Tukamuhabwa, B. R. (2012). Antecedents and Consequences of Public Procurement Non-compliance Behavior. *Journal of Economics and*

Behavioral Studies, Vol. 4, No. 1, pp. 34-46, Jan 2012 (ISSN: 2220-6140).

UNDP (2010). Accountability in Public Procurement: transparency and the role of civil society

World Bank (1995a). Guidelines: Procurement under IBRD Loans and IDA Credits, World Bank, Washington, D.C.

World Bank Country Procurement Assessment Report, (2001).

World Bank Institute, (2005). *Social Accountability in the Public Sector.* Washington DC: WBI Working Paper No.33641.

Zubcic, J. & Sims, R. (2011). Examining the link between enforcement activity and corporate compliance by Australian companies and the implications for regulators. *International Journal of Law and Management,* 53(4), 299-308.

CHAPTER TWELVE

FINANCIAL CRISES AND CORPORATE GOVERNANCE IN THE PUBLIC SECTOR: UNDERSTANDING THE IMPACTS ON RISK MANAGEMENT AND ACCOUNTABILITY IN THE UK CITY COUNCILS

SARA ABDALESS, ISMAIL ADELOPO AND GEORGIANA GRIGORE

Introduction

Corporate governance has been "trending" for the last decade in the private sector, and many academics as well as professionals have had a particular interest in it. This can be linked to the different corporate failures that have taken place in the 2000s, and indicates that the durability of a corporation is synonymous with good governance.

However, the private sector is not the only sector that has been influenced by the concept of corporate governance, with it being prominent in the public sector as well. It has been noticed from relevant studies, that there is not the same level of interest from academics with regard to the public sector as there is for the private one. This is the reason why this chapter presents a brief look at the governance framework in the public sector, particularly in local government.

The public sector can be classified as not-for-profit, as it is driven by providing services to the community instead of making profit. This sector has many particularities, such as the nature of funding (ownership), the constraints on resources, the groups of stakeholders, and, most importantly, the non-commercial aspect of their activities (Crowther and Seifi, 2011).

The stakeholder theory will be discussed in this chapter as it is one of the most influential theories in this field of study, and is important for corporate governance. Then, corporate governance in the public sector will be defined and its principles emphasised, and a brief introduction to the governance framework for the public sector will be provided.

This research is concerned with assessing the impact that the financial crisis had on risk management and accountability within local councils. A gap in the literature has been detected regarding this area, and this study covers the subject of risk management and accountability within a sample of local councils based in the East Midlands in England.

A theoretical framework

Stakeholder theory

In order to build a framework that will help in understanding the orientation towards stakeholders of organizations in the public sector, this chapter presents the stakeholder theory and the ways in which stakeholders can be classified. Stakeholder theory was firstly mentioned in Johnson's 1971 definition of the concept of corporate social responsibility. In his view, a socially responsible company not only focuses on generating profit, but also balances a variety of interests for groups such as employees, suppliers, local communities and society as a whole. As such, identifying the relevant groups to be satisfied and establishing the nature of the relationship with them is fundamental for every company. Carroll (1999) argues that there is a natural link between the idea of corporate social responsibility and the stakeholders of a company.

Stakeholders represent a key element in the analysis of the environment of an organization, which can positively or negatively affect its activities (Murray and Vogel, 1997). The most popular definition of stakeholders advances the idea of "individuals or groups that may influence or be influenced by the scope of organisational objectives" (Freeman, 1984, pp. 46). Ferrell et al. (2010) point out that individuals or groups are considered to be stakeholders of an organization when they meet one of the several conditions: (1) when they are positively or negatively influenced by the activity of a company or when they are preoccupied by its impact on the organisation's welfare, (2) when they can supply or procure essential resources needed for its activity or (3) when they are highly appreciated within the organisational culture.

Stakeholder theory brings together economic and social interests, which implies the focus on a large and complex range of objectives and the integration of stakeholders' demands into companies' core activities. Crowther (2008) poses the idea that stakeholder theory is based on the social contract between an organisation and society, the main argument being that if companies affect stakeholders, they ought to be responsible to them. Organisations do not operate in isolation, but rather within a very wide and complex network with its own synergy. As long as companies become aware of this vision, there is an opportunity for developing harmonious relations with society.

While some researchers indicate that no groups of stakeholders dominate others and that they all have the same intrinsic value for organisations (Clarkson, 1995; Donaldson and Preston, 1999), there are others who find this approach misleading and illusory (Gioia, 1999). Polonsky (1995) suggests that, when stakeholder theory is employed as a marketing tool, it is necessary to identify specific groups that might affect a company's activities. He promotes the idea of internal and external stakeholders. The first category includes employees, managers and shareholders, and represents those entities with which the company develops direct and strong relationships. On the other hand, external stakeholders are composed of the government, non-governmental organisations, the media, the environment, and society.

The relevant academic literature is abundant in stakeholder classifications (Clarkson, 1995; Henriques and Sadorsky, 1996, 1999; Wheeler and Sillanpaa, 1997; Werther and Chandler, 2006). Clarkson (1995) distinguishes between voluntary and involuntary stakeholders. The author specifies that, while voluntary stakeholders freely choose to cooperate with an organisation (and, as such, include shareholders, employees, managers, consumers, and suppliers), involuntary stakeholders have no freedom in making a decision and they cannot avoid a connection with the company (this category includes local communities, the environment, and future generations).

Agle et al. (1997) developed a stakeholder typology considering several of their attributes: namely, power, legitimacy and urgency. By combining these characteristics, the authors proposed a model with seven categories which can affect an organisation in either a higher or a lower degree. It is also suggested that if a stakeholder has power, he is accepted in the relationship with the organisation, and his demands put pressure on a company, then this stakeholder requires priority and immediate attention in satisfying his needs.

There is a link between the principles of corporate governance and the stakeholder theory. Corporate governance manages the relationship between an organisation and its stakeholders, by making the managers accountable, having a process and control systems in place, having a relevant risk management, and providing governance from a mix of independent and internal professionals.

Corporate Governance in the Public Sector

Corporate governance in the public sector has been defined by CIPFA and SOLACE as "...*the system by which local authorities direct and control their functions and relate to their communities*" (ALARM, 2001, p.3). Having good corporate governance in place ensures a high-quality service delivery, as well as a high level of public trust in the public bodies (The Audit Commission, 2003).

According to Ryan and Ng (2000), corporate governance in the public sector consists of governing the organisation rather than managing it. It is about making sure – through procedures and control systems – that the managers of the organisation are making their decisions efficiently and effectively. Accountability is also part of the role of corporate governance (Ryan and Ng, 2000), as it is crucial to communicate to the stakeholders, in a transparent way, how the organisation is managed and how it is performing.

Corporate governance in the local government has become more formalised after the introduction of the Local Government Act 2000, which provided a clearer structure and framework of governance. Although it has been noticed that the embedding of governance in public sector institutions takes time and creates confusion, it was however apparent that local authorities are doing better than other public institutions, due to the direct openness of their system to the general public (The Audit Commission, 2003) .

In research conducted by the CPA (2003) aiming to assess the statistical relationship between corporate governance and the quality of services provided by public sector bodies, it was shown that there is a positive relationship between the two, and that most public failures were due to a combination of factors such as poor risk management and control systems and poor leadership.

In the public sector, the balancing of political, social and economic factors can often be a problem. It can be confusing to cooperate in an environment where different objectives need to be achieved. That is why a clear framework of corporate governance principles is vital for the balancing of these factors (Whitfield, 2003). In addition to that, there are an increasing number of partnerships with the private and voluntary sectors, which makes it difficult to trace governance across all these institutions (The Audit Commission, 2003).

Principles of corporate governance

The Combined Code of Corporate Governance in the UK as updated by the Financial Reporting Council (FRC), in 2010, is still a principle-based code rather than a rules-based one (FRC, 2010). This code is a "comply or explain" (FRC, 2010), which means that the companies, if they fail to comply with certain principles, can explain why this was the case. This flexibility might be seen as a positive factor in embedding the spirit of good governance in companies, but it also threatens more creativity in explaining the failure of compliance. The shareholders, though, have the right to challenge the explanations given by the board, when they seem unconvincing (FRC, 2010).

The principles outlined in the Cadbury report have since been slightly expanded, and went from three - Openness, Integrity and Accountability – (Cadbury, 1992) to five - Leadership, Effectiveness, Accountability, Remuneration and Relations with shareholders (FRC, 2010). The content of the code has been the same, and aims for the same purpose: achieving good and durable corporate governance.

Furthermore, following the Cadbury report (1992) and the Nolan Committee report (1995) on standards in public life, the CIPFA and SOLACE issued a corporate governance framework for public sector organisations. The framework provides guidelines on five key areas that are considered to be very important in local governance, and requires that every local council should have in place a system for identifying and evaluating all significant risk.

Openness: Being open to the full communication of information about how the organisation is managed and about the people working in it. This will enable the stakeholder to build confidence in the public sector entities and in the stewardship of public resources. (IFAC, 2001)

Integrity: This concerns the honesty of the organisation regarding its activities and the control systems it has in place. It is shown in the quality of its financial statements and the level of performance achieved (IFAC, 2001).

Accountability: This is, primarily, a process by which organisations must have a clear attribution of responsibilities, which will enable each person to be held accountable and responsible for their actions (IFAC, 2001).

These three principles are interdependent in such a close way that one cannot be achieved without the other. Being open to the public cannot be achieved if there is no accountability and integrity. In other words, it is not possible to communicate to the public information that does not exist in the first place.

Being honest and having good control systems in place, without attributing responsibilities, or without being able to communicate the effectiveness of the organisation to its stakeholders will not satisfy the conditions of good governance.

Having a good structure and a clear role distribution without good processes in place and without communicating them to the stakeholders is not good governance either.

As such, it is very important for the board of governors – in order to maintain a certain level of good governance – to give very special attention to the balancing of these three principles, and to make sure that they are met at all times.

The board of directors is responsible for the leadership and governance of the organisation (FRC, 2010; IFAC, 2001; The Audit Commission, 2003). It has to have a clear identification and division of responsibilities between the executive and non-executive directors (FRC, 2010; IFAC, 2001; The Audit Commission, 2003). The management of the organisation is not the responsibility of the board, but of the executive directors (managers) (FRC, 2010). The chairman is the leader of the board and has to ensure that it is operating effectively (FRC, 2010; IFAC, 2001). The non-executive directors can help the executives tailor their strategy in an effective way (FRC, 2010; IFAC, 2001), without intervening in the management of the organisation (Cadbury, 1992). In local governments, the non-executive roles are occupied by the elected councillors (The Audit Commission, 2003).

The effectiveness of corporate governance can be achieved through the board and its committees. The members of the board and committees

"should have the appropriate balance of skills, experience, independence and knowledge of the company to enable them to discharge their respective duties and responsibilities effectively."   (FRC, 2010, p.12)

The effectiveness of the board is closely related to the procedures by which new directors are appointed, the information received at their induction, the procedures of re-electing the directors, the time that these dedicate to the governance of the organisation, and, most importantly, the assessment of the board, the committees and each member's performance on a regular basis (FRC, 2010; IFAC, 2001).

Remuneration is one of the most critical principles of governance. A balance should be made when fixing the remuneration of the directors, in order not to discourage highly-skilled and competent people from accepting the job, while making sure not to over remunerate them, so that they can become biased in their governance (FRC, 2010; IFAC, 2001). The remuneration of the directors is fixed by a special committee, where the directors are not allowed to decide their own remuneration (Cadbury, 1992 and FRC, 2010; IFAC, 2001).

Risk Management

Corporate governance is about managing risk effectively. The effective management of an organisation cannot be achieved without proper risk management in place (ALARM, 2001); therefore, it is important first to define what it is meant by "risk management", which concerns "the identification, analysis and economic control of those risks which might prevent an organisation from achieving its objectives." (ALARM, 2001, p. 8). Having a good risk management process in place implies that it is embedded in the organisational culture and considered as a part of the holistic system of governance rather than one separate function (ALARM, 2001).

In the early 2000s, risk management was still confused with the concept of insurance; many insurance managers were allocated the task of risk managers (ALARM, 2001). This is an important issue, as it limits risk management to insurance, whereas, insurance is actually part of managing risks. The ALARM has issued a number of risk management recommendations for public sector bodies to follow. The list of recommendations is not exhaustive and variances may apply from one organisation to another (ALARM, 2001). These guidelines can be resumed as follows:

Risk management should be driven by the elected members in the case of local authorities (ALARM, 2001). These people are also responsible for defining a risk management policy for their organisation that needs to be signed by the CEO and approved by the board. The follow-up of the policy needs to be done yearly, in order to decide whether the policy requires updating (ALARM, 2001). It is also recommended that local authorities designate a "champion" for the program from the board of elected councillors and form a working group to provide general knowledge of the organisation's risks. A formal assignment of the risk management roles and responsibilities will make the managers more accountable and integrated, as well as facilitating the identification, analysis and monitoring of the risks facing the organisation.

The board needs to communicate to both managers and employees the risks and opportunities for the organisation, in addition to having a clear and tested contingency plan in case things go wrong (ALARM, 2001). The ALARM suggests an interesting framework, although it seems to lack many components and has a very top-down approach. A good risk management process that leads to a detailed identification of risks, analysing them and deciding which to eliminate, share, mitigate or accept, needs to be both top-down and bottom-up (Coyle, 2002). Communicating to employees what the risks are is not enough, as they might have a different perception of risks, and might have identified other risks that did not appear to the top managers. As such, it is very important for public and private sector organisations to have an interactive way of managing risks, where different parties, both internal (across all levels) and external, are allowed to have their say. It seems complicated, but it is better to be ready to face risks than to expose a whole community to governance failure.

Methodology

This chapter is based on an exploratory study aiming to explore the impact of the financial crisis on governance in local councils in the East Midlands of England. The data collected for this study is both primary and secondary qualitative data.

A semi-structured interview was conducted in order to collect the data, and was then sent by email to 47 local councils in the East Midlands, relying on the list of their contact details provided on the direct.gov website. Out of the 47 councils, 4 councils replied by email and one council provided information through a phone interview.

The respondents were holding key governance jobs within the councils and varied from the Head of Regeneration and Organisational Development, the Corporate Governance Officer to the Director of Delivery, Communications & Political Governance.

In order to complete the information generated through the interviews, the last two annual reports from the websites of the respondent councils have been analysed.

Data analysis

A thematic approach was adopted in the analysis of the response from the local councils. This was with the aim of highlighting risk awareness, planning and action, and secondly to assess the implication of the financial crisis. The analysis is embedded in the current findings in the literature on risk generally, especially those studies with relevance to the public sector.

Risk identification

How was the council affected by the austerity measures and the budget cuts operated by the central government?

This question centres round councils' risk identification processes - the fundamental starting-point of any risk management framework, including those of local governments (Crawford and Stein, 2004; Wood, 2009). Risk identification is the process of recognising potential situations or events that give rise to a situation that could inhibit an organisation from achieving its set objectives or lead to an organisation settling for a more sub-optimal outcome than planned. However, effective risk identification requires broad risk awareness which is influenced by risk perception. Risk perception is both socially, culturally and, in some cases, institutionally determined (Hofstede, 1980; Weinstein, 1989).

Organisations do not exist in a vacuum and are constantly exposed to events and situations both internally and externally (Aguilera et al., 2007; Di Maggio and Powell, 1983). While some of these events could be outcome-enhancing, others are not. For example, there appears to be a general consensus that the current economic climate exacerbated by the financial crisis presents a formidable risky situation for many organisations in both the private and public sector.

Our findings showed that all the councils studied exhibit a clear awareness of the potential risk arising from the financial crisis. This awareness is also reflected in a lucid quantitative assessment of the implications of the crisis on the councils' budgets. The following excerpts from the responses from the councils reflect this fact. One of the district council, council B stated that:

"We lost 32% of our central government grant. As a result, we cut £1.3 million from our budget in 2011/12 and we have a further £0.8 million of savings planned. We still need to find another £0.4 million in savings."

Council E, the borough council, suggested that:

"The austerity measures, along with other factors led to £1.5m of expenditure cuts. This included the loss of approximately 25 posts."

The third, council D, suggested that:

> "since the austerity measures were introduced under the Comprehensive Spending Review 2010, the Council's Revenue Support Grant has been cut from £10.366million in 2010/2011 to £8.185million in 2011/2012 (a reduction of £2.181million from the previous year) and to £7.282million in 2012/2013 (a reduction of £903,000 from the previous year)."

Risk analysis and implications for governance, risk management and auditing in the council

However, while there is evidently a clear awareness of an event that represents a potential risk to the councils, this is merely a step in the risk management process itself. It is important that the risk is analysed and categorised appropriately. This would allow the implication to be effectively assessed, which would then inform the response to the risk. To find out about this, we asked the councils in the study how the current crisis has affected governance, and in particular its impact on risk management and auditing. We posed the question below:

How did these measures affect governance (including risk management and auditing)?

Our findings suggest a lack of clarity among the councils on the likely effects of the financial crisis on their governance and risk management and internal auditing processes. Thus, while some councils have a clear appreciation of the likely effects, others are less sure. Although we accessed the information about this online, we were interested in learning about the practical appreciation of the situation of the councils through their spokespersons on the issue. Thus, our analysis is based on the official response received from the councils under the Freedom of Information Act. This is because it reflects the official position of the councils and represents a carefully considered response. The following findings are indicative of our conclusion on the apparent lack of effective appreciation of the impact of the crisis on governance and risk management in the councils studied. For example, the city council, council A, suggested that:

> "A real practical issue, as there is a fear of fraud by the current employers in the council before they are made redundant for instance. In this case, the auditors are asked to look at particular areas that are at risk of fraud. Also, tighter controls are made on recruitment (do we really need to recruit this person? Therefore, more checks are done in the process and more

questions are asked in order to avoid spending money. We have a standard risk assessment and an equality impact assessment: as such, when we have to make a spending cut, we ask questions about how it is going to impact the communities and who the groups are that are going to be affected, then decide whether to accept the risk or mitigate it."

This response showed a very narrow and misguided view of the implications of the financial crisis on governance and risk management at the council level. Whilst internal control should ensure the protection of the resources of the stakeholders, it is far more extensive, and includes the process of establishing policies, procedures and control checks that ensure an adequate overall risk management process. We also got the sense that the financial crisis could compromise risk management in some councils, as it is possible that the risk management function could be subsumed into other functions as councils try to find savings in order to balance their budget as statutorily required. For example, in response to the question, the only borough council in the sample claimed that:

Council E:

"The responsible post was deleted but Risk Management was not affected as this function was absorbed into other roles."

District council B simply stated that:

"Governance has not been affected."

This response is reminiscent of the lack of clarity on the specialised nature of the risk management role within the public sector, and risks conflating the role of the risk managers with the insurance officers of the council (Crawford and Stein, 2004). There is a real danger that a proper analysis of the effects of the spending cuts on governance and controls within the councils is not undertaken as responsibilities for this are decentralised.

On the other hand, we have two district councils that showed a better appreciation of the effects of the cuts on their governance and risk management processes. This is suggestive of a proactive approach to risk and governance in these councils. For example, an appreciation of the risk management implications of the cuts has led to the reorganisation of service delivery, and the development of new portfolios and positions with specific remits on attending to governance and the risk that may result from the cuts. There is also evidence of operational reviews and improved briefing in order to enhance front-line service delivery and thereby minimise risks. For instance, district council D responded to our question as follows:

> "The Council has undergone a reorganisation to help us to deal with the austerity measures and to focus on meeting the needs of the Localism agenda. The main focus of the reorganisation was to meet the needs of our communities on an area basis, allocating resources to priorities agreed with the community. This has meant that we now have area managers and an area focus for the provision of services, organised around community rather than service needs. This approach has also allowed us to take on board the need to work in partnership with other public, private and voluntary sector partners to be able to make the most of the resources available.
>
> The reorganisation has also taken into account the need to make sure that governance arrangements are effective, and to appoint an Assistant Chief Executive responsible for a Governance Unit. The Unit is responsible for project management, governance, risk management, business improvement, information management, consultation, performance management and horizon scanning. Other than the changes to the Audit Commission, there are no changes in auditing – our internal audit service is provided by Audit X – the internal auditors for the County Council and the external auditors are currently the Audit Commission."

District council C provided the most refreshing and reassuring response which detailed policy and operations guidelines and indicated an administration that has given due consideration to the effects of the current financial crisis on its governance and risk management procedures.

> "When implementing savings, Managers are expected to regard potential control issues which could impact on their service; this is a requirement set out in the Council's Financial Regulations. Managers are required to discuss any potential control issues they may have with Internal Audit which could impact on the Council's governance arrangements.
>
> Internal Audit may increase testing if they feel there are any governance issues raised when their planned audit work is carried out.
>
> The annual Audit Plan and Terms of Reference for individual audit are reviewed in light of any changes to service or staff structures.
>
> In order to strengthen Corporate Governance, C District Council is looking at implementing an Audit Assurance Framework, which would consider all areas affecting governance at the Council and putting in place a process for monitoring these against a predetermined standard.
>
> The Council has recently reviewed and strengthened its Strategic Risk Register, especially in the area of financial management."

It is clear from the findings that councils have different appreciations of the effects of the cuts on their governance and risk management procedures. A standard guideline on this will be hugely useful for councils in their stakeholder management functions.

Stakeholder relationship, governance and risk management

An important aspect of the local councils' governance and risk management processes relates to their interaction with their stakeholders. A lack of appreciation of who the key stakeholders are and how the current financial crisis could impact on the relationship with them could be indicative of poor corporate governance and risk management processes. O'Donovan (2002) suggests that organisations need to continuously renew their legitimacy with their dynamic conferring public. Bridging the gap with dynamic stakeholders requires an effective governance structure that places risk management at the centre of its operations. This is important in order to understand the nature of the changes that may have occurred to the conferring public (Adelopo et al., 2012) and to understand how to effectively respond to this change so as to maintain legitimacy by reducing legitimacy gaps.

Managing legitimacy gaps during periods of uncertainty typified by the current financial crisis may require new partnerships and the building of new networks to ensure the effective utilisation of available resources to deliver optimum value to various stakeholders. This is underpinned by the idea of an enlightened stakeholder approach which the UK is renowned for. In order to find out how the councils' stakeholders have changed and how the councils are responding to their stakeholder management in this uncertain financial situation, we posed two sets of related questions to the councils as follows:

Who are the most significant stakeholders for your Council? How does the council fulfil their demands and needs? Who are the most affected stakeholders by the cuts and why?

What is the corporate governance vision of your council? How was the vision of your council affected by the cuts?

The first set of questions addresses the issue of stakeholders and the way they may have been affected by the cuts, while the second set of questions seeks to explore how the cuts have affected governance structures within the councils.

As would be expected, the responses to these questions vary from very superficial replies with no substance to more specific and detailed answers. There is a fairly unanimous response to the question about the key stakeholders. All the councils identified the service users, residents and the community as their key stakeholders. This is reflected in all the responses by the councils as presented below:

District council B

"Residents are our most significant stakeholders, and we fulfil their needs by providing services. The most affected stakeholders with regard to cuts have been our own employees, because we have tried to protect services to residents."

District council D

"The County Council and adjoining Councils are our most significant stakeholders as we have an agreement with the county council to be strategic partners, focusing on our strategic aims and working together on shared aims. Taking an area approach has also meant that the communities themselves and community groups are included as the stakeholders for their areas, helping to formulate plans and priorities for partners to address."

Borough council E

"Members of the Public and Partners. Fulfilling their needs and demands is what the council is here for. No front-line services were significantly affected by the cuts."

City council A

"We are here for the public: people of xxxx, business in the city and other partner organisations. One of my team's jobs is to have data on who is in the community, what their needs are, etc., which is fundamental in making the right decisions. On top of that, communities are consulted when there is a major issue. For instance, the council is currently consulting with people about council tax benefits."

However, we noticed that district council D and borough council E suggested that they also considered their partners and adjoining councils as important stakeholders in order to focus on shared strategic objectives, and worked together with communities and community groups in "helping to formulate plans and priorities to partners". This approach is also seemingly at the heart of the "big society" agenda of the coalition government at the inception of the administration which effectively suggests the devolution of resource allocation to community groups and stakeholders. This marks a watershed in stakeholder management as we know it. However, the idea appears to have been somewhat short-lived as not a lot has changed since.

Local Governance and cuts

Another important theme that featured in our interview with the councils was the effects of the cuts on governance at the local council level. Essentially, we were interested in finding out if the cuts have led to changes in governance vision and how this was being handled. We were also seeking to unravel the effects on the board and governance structure. This is particularly relevant given that some councils now have an elected and/or executive council structure, compared to environments where the business of the council is at the mercy of the whole politically motivated machinery. For these reasons, the following questions were posed to our interviewees.

What is the corporate governance vision of your council? How was the vision of your council affected by the cuts?

Overall, we got the sense that all the councils surveyed have a similar governance vision, which is mainly to deliver first rate services to their stakeholders and ensure accountability. The majority of these visions have not changed despite the financial crisis. Table 1 provides a snapshot of some of the responses from the councils.

Councils	Governance visions	Effects of cuts on vision
City council A	Things have been overtaken. The vision has slightly changed as the economic climate has changed and governance has changed: we now have an elected mayor who is the decision maker. This is very helpful as there is one decision maker to direct the council. He has clear ideas about priorities, where we should invest and where we should not.	Changed. Also governance structure has changed.
District council B	The vision is unchanged, but in 2011 we reduced the number of corporate priorities from four to three.	No change but adjustment of priorities.
District council C	Although there are changes to the CIPFA governance framework, the council's governance visions are unaffected.	Unchanged
District council D	We have a vision for our corporate plan that is for the district to be a place where people want to live, work and visit – this vision has not changed and is still our aim.	Unchanged
Borough council E	See corporate plan (attached) for full vision. The vision was not affected by cuts.	Unchanged

Table 12.1: Governance vision within local councils

The next section of the chapter presents discussions of the findings and makes suggestions for future research.

Discussion and conclusion

The current financial crises which started in 2007 have had far-reaching effects on many social actors. Both public and private enterprises have been adversely affected. Whilst private sector enterprises seem to have realised the real implication of the crisis and are seen to be adjusting their operational and financial dispensation accordingly, through downsizing, pragmatic risk management and enhanced corporate governance approach, it is not quite the same in the public sector.

The spending review is likely to lead to significant constraints on service delivery in a number of public sector organisations, especially the local councils which form the focus of this current study. Local councils provide the closest link to citizens and have essential roles to play in the everyday life of these citizens. Reductions in their financial grants mean that local councils have to find savings in order to prop up their finances and balance their books as statutorily required. This may affect frontline services as staff are made redundant with resultant effects on service delivery. The adverse consequences of these could worsen the financial situation of the councils further as they may be faced with significant litigations arising from poor service delivery and complaints.

Consequently, effective corporate governance and risk management are essential for local councils in dealing with the uncertainty brought about by the financial crisis. In order to provide answers to some related questions, this study conducted a semi-structured interview with five local councils in the East Midlands region of the UK. The study found that, although all the councils studied have evidence of risk identification arising from the financial crisis, their appreciation of the implications of the crisis on their risk management and governance strategies is somewhat inconsistent and shallow in some instances. While there are councils that show a significant appreciation of the dangers brought about by the crisis and are proactively taking steps in the form of re-organisation and the appointment of risk management and governance officers, others are rather laid-back about such uncertainty. We have, however, found evidence of quantification of the potential savings that would need to be generated in order to balance their books. This needs to be translated into a real impact on service delivery and a clear assessment of the risk management implications of this. In doing this, the idea of local councils buying audit assurance services may become appealing in the near future. This will prevent litigation and provide some limited guarantees on the ability of the council to meet its obligations. It will help the councils to identify risk areas, set predetermined standards, and monitor performance.

We have documented evidence of changing priorities in the local councils as a resource of the cuts; although the majority of the councils appear to suggest that their corporate vision and objectives have not been affected by the current cuts, they admitted that priorities are changing. Furthermore, we found that councils are having to expand their stakeholders' spectrum and are employing strategic alliances and partnerships with other stakeholders through focusing on areas for the delivery of their services. Community and community groups are also becoming involved in formulating governance policies at local councils, enhancing ownership and facilitating governance at the grassroots.

A strategic regulatory framework is needed for the public sector, with a focus on a small number of clear targets to enable organisations across the country to prioritise them (The Audit Commission, 2003). As a result, the control of performance will be made easier for auditors and inspectors to assess. The ultimate objective for public bodies is still to provide high quality public services (The Audit Commission, 2003), but in order to achieve this, some strategic targets need to be set and met.

The findings in this chapter show that corporate governance in the public sector is a vital process for a truly democratic and sustainable society. It is also shocking that, back in 2003, the public satisfaction and trust in the public bodies was very low, while conjuncture was not as bad as it currently is. Cutting public spending in frontline jobs across sectors will only decrease the level of trust that the public have in public bodies, from hospitals to city councils. Further research about how the current political system affects the level and quality of corporate governance, and how it tests the strength of the governance procedures already in place would prove to be extremely interesting and fruitful. It is also shocking to know that in a developed country like the United Kingdom, the quality of services delivered by the public sector is still considered as unsatisfactory, making one consider how abject it may be in poorer countries, where corporate governance remains an unknown, or at the very best a theoretical, concept.

Governance, in order to be implemented properly, needs to be carried out by people who believe in it, and must have clear procedures and rules. Neither can achieve good governance separately (ALARM, 2001). Therefore, the key element to the success of governance is the stakeholders (the people), whether these are managers, communities, customers or auditors.

References

Aguilera, R., Rupp, D. and Ganapathi, J. (2007), Putting the S back in corporate social responsibility: A multilevel theory of social change in organizations, *Academy of Management Review*, Vol. 32, pp. 836–63.

ALARM (2001), *Corporate Governance in the public sector: the role of risk management*, [Online] Available at: http://www.alarm-uk.org/PDF/corpgovsum.pdf [Accessed on 27 April 2011].

Audit Commission website (2011), *Assessment Area: Leicestershire (2009)*, [Online] Available at: http://oneplace.audit-commission.gov.uk/SiteCollectionDocuments/pdf/2009/AreaAssessment/AreaAssessment2009Leicestershire_Summary.pdf [Accessed on 15 April 2011]

Audit Commission, (2003), *Corporate Governance : Improvement and trust in local public services*, London.

Cadbury Report (1992), [Online] Available at:

http://www.jbs.cam.ac.uk/cadbury/report/index.html [Accessed on 15 April 2011]

CIPFA, (2011), Delivering Good Governance in Local Government: Briefing note, [Online] Available at: http://www.cipfa.org.uk/panels/corporate_governance/good_gov_briefi ng.cfm [Accessed on 20 April 2011]

Coyle, B., (2004), *Risk Awareness and Corporate Governance*, 2nd Edition, Kent: ifs School of Finance.

Crawford M. and Stein, W., (2004), Risk Management in UK Local Authorities: The effect of current guidance and practice, *International Journal of Public Sector Management*, Vol. 17, pp. 498-512.

Crowther, D. and Seifi, S., (2011), Corporate governance and international business, David Crowther, Shahla Seifi and Ventus Publishing, ApS.

DiMaggio, P.J. and Powell, W.W. (1983), The iron cage revisited: Institutional isomorphism and collective rationality in organizational fields, *American Sociology Review*, Vol. 35, pp. 147-60.

Donaldson, T., and Preston, L., E., (1995),The Stakeholder Theory of the Corporation: Concepts, Evidence, and Implications, *The Academy of Management Review*, Vol. 20, No. 1, pp. 65-91.

Financial Reporting Council website (2011), The UK Corporate Governance Code 2010, [Online] Available at: http://www.frc.org.uk/corporate/ukcgcode.cfm [Accessed on 15 April 2011].

Freeman, R., E., and McVea, J., (2001), *A Stakeholder Approach to Strategic Management* Social Science Research Network Electronic Paper, [Online] Available at: http://papers.ssrn.com/paper.taf?abstract_id=263511 [Accessed on 22 April 2011].

Hofstede, G. (1980), *Culture's Consequences,* Sage Publications.

IFAC (2001), Governance in the public sector, [Online] Available at: http://web.ifac.org/media/publications/9/study-13-governance-in-th/study-13-governance-in-th.pdf [Accessed on 27 April 2011].

Leicester City Council website, (2011), *Annual Report 2010,* [Online] Available at: http://www.leicester.gov.uk/your-council-services/council-and-democracy/key-documents/annual-report/ [Accessed on 15 April 2011].

Leicester City council website, (2011), One Leicester Vision, [Online] Available at: http://www.oneleicester.com/one-leicester-vision/ [Accessed on 15 April 2011].

Mainardes, E., W., Alves, H., Raposo, M., (2011), Stakeholder theory: issues to resolve, *Management Decision*, Vol. 49, No. 2.

Mitchell, R., K., Agle, B., R., and Wood, D., J., (1997), *Toward a Theory of Stakeholder Identification and Salience: Defining the Principle of Who and What Really Counts,* The Academy of Management Review, Vol. 22, No. 4, pp. 853-886.

Moure, R.C., Adelopo, I., Vargas, L.P. and Obalola, M., (2012), Determinants of Web-accessibility of Corporate Social Responsibility (CSR) communications: Evidence from Six Western European Countries, *Journal of Global Responsibility*, Vol 3, No 2.

O'Donovan, G. (2002), Environmental Disclosures in the Annual Report: extending the applicability and predictive power of legitimacy theory, *Accounting, Auditing and Accountability Journal*, Vol. 15 No 3, pp. 344–371.

Ryan C. & Ng. C. (2000), Public sector corporate governance disclosures: an examination of annual reporting practices in Queensland, *Australian Journal of Public Administration,* Vol. 59 No 2, pp. 11-23.

Whitfield, T., (2003), *Achieving Best Practice Corporate Governance in the Public Sector*, The Audit Office of New South Wales.

Woods, M. (2009) A contingency theory perspective on the risk management control system within Birmingham City Council, Management Accounting Research, Vol.20, pp.69-81.

Chapter Thirteen

Conclusions:
Developing a Theory of Governance
and Sustainable Development

Sara Abdaless, David Crowther,
Mourad Oubrich and Redouane Barzi

Introduction

The contributions to this book have applied the full range of meanings to the notions of governance, responsibility and accountability. Arguments have concerned retrospective accountability, the allocation of blame, and reasons for the state of relations between stakeholders. There has also been concern for prospective accountability, that corporations and governments have obligations and duties to exercise. Some of the debates have also questioned the capacity of corporations to make moral judgements. This book has not sought to assess causal issues, recognising that not all failures or accidents attract blame. Nevertheless, much of the debate on corporate social responsibility, within this book and elsewhere, suspects some linkage between corporate actions and a wide range of undesirable social and ecological outcomes.

Together, we have ranged far and wide in exploring the terrain of organisational governance and more generally the topic of business ethics. Some contributions have pursued a macro perspective in discussing the relationship between the corporation and society, but locate their discussions within differing frames. Other contributions have focused on technological changes and concomitant corporate behaviour. Crowther (2004) finds that the burden of social responsibility has shifted from the corporation to society. Other contributions have narrowed their perspective to examine processes within particular sectors, focus on corporations constructing social relations, and outline how managers should behave within the corporation. A number of important and unresolved debates remain embedded within most of these topics. At one level, this book may be regarded as a social barometer. The diversity of fears, hopes and propositions being aired about governance and corporate social responsibility broadly reflects the concerns of large sections of society, including ordinary citizens, sectional pressure groups and activists (particularly with regard to environmental concerns, individual rights, and investor exposure) and policy makers. At another level, this book highlights the persistence of a number of underlying debates that reinforce the difficulties facing stakeholders (including governments and corporations), seeking to shape a better world. One of these debates centres on the acceptability of corporate self-interest as a driving force of a capitalist economic system. Another area of difficulty with which this book has grappled is the very notion of sustainability.

Sustainability

Sustainability is just a general term. A quick look at a dictionary may lead us to a list of definitions, such as the ability to suffer (loss or injury); the ability to be supported (emotionally or physically); the ability to keep going for a long time (in business); the ability to be kept going; the ability of being sustainable; the ability to survive without human interference; and to keep in existence (in botany). So, on the whole, such definitions provide a clear understanding that sustainability relates to survival. "Sustainability" is often misleadingly used as a synonym for "sustainable development", despite the fact that sustainability is actually the target for sustainable development. Sustainable development, as indicated in ISO 26000, is "development that meets the needs of the present without compromising the ability of future generations to meet their own needs". All that is done under the title of sustainable development only aims at sustainability, or the ability to survive.

Different theoreticians have different ideas regarding the relevance of sustainability and social responsibility. For example, Crowther (2002) believes that sustainability in conjunction with accountability and transparency comprises the principles for social responsibility. ISO 26000 defines the principles of social responsibility as accountability; transparency; ethical behaviour; respect for stakeholder interests; respect for the rule of law; respect for international norms of behaviour; and respect for human rights. It is notable that "sustainability" is not included in this list of so-called principles. On the other hand, the WBCSD has counted three pillars for sustainable development, namely economic growth, ecologic balance and social responsibility. This means that sustainable development is predicated in social responsibility.

Therefore, one may conclude that there is an interwoven relationship between sustainability and social responsibility. One group believes that sustainability ensures social responsibility and the other group believes the reverse. We believe in the precedence of social responsibility, as sustainability is a phenomenon which takes place in the long run - we can say that sustainability is the offspring of social responsibility. One can also assume that sustainable development is a strategy, whereas social responsibility is a mission. A strategy cannot be achieved in the short run; instead, it is a long-term plan. Furthermore, because sustainable development is the aspiration of an entire nation, it is here defined as a macrostructure, whereas social responsibility, comparatively, is a microstructure, as it deals with the conditions of a single enterprise.

Current issues in organisational governance

There are a number of issues which are currently of concern to both businesses and individuals. Broadly speaking, these issues are generally concerned with the environment, human rights protection, and governance.

Global warming

The changes to weather systems around the world are apparent to most people, and are manifest in such extreme weather as excessive rain or snow, droughts, heatwaves and hurricanes, which have affected many different parts of the world. Indeed most of us remember, for example, Hurricane Katrina which devastated New Orleans. Global warming and climate change, its most noticeable effect, are subjects of discussion all over the world, and it is generally, although by no means universally, accepted that global warming is taking place and, therefore, that climate change will continue to happen. Opinion is divided however as to whether or not climate change which has already taken place can be reversed. According to Lovelock (2006), climate change, with its inevitable effects on the environment, will also have consequences for human life and economic activity.

Although there are many factors which contribute to global warming, it is clear that commercial and economic activity plays a significant part. Indeed, many people talk about 'greenhouse gases', such as carbon dioxide, being a direct consequence of economic activity. Many people see the reduction in the emission of such gases as being fundamental to any attempt to combat climate change. This, of course, requires a change in behaviour – both of people and of organisations. Such a perceived need for change is one of the factors which have caused the current concern with sustainability.

Ecological Footprinting

Another factor which currently occupies the mind of the general public is that of their "ecological footprint" – the amount of physical area of the earth needed to provide for each person. Ecological footprint analysis compares human demand on nature with the biosphere's ability to regenerate resources and provide services. It does this by assessing the biologically productive land and marine area required to produce the resources a population consumes and absorb the corresponding waste, using prevailing technology. This approach can also be applied to an activity such as the manufacturing of a product or the driving of a car. A possibly more fashionable term for this at the moment is "carbon footprinting".

For an individual the definition of their carbon footprint is the total amount of carbon dioxide attributable to the actions of that individual (mainly through their energy use) over a period of one year. This definition underlies the personal carbon calculators that are widely used. The term owes its origins to the idea that a footprint is what has been left behind as a result of an individual's activities. Carbon footprints can either consider only direct emissions (typically from energy used in the home and in transport, including travel by cars, aeroplanes, rail and other transport), or can also include indirect emissions (including carbon dioxide emissions as a result of goods and services consumed). Bottom-up calculations account for such emissions that result from individual actions; top-down calculations take total emissions from a country (or any other high-level entity) and divide these emissions among the residents (or other participants in that entity). A number of studies have calculated the carbon footprint of organisations and nations. One such UK study (2007) examined age-related carbon emissions based on expenditure and consumption. The study found that, on average, people aged 50-65 years have a higher carbon footprint than any other age group. Individuals aged 50-65 years old have a carbon footprint of approximately 13.5 tonnes/capita per year compared to the UK average of 12 tonnes.

It is commonly understood that carbon dioxide emissions (and the emissions of other greenhouse gases) are almost exclusively associated with the conversion of energy carriers such as wood burning, natural gas, coal and oil. The carbon content released during the energy conversion process reaches the atmosphere and is deemed to be responsible for global warming and, therefore, climate change.[1] General concern about climate change has been expressed worldwide, leading to the Kyoto Protocol.[2] The Kyoto Protocol defines legally binding targets and timetables for cutting the greenhouse-gas emissions of the industrialized countries which ratified the protocol.[3]

Although scientific opinion has more or less reached a consensus that global warming is taking place, and therefore that climate change is happening, there are still a considerable number of sceptics and people who deny that it is occurring.[4] There are others who argue that the human contribution to global warming is negligible; they argue, therefore, that it is useless or even harmful to concentrate on individual contributions.

Water supply and distribution

In many parts of the world, water is becoming a serious problem. Irrigation has led to serious problems in such parts of the world as California, while in Uzbekistan it has led to the shrinking of the Aral Sea[5] to a fraction of its previous size. Furthermore, many rivers, throughout the world, have had so much water extracted from them that they no longer reach the sea. At the same time, millions of people do not have access to safe drinking water, and countries are entering into disputes with each other regarding access to water that they share between them. Indeed, access to water is forecast to become a major source of conflict in the 21st century.

---

[1] This is of course overly simplistic, if not completely wrong. Thus, people (and animals) produce carbon dioxide when breathing, cows (and other ruminants) produce methane, and the process by which vegetation produces, captures and subsequently releases carbon dioxide is complex and not fully understood (see Lomborg, 2001).

[2] This was agreed in 1997 and came into effect in 2005.

[3] In late 2007, Australia ratified the protocol, leaving only one large developed country which has not done so. This country is, however, the USA, probably the largest producer of such greenhouse gases.

[4] The European consensus is by no means applicable worldwide in this respect.

[5] This is in addition to the generally acknowledged human rights abuses.

Resource depletion

Obviously the resources of the planet are finite and this is a limiting factor to growth and development which we have considered to a considerable extent in this book. The depletion of the resources of the planet, however, is one of the factors which have helped create the current interest in sustainability. Of particular concern are the extractive industries, and such things as aluminium are becoming in short supply. In the UK, mineral resources such as tin and lead were fully extracted long ago, and the thriving industries based around them are long gone. As other resources – such as coal – are being exhausted, the companies based upon them disappear, as do the jobs in those industries. This is an obvious source of concern for many people.

Of particular concern is the extinguishing of supplies of oil, because a great deal of economic activity is only possible because of energy created by the use of oil. Indeed many would argue that the wars in the Middle East[6], particularly the problems in Iraq and Iran, were caused by oil shortages, actual or impending, and the problems thereby caused, rather than by any concern for political issues. Most people have now heard of Hubert's Peak, and have engaged with the debate as to whether or not it has been reached. It certainly has in parts of the world, such as the USA and the North Sea, but it is less certain if it has been reached for the world as a whole. Nevertheless, the whole crux of sustainability – and sustainable development – is based upon the need for energy, and there are currently insufficient alternative sources of energy to compensate for the elimination of oil as a source of fuel. As such, resource depletion, real or imagined, and particularly that of energy resources, is one of the most significant causes of the current interest in sustainability.

The supply chain

Another thing which has become prominent in current discourse is the concern with the supply chain of a business; in other words, the concern with what is happening in the other companies with which a company does business – such as their suppliers and the suppliers of their suppliers. In particular, people are concerned with the exploitation of people in developing countries, especially with child labour and sweat shops.

---

[6] And most probably any other parts of the world also – it would be instructive to correlate the presence of oil with conflicts.

As such, no longer is it acceptable for a company to say that the conditions under which their suppliers operate are outside of their sphere of control and responsibility. Customers have realised that this is not acceptable and have called companies to account. There have recently been a number of high-profile retail companies which have held their hands up to acknowledge problems and then taken very public steps to change such situations.

Interestingly, the popularity of companies generally increases after they have admitted problems and taken steps to correct these problems. In doing this, they are thereby showing both that honesty is the best practice and also that customers are reasonable. The evidence suggests that individual customers are understanding and that they do not expect perfection, but do expect honesty and transparency, and also expect companies to make efforts to change their behaviour and to try to solve their CSR problems.

Companies themselves have also changed. No longer are they concerned with greenwashing – the pretence of socially responsible behaviour through artful reporting. Companies are now taking CSR much more seriously, not just because they understand that it is a key to business success and can give them a strategic advantage, but also because people in these organisations care about social responsibility.

As such, it would be reasonable to claim that the growing importance of CSR is being driven by individuals who care – although it should be noted that those individuals are not just customers, they are also employees, managers, owners and investors. It is apparent, then, that companies are partly reacting to external pressures and partly leading the development of responsible behaviour and reporting.

A crisis of governance

When we are thinking about alternatives, we need to spend a short time considering "governance". All systems of governance are concerned primarily with managing the governing of associations, and therefore with political authority, institutions, and, ultimately, control. Governance, in this particular sense, denotes formal political institutions that aim to coordinate and control interdependent social relations and that have the ability to enforce decisions. Increasingly, however, in a globalised world, the concept of governance is being used to describe the regulation of interdependent relations in the absence of overarching political authority, such as in the international system. Thus, global governance can be considered as the management of global processes in the absence of forms of global government. There are some international bodies which seek to address these issues, and prominent among these are the United Nations and the World Trade Organisation. Each of these has met with mixed success in instituting some form of governance in international relations, but they are both part of a recognition of the problem and an attempt to address worldwide problems that are beyond the capacity of individual states to solve.

Global governance is not, of course, the same thing as world government: indeed it can be argued that the former system would not actually be necessary if there was such a thing as a world government. Currently, however, various state governments have a legitimate monopoly on the use of force and on the power of enforcement. Global governance, therefore, refers to the political interaction that is required to solve problems that affect more than one state or region when there is no power of enforcing compliance. Improved global problem-solving need not of course require the establishment of more powerful formal global institutions, but would involve the creation of a consensus on norms and practices to be applied. Steps are, of course, underway to establish these norms; one example of this being the creation and improvement of global accountability mechanisms. In this respect, for example, the United Nations Global Compact[7] – described as the world's largest voluntary corporate responsibility initiative – brings together companies, national and international agencies, trades unions and other labour organisations and various organs of civil society in order to support universal environmental protection, human rights and social principles. Participation is entirely voluntary, and there is no enforcement of the principles by an outside regulatory body. Companies adhere to these practices both because they make economic sense, and because their stakeholders, including their shareholders (most individual and institutional investors), are concerned with these issues and this provides a mechanism whereby they can monitor the compliance of companies easily. Mechanisms such as the Global Compact can improve the ability of individuals and local communities to hold companies accountable for their activities.

The role of companies in effecting change

As we have seen, there are a number of important issues which need to be addressed, and are being so, as companies develop in their understanding and application of CSR. Sometimes companies take action

---

[7] See www.unglobalcompact.org

because of the pressure exerted upon them, and sometimes they take action because they are concerned. We use the following two cases to illustrate this. The first concerns the actions of oil companies in the Niger Delta, where action is being taken because of the pressure brought to bear on those oil companies by consumers. The second concerns the cotton industry in Uzbekistan. The problems here are not so generally well-known, and so pressure from consumers is not being exerted. Nevertheless companies themselves are using their influence to bring about change.

Shell in the Niger Delta

Nigeria has a population of around 140 million, with 30 million located in the Niger Delta region. This is a particularly oil-rich part of the country, but this is in conflict with the needs of the local people, who rely largely upon agriculture and fishing for their livelihood. Oil is very important to the Nigerian economy: the country supplies around 3% of the world's crude oil. Nigeria depends on the oil and gas industry for 95% of its export earnings and 80% of its government revenue. Joint ventures are a major revenue generator for the country, contributing more than $25 billion to the government over the last three years. Nigerian National Petroleum Corporation (55%), Shell (30%), Total (10%) and Agip (5%) constitute Nigeria's joint venture partners. In 2007, Shell-operated ventures produced an average of almost 934,000 barrels of oil equivalent per day, half of the country's total oil and gas production.

A well-known incident concerning the oil industry in Nigeria involved Kenule "Ken" Beeson Saro Wiwa (1941–1995) who was a Nigerian author, television producer and environmental activist. He led a non-violent campaign against the environmental degradation of the land and waters of Ogoniland by the operations of the oil companies, especially Shell. He was also an outspoken critic of the Nigerian government, which he viewed as reluctant to enforce environmental regulations on the foreign petroleum companies operating in the area. At the peak of his non-violent campaign, Saro-Wiwa was arrested, hastily tried by a special military tribunal, and hanged by the military government of General Sani Abacha, on charges widely viewed as entirely politically-motivated and completely unfounded.

Shell as a company, is deeply unpopular among Nigerians due to its environmental records in the Ogoni area of the Niger Delta. In a landmark ruling in a Nigerian court, the company was ordered to pay about £2bn in compensation to the Ogoni people. However welcoming the news might have been at the time of the ruling, it seems unlikely to be achieved as the

Nigerian press have cited corruption, injustice and brutality (by the government) as major barriers that may ultimately prevent this compensation from ever actually being paid. As the Niger Delta saga seems to continue without end (even after the death of Ken Saro-Wiwa), Shell is also unpopular in other areas of the globe (such as, for example, Rossport, Ireland, and British Columbia, Canada).

The oil companies are largely castigated for their behaviour in the Niger Delta with Shell, as the largest operator, being particularly singled out. It is certainly true that the people of the delta have seen their environment degraded, with little benefit from the oil revenue. If you were to ask the Ogoni people, however, they would mainly blame the Nigerian government, one of the most corrupt in the world, for its tribal preferences, which prevent them from benefiting. Shell, on the other hand, are quite open and most of this information can be found on their website. Such transparency, based upon full disclosure, is, of course, an essential feature of CSR.

Cotton from Uzbekistan

Uzbekistan is a largely arid country, but the Soviets decided that it would be a good place to grow cotton. They therefore commenced large-scale irrigation projects by diverting river water which previously flowed into the Aral Sea. Canals were built to use this water, though they were built so inefficiently that between 30% and 75% of the water is wasted. This has had serious consequences for the Aral Sea, which was once the 4th largest inland sea in the world, but has been shrinking so steadily since the 1960s that it now consists of a couple of small lakes. This has devastated the local fishing business and other industries which were dependent on it. The northern lake is located in Kazakhstan, which has instituted conservation measures to attempt to restore the sea, with some success. The southern lake is in Uzbekistan, a much poorer country, which is dependent upon cotton for 20% of its exports (it is the second largest exporter of cotton in the world, exporting most of its production to Europe). No action has been taken by Uzbekistan concerning the sea or about increasing the efficiency of the irrigation.

There are, however, much greater problems associated with the production of Uzbek cotton. The first is related to its harvesting: most countries make use of machines to harvest cotton, while Uzbekistan uses manual labour, specifically child labour. Every autumn, state officials shut down schools, and send students, together with their teachers, to the cotton fields, along with university students and public officials. Many thousands of children, some as young as seven, are forced to undertake weeks of this arduous labour, with no financial reward. As a result of cotton quotas, teachers are made to ensure that students pick the required daily amount. Children who fail to pick their target of cotton are reportedly punished with detentions and are told that their grades will suffer. Those who refuse to take part can face academic expulsion.

Uzbekistan's cotton farmers do not benefit from this system. Officially, they receive the market price for their crops. In practice, they are forced to sell their cotton to the state agency and receive less than one third of the world market price. As such, they are barely receiving subsistence level returns for their hard work. The government, however, sells the cotton on commodity exchanges at the market price – thereby guaranteeing huge profits, primarily for President Karimov and his associates. Uzbekistan is, unsurprisingly, deemed to be one of the most corrupt countries in the world.

There are, therefore, serious environmental issues and serious human rights issues associated with the production of Uzbek cotton. Indeed, the production methods used make it clear that it is not sustainable as a crop. Nevertheless, it is bought extensively by European cotton manufacturers who do not disclose the sources of their cotton in the goods manufactured from it and sold to domestic consumers. Pressure has, however, mounted on manufacturers, who are gradually refusing to use Uzbek cotton, thereby exerting pressure for reform upon the Uzbek government, demonstrating the push towards socially responsible behaviour across the world.

Failures and crisis

The 2008 financial and economic crisis[9] has shown that there are failures in governance and problems with the current market system. In the main, these have been depicted as representative of systemic failures of the market system and the lax application of systems of governance and regulation. Naturally, many people have discussed these failures and the consequent problems, and will continue to do so into the future, arguing for improved systems to combat them. It is not, of course, the first such crisis, and the market economy has been proceeding on a cycle of "boom and bust" for the last 20 years, which is not dissimilar to that of the sixties and seventies, which neo-conservatives claimed to have stopped. The main differences are that recent cycles are driven by financial markets, and that

---

[9] Actually it began in 2008, but is still continuing at the time of the editing of this book.

the era of globalisation means that no country is immune from the effects felt in other countries.

Issues arising

There are a number of issues which are apparent from our analysis. Firstly we must recognise that the future is going to be difficult. We have an economic recession to recover from, while also dealing with such issues as climate change and resource depletion. No longer are people ready to accept injustice – and no longer can bad practice be hidden. Today, the web has meant that corporate activity is visible to the whole world – and people are watching.

There are undoubtedly a lot of problems which need to be managed - but this can be done. Financial and economic recovery is starting to take place, and it may not be merely a simple repeat of the past. A new economic model is currently emerging which will be different to that used in the past. The new power and activities of stakeholders must also be regarded as an opportunity and not a threat, which will, in turn, allow the issue of resources depletion to be dealt with through R&D, better design and increased efficiency in our activities. At the same time, climate change can be addressed through the minimisation of our collective carbon footprint. It is clear that the future will be far more complex and fraught with issues than the past, but it can be manageable.

As the financial and economic crisis continues to unfold and to roll on through recession and towards recovery, various issues have been brought to the fore and have been discussed extensively in the media. It is time, therefore, to focus on what we have learned from the crisis. It is certainly true that wealth is not created by speculation. The real issue is that we truly live in a global world or – as Marshall McLuhan termed it in 1968 – a global village. In this global village, none of us are immune from problems in other parts of the world, and we must all take responsibility for what is happening, or has happened, in the world around us. This is the principal lesson from globalisation that we all need to learn: the good and bad effects – and there are always both – are shared equally by all of us. Furthermore, we, as individuals, must also accept both collective and individual responsibility for what has happened and what will happen. One of the recurrent messages in today's world is that social responsibility begins with individual responsibility. Sadly, however, this is a message that many people do not want to hear.

Given that we are all responsible for the problems of the world, it obviously follows that we all have a responsibility for developing solutions to these problems. It is particularly important to understand how the crisis originated, and to take action to make sure that the same sequences of events will not happen again in the future. This requires a radical rethinking of our economic system, just as much as it requires a radical rethinking of our food production and distribution system. At the moment, however, this does not appear to be happening. The danger of this is that the world will recover from these crises and continue as if nothing happened – with similar future consequences. We must not let this happen. We must recognise and act upon the things discussed here.

The future of governance

This concern with social responsibility faded out at the end of the 1970s with the rise of the New Right politics of Thatcher and Reagan and the consequent legitimation of selfish behaviour and greed in the acquisition of wealth. This was positively encouraged at an individual level and spilled over into the corporate world as governments facilitated the free market orientation to the provision of goods and services. Thus, markets were progressively opened to competition, corporate taxes were reduced and regulations relaxed in the spirit of the times and the belief in the 'trickle-down theory', the idea that this would benefit all levels of society[11]. It is only recently that concerns with social responsibility have re-emerged to play a role in such discussions. It remains, therefore, to consider the extent to which any concern for corporate social responsibility is a cyclical phenomenon which surfaces in times of economic prosperity and disappears when the economic cycle turns downwards. In other words, is the future of this concern with social responsibility one in which this cycle will be repeated and any concern for social responsibility becomes manifest periodically?

It is always tempting to argue that the current period is different from previous periods and that any welcome changes will be sustainable this time around, even without evidence. This time however there is evidence that the concern with corporate social responsibility might be different, as it can be seen to be related to various other global and local movements taking place in the context of the increased activism of citizens concerned with what is happening in the global corporate arena. Such evidence comes from the pressure placed upon the accounting profession through

---

[11] Some would argue instead that there was a callous disregard for the majority of society in the promulgation of these policies. Indeed, Thatcher is on record as stating that there is no such thing as society.

the establishment of groups such as the Association for Integrity in Accounting[12] in the USA, the Association for Accounting and Business Affairs[13] in the UK, and the Tax Justice Network[14], providing examples of a challenge to the hegemony of corporate activity.

Other evidence comes from such things as the feminist movement and more specifically from the pacifist and anti-militarist strand of this movement (Liddington 1989). Although they initially started out as part of a protest against nuclear weapons, the Greenham Common peace ideals were adopted by large numbers of women, many of whom were conventional citizens and consumers. The ideals of breaking with the mores of society assumed prominence for these women. This led initially to the establishment of peace camps at Greenham Common and elsewhere, but subsequently to a movement which espoused violence and sought to establish different ways of living. Further evidence comes from the various protest movements which exist at present and are concerned with such things as environmental pollution, animal experimentation, road use and genetically modified crops. Such pressure groups include among their membership many members of society who express their concern not just through belonging to such groups, but also through their selection of goods and services which they consume. As such, various supermarkets have suffered from people's refusal to purchase goods containing genetically modified substances to such an extent that some have withdrawn such products entirely. They have equally been affected by other campaigns, such as the boycott of fish when it has been thought that dolphins have been disadvantaged. Similarly, Shell suffered from bad publicity surrounding their proposed solution for the disposal of the Brent Spar oil platform.

Various other activities have been more radical and illegal and have sought to affect society at large. This has been manifest in the violent and destructive tactics of organisations such as the Animal Liberation Front, the obstructive tactics of groups such as ecoprotestors in their opposition to road building programs, and the disruptive tactics of the "Reclaim the Streets" collective in gaining maximum media coverage from their non-violent program of closing major streets in London for periods of time or in affecting the 1998 G8 summit in Birmingham. There are examples of other actions of anti-global movements that have been less peaceful, such

---

[12] Information on the Association for Integrity in Accounting is available at http://www.citizenworks.org.
[13] see http://visar.csustan.edu/aaba/aaba.htm.
[14] See Http://www.taxjustice.net. This organisation is supported by such organisations as War on Want.

as what became known as the battle of Seattle, but equally demonstrate a growing concern with the activities of global corporations. The discourse surrounding such environmental terrorism is one of illegitimacy, depending upon whether one considers that the ends justify the means or not. The impact of such activities upon legitimate organisations tends to be one of increasing transaction costs for the firms targeted, or for society at large, rather than any long-term change in performance measurement and reporting. Chaliand (1987) has argued that a successful terrorist organisation needs a base in society which extends beyond its membership and needs popular support in order to exist and achieve results. Such popular support can be particularly seen in the actions of ecoprotestors (Crowther & Cooper, 2001), where their activities can be viewed as the direct action component of a popular movement which concerns large numbers of people.

A potentially more significant activity as far as organisations are concerned is the increasing use of community-based economic activity (Brass & Koziell, 1997). Such activity is manifest in alternative modes of economic exchange and the carrying out of economic activities such as the growing number of LETS schemes and the growing number of economically active organisations such as workers' co-operatives and community banks. Such activity reflects a disillusion on the part of individuals within society with its current mode of organisation, and is part of a search for alternatives. This kind of activity is relatively small in scale at present, but is growing in size and can be expected to have a significant impact upon numerous organisations to which a response needs be sought.

Further evidence of changes in societal mores can be gathered from the existence of the New Age Traveller movement (Earle, Dearling, Whittle, Glasse & Gubby, 1994). Such communities of travellers have specific strategic objectives. These objectives are not explicitly stated and have not been arrived at by any overt decision-making process, but, rather, have developed over time through an unconscious process. Nevertheless, these strategic objectives are clearly defined and openly expressed by such travellers (Crowther & Cooper, 2002), and are expressed by these travellers as seeking to achieve two distinct objectives, namely learning to live differently and developing a community spirit and identity.

By "learning to live differently", these people mean both that their relationship with nature must be different and that their ability to exist in a peaceable manner must not be driven by the normal societal motives of economic consumption and wealth creation. In this respect, therefore, they refuse to recognise the proprietary ownership mores of mainstream society as a basis for resource utilisation. This applies particularly to land, which is viewed as a common resource to be used rather than owned. This view of land and its use is of course one of the principal reasons why the traveller movement has so often been in conflict with conventional society and why mainstream publicity about them has been uniformly bad. As with the Leveller movement in the seventeenth century, their very existence, and possible survival, can be considered to be a threat to the economic basis of societal existence. The travellers themselves would be pleased to be perceived in this way as this provides a level of support for their ideas of existence. The other main strand of traveller philosophy, which can be seen from their way of life and their general involvement in the ecoprotest movement, is a general concern with the environment and its degradation through developments. This is particularly true when the proposed developments are for the purpose of increasing road transport, or air transport, at the expense of nature.

All of this suggests that concern with governance is part of a wider social movement in which citizens are seeking to wrest power back from the global corporate world and to demand a share in the benefits of civilisation. Evidence from throughout this book suggests that these corporations are slowly responding to this pressure. As such, there is ground for optimism, but only if the pressure from citizens and concerned stakeholders continues.

References

Brass, E. & Koziell, S. P. (1997), *Gathering Force*, London, The Big Issue Writers

Chaliand, G. (1987), *Terrorism – From Popular Struggle to Media Spectacle*, London, Saqi

Crowther D (2002); *A Social Critique of Corporate Reporting*; Aldershot; Ashgate

—. (2004); Corporate social reporting: genuine action or window dressing?; in D Crowther & L Rayman Bacchus (eds.), *Perspectives on Corporate Social Responsibility*, Aldershot; Ashgate, pp 140-160

Crowther, D. & Cooper, S. (2001), Innovation through postmodern networks: the case of ecoprotestors, in O. Jones & S. Conway (eds.), *Networks and Innovation*, London, Imperial College Press pp 321-347

Crowther, D. & Cooper, S. (2002); Rekindling community spirit and identity: the case of ecoprotestors; *Management Decision* Vol. 40 No 4 pp 343-353

Earle, F., Dearling, A., Whittle, H., Glasse, R. & Gubby (1994), *A Time to Travel?*, Lyme Regis, Enabler Publications

Liddington, J. (1989), *The Road to Greenham Common*, New York, Syracuse University Press

Lomborg B (2001); *The Skeptical Environmentalist*; Cambridge; Cambridge University Press

Lovelock J (2006); *The Revenge of Gaia*; Harmondsworth; Penguin

INDEX